[d i g i t a l]
CHARACTER
ANIMATION

W9-ART-213

george maestri

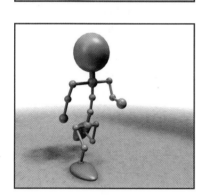

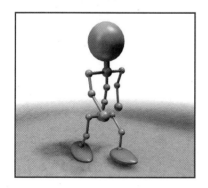

New Riders

New Riders Publishing, Indianapolis, Indiana

Acquisitions Editor
Steve Weiss

Software Specialist
Steve Flatt

Senior Editor
Sarah Kearns

Development Editor
Tim Huddleston

Project Editor
Stacey Beheler

Copy Editors
Gina Brown
Jennifer Eberhardt
Laura Frey
Lawrence Frey

Technical Editor
Bijan Tehrani

Acquisitions Coordinator
Stacey Beheler

Administrative Coordinator
Karen Opal

Cover Designer
Sandra Schroeder

Cover Illustrator
George Maestri

Cover Production
Aren Howell

Book Designer
Sandra Schroeder

Production Manager
Kelly Dobbs

Production Team Supervisor
Laurie Casey

Graphics Image Specialists
Steve Adams
Brad Dixon
Clint Lahnen

Production Analysts
Jason Hand
Erich Richter

Production Team
Daniel Caparo, Aleata Howard,
Christopher Morris, Pamela Woolf

Indexer
Sharon Hilgenberg

Digital Character Animation

By George Maestri

Published by:
New Riders Publishing
201 West 103rd Street
Indianapolis, IN 46290 USA

Printed in the United States of America 1 2 3 4 5 6 7 8 9 0

Library of Congress Cataloging-in-Publication Data

Maestri, George, 1960-
    Digital character animation / George Maestri.
        p.   cm.
    ISBN 1-56205-559-3
    1. Computer animation.   I. Title
TR897.7.M34 1996
741.5'8--dc21   96-47533
                                                             CIP

Warning and Disclaimer

This book is designed to provide information about digital character animation. Every effort has been made to make this book as complete and as accurate as possible, but no warranty or fitness is implied.

The information is provided on an "as is" basis. The author and New Riders Publishing shall have neither liability nor responsibility to any person or entity with respect to any loss or damages arising from the information contained in this book or from the use of the disks or programs that may accompany it.

Publisher	Don Fowley
Publishing Manager	David Dwyer
Marketing Manager	Mary Foote
Managing Editor	Carla Hall

About the Author

George Maestri is a Los Angeles based writer and animator with experience in both traditional and computer animation. He has written for a number of animated shows, including the Cable Ace nominated series "Rocko's Modern Life." George has developed original shows for several major networks, including Nickelodeon, Fox, ABC, and Carlton UK. He has also written numerous articles on computer animation for magazines such as *Digital Video*, *Computer Graphics World*, *Publish*, *New Media*, and *Animation Magazine*. As a visual artist, he has animated and directed both traditional and computer animation for a number of major studios, including Nickelodeon, Film Roman, and MGM.

Trademark Acknowledgments

All terms mentioned in this book that are known to be trademarks or service marks have been appropriately capitalized. New Riders Publishing cannot attest to the accuracy of this information. Use of a term in this book should not be regarded as affecting the validity of any trademark or service mark.

Dedication

This book is dedicated to my beautiful daughter, Moyet Maestri, who put up with an absent father for the months it took to write this.

It is also for my father, George Harvey Maestri, who I know would have been very proud of his son's first book.

Acknowledgments

My heartfelt appreciation goes to Toni Petniunas for being my best friend during this very difficult task.

Many thanks to David Dwyer, Steve Weiss, Tim Huddleston, Bijan Tehrani, Kim Tempest, and everyone else at New Riders who gave me tons of constructive feedback that helped make this book better.

Lynda Weinman for blazing the trail and being my peer.

Maestri Smith (photographer) and Joan Barlow (model) for the photographs used in Chapter 11.

Rick Connor for bits of music to accompany the animation on the CD.

The people on the CG-CHAR mailing list who gave me many tips and pointers.

Special thanks to Intergraph Computer Systems and Dynamic Pictures for providing incredibly fast OpenGL cards that made my machine hum.

Viewpoint Datalabs for many of the models I used in the book.

Microsoft, along with Andrew Mackles, Heidi Lowell, and Heather Talbott of MacKenzie Kesselring for providing me with Softimage|3D and training.

Kinetix, who gave me 3D Studio MAX and Character Studio.

The people at Newtek, for providing me with LightWave.

Digimation for allowing me to beta test Bones Pro and Sandblaster during the writing of this book.

The guys at Meme-X for Lock & Key.

Franca Miraglia at Alias for images created with their terrific package.

The people at REM-Infografica for images of MetaReyes.

Finally, my dog Alex, for accepting fewer walks in the park and for keeping my feet warm by sleeping under the desk as I wrote this book.

3D models provided by Viewpoint Datalabs International, Inc., Orem UT 801-229-3000, http://www.viewpoint.com.

Publisher's Note

New Riders offers our heartfelt congratulations to Mr. Maestri for bearing up like a champion through what was at times a distinctively challenging process. The creation of this book was a true labor of love for George; a first effort made more difficult by seemingly insane deadline pressure, oodles of niggling details, and the affectionately respectful badgering of a small pack of publishing people.

We salute your mettle, George; it has been a pleasure and an honor. And we are very, very proud of what we have accomplished together.

A special debt is also owed to three amazing individuals: Stacey Beheler, Jennifer Eberhardt, and Laura Frey, who moved Heaven and Earth to make this book a reality when all evidence pointed to the contrary. You are the best.

Contents at a Glance

vi

Table of Contents

Introduction

Animating with a computer is very similar to writing with a word processor. Both are creative tasks that just happen to involve technology. In both cases, the creativity is what matters. People—not computers—are creative. Technology is simply a tool to assist that inventiveness.

A word processor may make your documents look stunningly beautiful, with a dozen fonts in full color, but it does not make you a better writer. Writing is a creative task that comes mostly from the right side of a person's brain. The word processor doesn't read the classics, it doesn't study poetry, and it can't create a brilliant novel, script, or research paper. It takes a creative person to do that. The word processor simply makes it easier to get the words out of your head and on a printed page so people can read them.

The same goes for computer animation. You may have the best animation software in the world, and it may render each frame of your animation beautifully and quickly, but the content of those frames is driven by your creativity. Character animation is a study of motion, timing, and acting, and it is just as creative an art as writing, acting, drawing, or painting. Like the word processor, the computer is a tool that makes it easy to get the animation that's in your head on to film or videotape so that people can see it.

Regardless of whether you use pencils or pixels, the fundamentals of animation are the same. Bringing Homer Simpson to life in 3D requires many of the same character animation techniques that classical animators learn.

Just because you animate with a CPU doesn't mean you're some sort of trailblazer in the world of animation. Digital animation may be relatively new, but people have been animating since motion pictures were invented. The skills and knowledge that animators discovered long ago make the very strong foundation on which newfangled computer animators stand. The computer does make the creation of animation easier and quicker, but it also makes it quicker and easier to create garbage. In order to produce quality animation, you need a firm grounding in the basics of animation, which have not changed much since the golden age of animation, more than 50 years ago. The same principles and techniques that went into making the classic cartoons of the 1940s are principles every animator should know, regardless of the medium.

Animation is the art; computers are the medium. Whether you animate with pencils, clay, or pixels, you still need to know the basics of animation. You need to understand anatomy, motion, weight, and timing—the foundational elements of animation. Some animators may know how to draw, some may sculpt, but they all stand on this same foundation.

What You Can Expect from This Book

This book is meant to give you two things. The first is an understanding of the fundamentals of character animation. These techniques are the foundation from which all animators draw, regardless of their creative medium. This book also updates these age-old techniques just a bit so that they apply to the computer animator.

A traditional animation book may start out with a few chapters on drawing; this book spends the first few chapters on designing and building characters in the computer and then focuses on the fundamentals of animation using characters that you've built. (I've also provided a few characters on the CD for you to use.) Finally, the later chapters tackle some of the more difficult areas of animation, including walking and talking.

What You Should Know

Before you begin this book, you should have a fundamental understanding of computers, computer graphics, and 3D software. I am not going to bore you with a dissertation on CPUs, RAM, and hard disks. Nor will I bother you by explaining such things as pixels, alpha channels, and rendering. If you don't know these terms, I suggest you seek out resources in your community such as books or classes. You should also be familiar with the 3D package you decide to use. Read your software's manuals and work through the package's tutorial to understand its features.

What You Will Need

All you need to animate characters digitally is a computer and a 3D animation package. That said, there are specific packages that lend themselves to character animations more readily than others, supporting shape animation, skeletal deformations, hierarchies, Inverse Kinematics, metaballs, and constraints. Packages in this group include:

- Alias/Wavefont
- Softimage|3D
- 3D Studio MAX
- LightWave
- Animation Master
- Prisms

There are also packages that support many, but not all the capabilities needed for full-featured character animation. These packages can all do character animations, but not quite as easily as those in the preceding list:

- ElectricImage
- RayDream
- Truespace
- Extreme 3D
- Strata
- InfiniD

All the vendors of these software packages, however, are working diligently to make their offerings more character friendly, and many of these second-tier packages will be able to do decent characters in the near future. To go along with these advances in software, hardware is getting faster and cheaper every day.

4

Beginning animators should decide on the software they want to use before buying any hardware. The PC, Mac, and SGI platforms all have their selling points, and all can animate characters. When configuring a system, a good rule of thumb is to take the software manufacturer's minimum requirements and double them. If the vendor recommends 32 MB of memory, try to buy 64 MB. If the manufacturer recommends a 100 MHz processor, try to get a 200 MHz processor. Hardware is advancing quickly, making today's machines obsolete in about 18 months, so getting the fastest machine you can afford will forestall the inevitable upgrade—if you have the money, of course. It is entirely possible to produce terrific animation on a budget, and used equipment can be the basement animator's secret weapon. Quality is not a function of processor speed.

The real lure of digital animation is interactivity, or the ability to play back your animations on the fly and make changes immediately. The faster your machine, the higher the level of interactivity and the smoother the creative processes flow. To help speed things along, a 3D accelerator card helps you play back shaded animation tests immediately without having to first render the animation. Being able to view and manipulate your models fully shaded as you create them also speeds productivity. Not all 3D cards are created equal, however, so check with your software vendor for a list of supported 3D cards before you buy.

3D accelerator card

Another important issue is output. The PC, Mac, and SGI platforms all enable you to play back thumbnail-sized animations directly from your computer. For your own tests, this type of animation is perfectly acceptable. If you want full-motion video, however, you usually need to add a third-party card for this task, along with a fast hard disk or disk array. The capability of printing your animation in full motion to videotape is a good idea because it enables you to show other people your work. A full-motion video card is a good idea for anyone who's serious about animation as a career.

full motion video

About This Book's Approach to Software

It would have been easy to write this book using a specific software package. A book on Brand X software, however, would prove somewhat useless to the person owning Brand Y software.

Added to that is the fact that as soon as Brand X got a slew of new features or a new interface, this book would be headed for the trash. Besides, there's already a book about the software you own; it's called the owner's manual.

This book takes on a bigger challenge—a guide for anyone with a computer and a 3D package. The principles presented in this book will be applicable over a broad range of platforms. The techniques are presented from every angle, from the professional with the cutting-edge workstation to the student with barely enough computer to squeak by. As a result, there should be something in this book for everyone.

As mentioned previously, there are at least a half dozen packages on three separate platforms that can animate characters. Add to that all the second-tier software, and you can see how many packages from which you can choose to do character animation. Still, it's not the software, it's how you use it that counts. You need to know your software inside and out, to read your owner's manual, and to work through the tutorials that came with your package. Ignorance of your tools is not an excuse. Just as a painter needs to know his brushes and his canvas, you need to know your software and its features.

Studying these half dozen packages indicated that they are typically more alike than different in most respects, and this book concentrates on the similarities and does not to present too many exercises that are unique to only one package. Still, there are differences, and there may be techniques presented that simply don't apply to your personal situation. When possible, the book points out the discrepancies, but if you know your software's features and capabilities, the differences are usually obvious. If your modeler does not handle splines, for example, then the sections on spline modeling might be interesting reading, but not directly applicable. Also, software is changing rapidly. A feature that is currently missing from your software will most likely be found in the next release or two.

This book also has to jump through hoops when it comes to terminology. The exact same feature on two packages may have two completely different names. The most common terminology is used, and the differences are explained as you go along. If you know your software and its capabilities, however, you should be able to make the connections yourself.

About the CD

The CD contains as many models, textures, and animations as I could create in the time span allotted. The models are in DXF and 3DS format, simply because these formats can be imported by almost every 3D package. Most of the major exercises have an animation that you can watch as reference. I've saved these in both QuickTime and AVI formats for maximum compatibility.

Finally, Viewpoint Datalabs has graciously allowed us to put some of its models on the CD. Many of these models will be characters you can animate, and some of the models will be parts of bodies, such as a hand that you can attach to any body.

About New Riders Publishing

The staff of New Riders Publishing is committed to bringing you the very best in computer reference material. Each New Riders book is the result of months of work by authors and staff members who research and refine the information contained within its covers.

As part of this commitment to you, New Riders invites your input. Please let us know if you enjoy this book, if you have trouble with the information and examples presented, or if you have a suggestion for the next edition.

Please note, however, that the author and New Riders' staff cannot serve as a technical resource for your 3D modeling and animation software or hardware. If you have questions about your software or system, please refer to the documentation or Help files that accompanied them.

If you have a question or comment about any New Riders book, there are several ways to contact New Riders Publishing. We will respond to as many readers as we can. Your name, address, and phone number will never become part of a mailing list or be used for any purpose other than to help us continue to bring you the best books possible. You can write to us at the following address:

New Riders Publishing
Attn: Publishing Manager, Graphics
201 West 103rd Street
Indianapolis, IN 46290

If you prefer, you can fax New Riders Publishing at
317-817-7448.

To send us e-mail via the Internet, use the following address:

ddwyer@newriders.mcp.com

Or check out our World Wide Web site at this address:

http://www.mcp.com/newriders/

New Riders Publishing is an imprint of Macmillan Computer
Publishing. To obtain a catalog or information or to purchase any
Macmillan Computer Publishing book, you can visit our World
Wide Web site at the preceding address or call 800-428-5331.

A Final Note

Animating characters is a life-long journey, and this book will
help you take the first few steps. Animation can be incredibly fun,
but it's also a very difficult art to master; after finishing this book,
it will take many years of practice for you to become an animator. Hopefully, you will rely on this book as a reference throughout your journey.

CHAPTER 1

Basic Character Design

This book is about creating and bringing characters to life. Before you model and animate a character, however, you need to think about its design. A character design can be as simple as a sketch or as complex as fully rendered sculpture. The design serves as a simple road map, a plan of action for creating a digital character.

Here, the term "design" means making decisions about your characters. You need to decide how tall or short they'll be, the textures you'll use for their skin, and what type of clothes they'll wear. You also need to decide how realistic or stylized you want to make your characters. These decisions are all interrelated. If you want to model a realistic character, you will probably have to animate it realistically, as well.

If you design your characters properly, their personalities jump off the screen. Your audience knows who your characters are immediately and likes them. A well-designed character also will be easier for you to animate. If you can animate your character without fuss, it makes the animation process easier and far more creative. Designing characters that animate well requires a knowledge of anatomy as well as a thorough understanding of the strengths and weaknesses of your software tools. Both of these topics are discussed in detail throughout this book.

A simple character made from spheres and cylinders can be animated easily in any 3D package. Animate him well, and the audience will accept his simple design.

A character with a seamless body needs to be animated with a skeletal deformation system (discussed in later chapters). The designer has used a helmet to obscure the face, eliminating the need for facial animation. This makes the character a prime candidate for an action sequence, but not a love scene.

To animate a complex head you need more sophisticated tools, including software that can handle the shape animation needed to manipulate the flexible mouth. If you don't have these tools, you should design your character differently.

Approaching Design as an Artist

Design is an art, as is animation. When great design is coupled with great animation, the result is much larger than the sum of its parts. You can approach the design of your characters from many different ways. Because design is a creative process, everyone approaches the task using his or her own artistic strengths and weaknesses. Some people work out their designs with pencil and paper, others prefer clay, some prefer pixels. All these methods can inspire new and innovative designs.

Those who want realistic characters may simply place a human in a laser scanner and snap a digital picture of the real thing. Deciding who steps into the scanner, however, is a design decision. What's important is that you consider your character from a design standpoint before your hand ever touches a mouse.

First and foremost, a well-designed character conveys personality. Your characters should also be well-proportioned and appealing to the eye. In addition to your character's outward appearance, you also need to design with animation in mind—understanding your software and what it needs to animate a character successfully.

Some of your design decisions are dictated by the limitations of your software. If your software doesn't enable you to create hair, for instance, then you might want to avoid animating an English sheep dog. You should use the strong points of your software to your advantage and design around the weak spots. The audience won't know that you didn't have that whiz-bang new hair plug-in. Instead, they'll simply see a character on the screen. If it looks good and has personality, the audience really won't care how you created it, even if your character is bald.

Believe it or not, simplicity is the key to designing good characters. Many times, the most amazing character turns out to be the simplest to construct. You should always think about your character's construction and try to keep your models simple and light. Simple characters also animate faster and easier. If your character has too many parts or more detail than it needs, you will have more elements to keep track of when animating. Problems that slow you or your system down also detract from the creative process, and your animation suffers.

Categories of Design

Designs fall into two broad categories: realistic and stylized. Realistic designs try to mimic reality. If you want to create realistic characters, you need to design your character in accordance with nature. Stylized designs, on the other hand, are caricatures or parodies of reality and give you far more design choices.

Realistic Designs

Digital character animation has been successful in the area of special effects for feature films. Computer animators and special effects teams have been able to make characters, such as dinosaurs, look completely real and integrate them into live-action environments. Many of the larger studios are working toward creating digital humans, and, most likely, they will succeed. Digital stunt doubles have already been employed to complete stunts that would have been too expensive or impossible for a real stunt double to do.

If you want to create characters that closely mimic reality, digital animation is the medium you should choose. You must understand, however, that reality is a hard thing to simulate, regardless of medium. Creating an effective animation of a realistic character requires a thorough knowledge of anatomy and motion. Many studios simply resort to motion capture. Motion capture, however, is a direct descendant of puppetry, and animation plays little role in this process.

A realistic human can prove vexing when it comes to animation. This character was produced using Softimage.

If you want to design and animate a realistic character, reference of the real thing is essential. In traditional animation, many of the large studios have been known to bring animals to the studio for the animators to study. If you can't afford to hire an ostrich or an elephant for the afternoon, a trip to the zoo or a videotape of a nature documentary can provide equally good reference. If you want to create a realistic human, a trip to the zoo could also be in order. Of course, for humans, the cities are the zoos. In a big city, step out the front door and watch the passersby for reference.

Stylized Designs

Creating a caricatured world is usually more fun and gives you much more freedom in your designs. Computer animation can mimic reality, but animation is always at its best when it goes far beyond reality and into the surreal. Think of those classic cartoons from the 1940s. Daffy Duck was a wild and wacky character, but he was a duck. In real life, ducks swim, eat, and breed, but that's about it. Ducks certainly don't talk, and they don't hold grudges against smart-alecky rabbits. It's way beyond the realm of reality, but a talking duck is still entertaining. The audience accepts the animated universe as you define it. If your character pulls off its head and dribbles it like a basketball, the audience doesn't question it; they simply laugh.

The audience's preconceptions are important, and you should consider those preconceptions as you design your characters. If your audience sees a picture-perfect digital human on the screen, they expect him to walk, talk, and act like a human. If your character is the slightest bit off from the way a real human acts, the illusion is lost. If you give the audience a caricatured cartoon hedgehog, however, they have absolutely no preconceptions. The audience is much more accepting of your stylized character. You, as the animator, have the freedom to make your character move and act however you want, even if it's not exactly the way a real hedgehog would act.

Animation is what brings a character to life. Even a design as simple as a box can be brought to life if you animate it well.

A caricatured design, however, is not a license to animate your characters poorly. Good animation makes even the simplest character appear to breathe. As you'll see in Chapter 8, "Anthropomorphic Animation," even a simple box can be animated quite easily by twisting and turning it and moving it so that it has weight, volume, and personality.

Understanding Anatomy

No matter what design style you choose, you need to understand anatomy. Even a simple box appears to have feet and shoulders if it is animated. If your character has real shoulders and feet, you need to know something about the way the body is put together. If you use digital skeletons, as we'll cover in the next chapter, this knowledge is doubly important. You will need to design and build your digital skeletons so that they simulate the actions of real bones.

A strong understanding of anatomy is important for anyone who uses the human figure in art. I would highly recommend life drawing classes for any animator. To help you understand the human figure, there will be several places in this book where I focus on anatomy. To start, here is the basic structure of the human body and the skeleton.

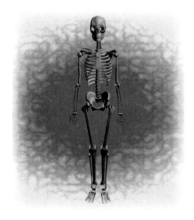

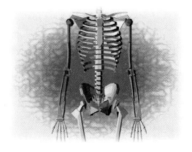

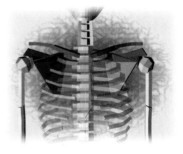

The Skeleton. If you want to design human-like characters that animate well, you need to understand the human skeleton and how it moves. The human skeleton has about 200 separate bones. Many of these, however, are small bones, such as the ones in the feet and the inner ear. As an animator, you need to concern yourself only with the bones that affect the body's global shape, especially the bones in the four major limbs, the vertebrae, the shoulders, and the hips.

The Arms. Three major bones comprise the arms: the humerus, the radius, and the ulna. The *humerus* is the upper arm. It is connected to the forearm at the elbow, a hinged joint. The forearm consists of two bones, the *radius* and the *ulna*. These bones twist about one another to rotate the hand at the wrist. Proportionally, the arms hang down so that the wrists are even with the hips.

The Shoulders. Two bones comprise the shoulders. In the front is the *clavicle*, a long thin bone that is commonly called the "collar bone." Along the back is the *scapula*, more commonly known as the "shoulder blade." Together, they connect the arms to the rib cage and, more importantly, the spine. The scapula holds the top of the arm in a ball-and-socket joint, giving the arm a wide range of movement.

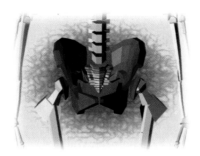

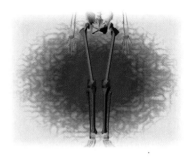

The Vertebrae. The *vertebrae* is the support system for the upper body. All the weight of the upper body is transmitted through the spine to the hips at the sacrum. Alone, each vertebra bends only slightly; however, all the vertebrae together make it possible for the upper body to twist as well as bend at the waist.

The Hips. Several bones comprise the hips, the most important of which is the *pelvis*. The hips are the foundation of the spine and transfer the weight of the upper body to the legs. As such, the hips are the center of weight distribution for the body. The pelvis connects to the legs with a ball-and-socket joint, much like the one found in the shoulders.

The Legs. Like the arms, three bones comprise the legs. These are the *femur*, which is also known as the "thigh bone." It connects through a hinged joint to the shin, which is actually two bones, the *tibia* and the *fibula*. Much like the forearm's radius and ulna, these two bones twist about one another to rotate the foot. Proportionally, the legs are almost half the height of the entire body.

Designing a Character

Now that you know the way the body is put together, you can think about the design of your character. The way the character is designed depends largely on the character itself. A character who's big and mean has broad shoulders and beady eyes. A character with big eyes and a pot belly seems meek by comparison.

Head and Body Proportions

When deciding on the height of your character, use the size of the head as your guide. An average human is about seven to eight heads tall. If the character is taller, it may appear more lithe and graceful.

Cartoony characters, on the other hand, can have much bigger heads in relation to the body. Mr. Potatohead, in fact, has no body; he simply has arms and feet. If your character has a body, it may only be as large the head itself. A larger head in proportion to the body tends to make a character look cute. Many characters are only two or three heads tall.

This realistic character is between seven and eight heads tall, not including the hat. This height is normal for an average human.

This cartoon character is a little more than two heads tall. The bigger the head in relation to the body, the cuter the character will look.

Eyes

The size of the eyes in relation to the face determines how the audience perceives a character. If the eyes are small and beady, the character may appear mean or angry. Big eyes convey innocence and look cute. The eyes of your character can also change shape. If your character has cartoon eyes (which are basically outside the head), you can bend and flex the eyes wildly with the character's emotions. If your character has eyes that are inside the head, and more realistic, you don't have as much freedom in changing the shape at animation time. If you want the eyes to be bigger than normal, you need to model them big to begin with. Eyes are covered in detail in Chapter 4, "Modeling Heads for Animation."

The shape of your character's eyes can also determine his personality. Round, symmetrical eyes can look pleasant.

Oblong, asymmetrical eyes can make your character look like he's begging for neurons.

For a character with eyes inside the head, you have less flexibility in changing the eyes' shape. If you wanted this character to have larger or smaller eyes, you probably would need to remodel the entire head from scratch.

Feet

On a real human, the feet are relatively small in relation to the body. Your character's foot should be almost exactly as long as its forearm. Many times your character will be wearing shoes. In animation, however, it is not necessary to model feet to place inside the shoes; the shoes can simply attach to the legs at the ankles.

A cartoon character, on the other hand, may have the feet exaggerated so that they are much larger than normal. If you decide to exaggerate the feet, remember that your character still needs to walk. Feet that are longer than the legs will prove difficult, if not impossible, to animate.

This stylized character's feet are bigger than normal.

If the feet are modeled too big, however, the character will have problems walking.

Hands

Like feet, hands on a stylized character can be slightly oversized to give it a cartoony look. If your design is more realistic, you might want to proportion the hands realistically as well. If realism is the goal, you may need to attach the hands seamlessly to the forearm, build your character as one solid mesh, or use an advanced seam-hiding technique, such as a blend or a fading texture, to keep the skin smooth. These techniques are discussed in the next chapter.

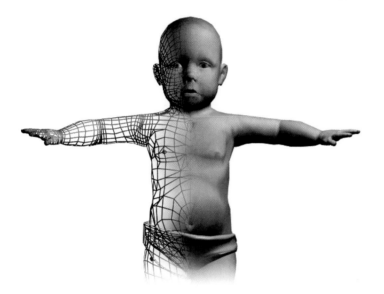

A character whose hands and body are one seamless mesh.

If you want, you can give your character cartoon gloves for hands. In the 1920s and 1930s, cartoon gloves were devised by animators so that hands and wrists would be easier to draw. The design stuck, mostly because it looks stylish and it works. For a 3D animator, cartoon gloves serve much the same purpose. They can be much easier to attach than a naked hand because the glove can have a seam where it attaches.

Clothing and Other Accessories

Clothes make the man, or so they say. If your character is an astronaut, he will probably be wearing a space suit. A caveman may need only a bear skin. Clothing tells the audience, to a large degree, who the character is and how it should perceive him. If you want a character to be mean and nasty, dress him accordingly. Not every villain you create, however, needs to wear black. When designing characters and their clothing, try to be original and avoid stereotypes.

A cartoon glove is stylish, and it helps you design around the tricky problem of seamlessly attaching your character's hand to the wrist.

18 Do clothes make the man? The character on the left may be perceived differently from the one on the right, simply because of his clothes.

Clothing can also help you design around the limitations of your modeler. If your modeler forces you to place a seam at your character's waist, a belt may be a good way to hide the seam. A dress or a long shirt can help to hide the hip area, which can be difficult to model and animate with some software.

This character has an unsightly seam at his waist.

Add a belt and the audience will never see the seam.

Exercise #1: Character Design

In this first exercise, try to be creative. Take a pencil and paper and sketch out some character designs that you might want to model in the next few chapters. (If you're more familiar with sculpting, you might want to do this in clay.) These designs should focus only on the outward appearance of the character, its proportions, and whether the character is small, large, skinny, fat, and so on.

After you have a number of designs, go through each character and think of how that character might be constructed in your chosen software. Because you are just getting started, these issues may not be readily apparent, but they will become clear as you learn more about how to build characters in the next few chapters.

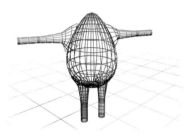

CHAPTER 2

Modeling Bodies for Animation

Now that you understand some of the basic concepts of character design, you can begin building a character that's not only appealing, but also animates well. There are countless ways to build and animate characters digitally, and many of the choices you make are dictated by your software's capabilities.

Remember that your characters don't only need to look good; they must animate well. There are many ways to set up a character for animation. You may need to break up your character into individual segments and reconnect them with a hierarchy. It also might mean setting up an Inverse Kinematics system to make the segments easier to animate. If you have a seamless character, you need to model it correctly, with extra detail in the joints, so that it deforms naturally. You also might need to set up a skeleton of digital bones to deform your character, much like the bones in human bodies.

A character that is easily manipulated in the computer makes animation a breeze. By building and configuring your character properly before you start animating, you avoid many headaches in the long run.

Deciding on the Correct Geometry

Before you create a character, you need to decide exactly how it will be constructed and animated. First, you must decide what type of geometry you'll use. Animation packages generally handle two main classes of geometry: polygons and splines.

Polygons

Polygons are simply triangles or squares that define small areas of the character's surface. Each polygon defines a little flat plane; by placing a series of these polygons together, edge to edge, you can create intricately shaped surfaces. To get a smooth surface, however, you need a lot of these little planes. If you use too few polygons, your objects break up into telltale flat surfaces, and their vertices become visible. Polygons require a lot of detail.

An important benefit of polygonal modeling is in the number of different surface types that can be defined. Many spline modelers are limited to surfaces that are topologically simple, such as cylinders or spheres. In order to create an object that's more complex, such as a body, you may need to make it out of several surfaces that are seamed together. Polygons don't suffer from this topological conundrum, however, and with a polygonal modeler, you're free to make your surface as complex as you desire.

Polygons are great for things that don't change shape, such as buildings and spaceships. When it comes to organic shapes, such as characters, the sheer number of vertices it takes to create a smooth polygonal surface can prove cumbersome compared to other modeling methods. If you have a large number of polygons, you can't move them individually and expect your model to remain smooth. Still, many vendors provide novel ways of manipulating groups of vertices quite effectively. Techniques such as lattice deformations, magnets, bones, and the like can smoothly manipulate even the most complex models.

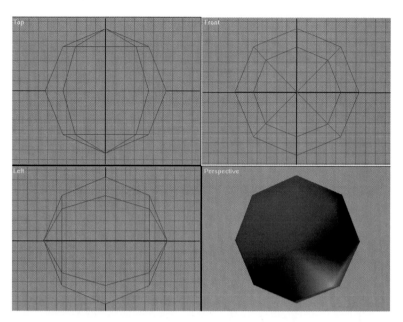

A simple sphere made out of polygons. With only eight subdivisions, you can see the edges of the planes defined by the polygons.

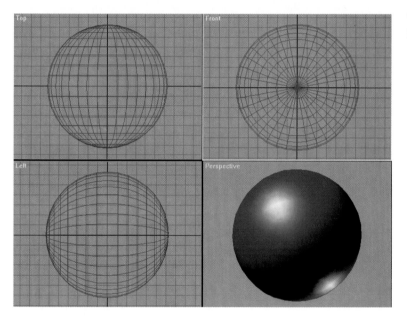

You must quadruple the detail before the sphere looks smooth.

24 This sphere is made out of splines. Even with only eight subdivisions, it remains completely smooth.

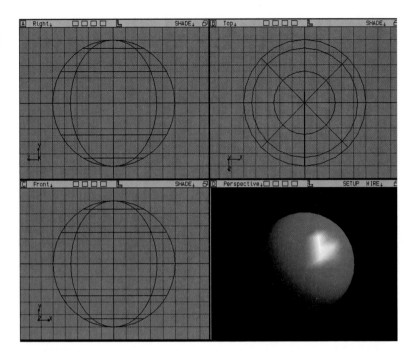

Splines

A *spline* is a curve; several splines can be put together to define a smooth curved surface, called a *patch*. A patch defines a far larger area than a single polygon, and this area is perfectly smooth, making splines a great way to create organic things such as characters. Most spline-based modeling programs are known as *surface modelers* because they define only the surface of the objects they create.

The good thing about splines is that they enable you to define a very complex surface with a few points, making the animation of complex shapes much easier than with a polygonal modeler. Splines resolve to polygons at rendering time, but these polygons are calculated only at rendering time. The surface always remains smooth, making splines advantageous for modeling organic objects. This calculation, however, can add to rendering time, making polygons more efficient for real-time interactions such as video games. For animations not rendered in real time, however, the slight increase in rendering time is well worth the results.

There are five basic types of spline surfaces:

- ■ Linear
- ■ Cardinal

- ■ Bézier
- ■ B-Spline
- ■ NURBS

Some modelers may not be able to handle all five types of splines. Each type of curve is different in the way it handles its control points.

This linear spline looks like a series of lines connecting the control points. The surfaces defined by these curves are flat.

A cardinal curve passes through the control points. Each point has a tangent control, as well.

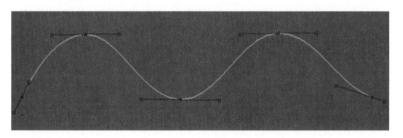

A Bézier curve is similar to those used in popular drawing programs, such as Adobe Illustrator. The curve passes through each control point, and each point has two tangential controls for adjusting the weight of the curve on either side of the vertex.

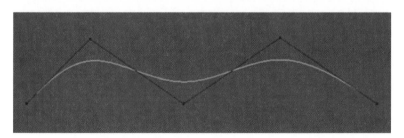

A B-Spline curve rarely passes through its control points, and having the control points far away can make manipulating a surface a bit confusing. In this type of curve, the points are called knots.

NURBS (Non-Uniform Rational B-Spline) curves function in much the same way as B-Splines, but each knot can have its own weight, so that you can affect the amount of pinch the curve makes at the vertex. A NURBS surface can define any of the other four types of curves, making it the most versatile spline.

Because splines generally define a four-sided patch, many spline modelers have problems with objects that have branches, such as the arms and legs on a body. Think of a patch as a piece of elastic wrapping paper. With wrapping paper, you can easily wrap a box or a cylinder, or you can twist up the ends to cover a sphere. If you have to wrap something that has branches, such as a human with arms and legs, you must use a separate piece of paper for the branches and find a way to attach it to the first. Adhesive tape is fine for birthday presents, but not for characters.

The wrapping paper problem applies to many spline modelers, as well. The patches defined by splines are usually four-sided surfaces, much like the wrapping paper example. Problems can arise at branching sections, where you may need to cut holes or glue the patches together. Today, a branching object is one of the defining problems of spline modelers, and the way a package handles, or doesn't handle, is what separates the wheat from the chaff. Advanced software, such as Alias and Softimage, are excellent in that they give you a number of tools to deal with this geometric limitation. Some strategies for resolving these problems are covered a bit later.

One package that deftly escapes this topological conundrum is Hash's Animation Master. It is a spline-based modeler that is unique in that it enables you to seamlessly create holes and branches without resorting to separate patches. It can also seam together patches easily.

Creating Segmented Characters

The easiest way to create a character is one joint at a time, each joint being an individual segment. To picture a segmented character, imagine the classic artist's mannequin, a character constructed from individual blocks of wood and fitted together with metal pins at the joints. Action figures, such as Hasbro's venerable GI Joe, are good examples of real world segmented characters.

The techniques used to create a segmented character apply equally to spline and polygonal modelers because each can create the individual body parts quite easily. Modeling the joints individually makes them easier to construct, and the character is easier to manage when animating. Because the individual segments don't change shape, a sophisticated animation system is not required. Most characters created for 3D video games are constructed from segments because they animate considerably faster in real-time applications than characters with a seamless skin that need to change shape. The same is true for modeling and animating segmented characters; manipulation is usually fast because the computer doesn't need to calculate shape changes on the fly.

An artist's mannequin found at any art store is a good example of a segmented character.

This character is constructed from simple segments, mostly boxes, cylinders, and spheres. He's easy to build and animate in almost any 3D package.

A more complex character made from segments. The segments themselves can be made from splines or polygons.

The downfall of the segmentation method is that, unlike characters with a single skin, segmenting a character creates telltale seams. Unless the joints are fitted perfectly so there are no gaps over a large range of rotation, seams are bound to show. If your camera never gets close enough to see the seams, the seams may not be a problem. You may want to avoid this limitation by designing a character where the seams don't really matter, such as a mechanical robot.

This exploded view shows his individual parts.

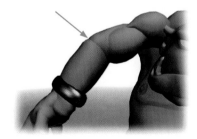

Even a character with well-fitted joints, however, can have faint seams.

Pivots and Joint Rotation

When creating a segmented character, you need to tell your software how the joints of your character's body rotate. The shin, for example, rotates at the knee. When you create an object, such as a shin segment, the software doesn't know that it's supposed to be a shin, and it has no idea that the shin rotates at the knee. It simply assigns the pivot to an arbitrary point, usually the physical center of the object. Arbitrary points are not acceptable. You need to check and reassign the pivot points on all your segments. The forearm rotates at the elbow, the thigh rotates at the hips, the head pivots at the neck, and so on.

The forearm is rotating around its default pivot point—the center of the object. Unfortunately (or should that be fortunately), real forearms rotate differently.

To make the forearm rotate properly, you need to manually reassign the pivot point so that the forearm rotates at the elbow.

Using Hierarchies to Glue Things Together

When building a segmented character, you'll create a dozen or more segments, or individual objects. You need to find some way of gluing the character together so that all these individual objects move as a unit. Further, you want the hand to move with the arm and the legs to move with the hips. You can glue a character's segments together in this manner by using a hierarchy.

A *hierarchy* is a way to tell the computer how your character is connected together. Taken literally, the hierarchy tells your software that the foot bone is connected to the ankle bone, the ankle bone is connected to the shin bone, and so on. Technically, the hierarchy looks a bit like a tree, with each connection forming a branch. The trunk is the parent of the branches, and the branches are parents of the twigs. If you move a child object, say a twig, you won't move the parent, say a branch or the trunk. If you move the trunk, however, all the children, the branches and twigs, follow.

Just like a tree, a hierarchy must have a trunk, a single parent that controls all the other branches. In a human skeleton, the trunk is usually the hips or pelvis. The pelvis is close to the center of gravity. More importantly, the pelvis is where the spine and legs are anchored, making the spine, the shoulders, head, arms, legs, and feet all children of the hips. As with the tree example, each segment of the body's hierarchy has a parent, child, or both. The shoulders parent the biceps, which in turn parent the forearm, and then the hand and fingers.

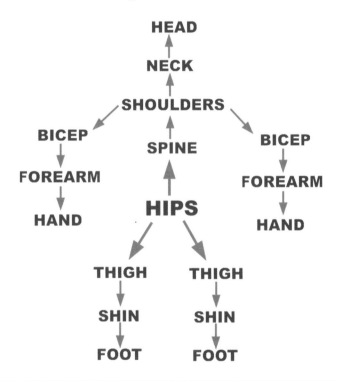

The basic hierarchy of a human body. The hips are the parent of all joints. If you move the hips, everything moves along with them.

Exercise #1: Creating a Simple Segmented Character

In this exercise, you create a simple segmented character out of only spheres and cylinders. This procedure can be accomplished in just about any package, and the spheres and cylinders can be made of splines or polygons. The character, although simple, shows you the way a body is put together.

continues

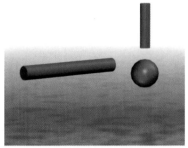

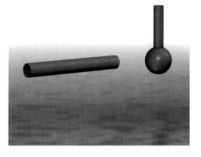

1. First, create a simple cylinder that runs horizontally, like the one shown here. The cylinder will be the hips.

2. Next, create a sphere, and then create a cylinder about half as long as the first, but running vertically.

3. Using a Boolean operation, fuse the sphere to the vertical cylinder. This ball and stick combination will become the basic segment, or joint, used to build the skeleton. Build the spine first.

4. Adjust the pivot point of this segment so that it matches the center of the sphere.

5. Make two copies of this segment and place all three of these end to end as shown to create the spine.

6. Make another horizontal cylinder and place it horizontally across the top of the spine to create the shoulders. Shoulders need to be wider than the hips so that the arms will hang straight.

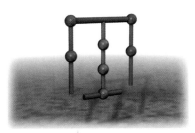

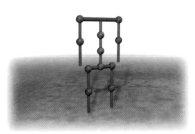

7. Hang two more ball-and-stick joints off each side of the shoulders to make arms. If you want, you can copy one of the segments from the spine and rotate it 180 degrees. You need to stretch both of these segments equally so that the wrists align with the hips.

8. Copy the arm segments to the hips to make the legs.

9. Copy a spine segment up to the shoulders to make a neck.

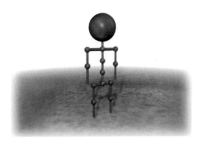

10. Add a simple sphere for the head.

11. The feet can be modeled out of flattened spheres. The hands can be spheres as well.

Now you have a huge number of bones that are completely unconnected. Set these up in a hierarchy so the character moves as one. The hips parent the thighs and the base of the spine. Use the previous figure of a hierarchy for reference.

On the CD

A copy of this character's model is on the CD. It is called TINKRBOY.3DS or TINKER-BOY.DXF.

If you've created a good hierarchy, moving the hips should move the rest of the body. If the pivots are set properly, rotating the thigh should move the shin and foot. Move your character around the screen and test the rotations on all the joints. Don't worry about animating the character, just make sure it can be moved properly. Animation will be covered starting with Chapter 5. You should save this body for use then.

Forward Kinematics

The hierarchy that you just set up for your simple ball-and-stick character can be manipulated by what's known as *forward kinematics*. Forward kinematics manipulates your character from the top of the hierarchy on down. If you move the pelvis, the whole body moves; if you rotate the elbow, the wrist moves. Most software packages enable this type of manipulation.

When you use forward kinematics, you soon realize that rotating your character's joints is the only way to move his body parts around. If you want to place the character's hand on a coffee cup, for example, you first rotate the shoulder, then the elbow, and then the wrist and fingers, working your way from the top of the hierarchy on down. Each rotation brings the hand closer to the cup. You can't simply move the hand to the cup and expect the rest of the arm to follow. The pelvis is the only exception to this rule. Because it is the parent of everything, you can move the pelvis anywhere and the rest of the body follows. If you want a character to walk across a room, for example, you first move the pelvis so the body floats across the room and then go back and rotate the joints of the legs and feet so it looks like the character is walking.

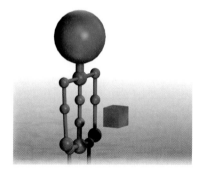

Try placing this character's hand on the block using forward kinematics.

First, you need to rotate the arm at the shoulder...

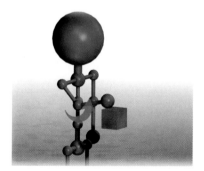

...and then at the elbow. When manipulating a character using forward kinematics, you work from the top of the hierarchy down.

The fact that you can't simply move joints the way you do in real life can make forward kinematics seem counterintuitive. As a remedy you must use Inverse Kinematics, or IK for short.

Inverse Kinematics

Inverse Kinematics is simply another way of manipulating a character. It is the exact opposite of forward kinematics, in that moving the children moves the parents. Inverse Kinematics is simple to use—you place the character's hand on the coffee cup, and the rest of the arm automatically follows. This simple action is more complex than you think, however, because the software must determine exactly how to bend the rest of the arm and body so that everything looks natural.

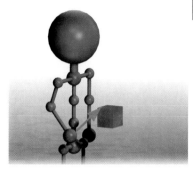

To make the character place his hand on the block using Inverse Kinematics, drag the hand to the block. The computer rotates the rest of the joints for you.

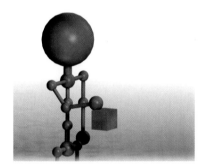
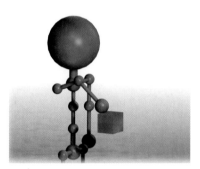
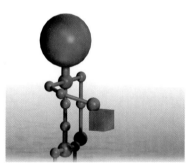

Here's three different ways to rotate the joints so that the hand rests on the block. Only one of these is correct, but the computer doesn't know that. You need to tell the computer exactly how you want your joints to behave.

The computer doesn't know how the joints of the body are supposed to move. If it's just as easy to bend the elbows backward to solve the problem, then that's fine with the computer. Unfortunately, bending elbows backward is not natural, nor is it an acceptable solution. Elbows are a hinged joint that can only bend forward. Without this information, the computer can't position the joints naturally.

You need to tell your software the exact way the joints are constrained, or limited in their motions, usually through an array of dialog boxes provided by your software. You can limit the rotations of the joints to certain axes and angles along those axes. The elbow, for example, only moves along one axis, like a hinge, and moves through an angle of about 150 degrees along its X axis, from the arm fully bent to fully extended. Conversely, the

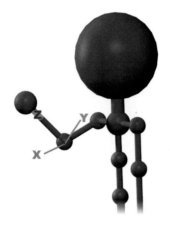

In table 2.1, it is assumed the Z axis is oriented along the bone of the joint. This illustration shows the orientation of the axes for the forearm. In this example, the forearm rotates around the X axis.

shoulder is a ball-and-socket joint, enabling the arm to move in three different directions. Table 2.1 lists the joints of the human body and their rotational limits.

Table 2.1					
Rotational Limits of Human Joints					
Segment	Joint	Type	X	Y	Z
Foot	Ankle	Rotational	65deg	30deg	0
Shin	Knee	Hinge	135deg	0	0
Thigh	Hip	Ball/Socket	120deg	20deg	10deg
Spine	Hip/Spine	Rotational	15deg	10deg	0deg
Shoulder	Spine	Rotational	20deg	20deg	0deg
Bicep	Shoulder	Ball/Socket	180deg	105deg	10deg
Forearm	Elbow	Hinge	150deg	0deg	0deg
Hand	Wrist	Ball/Socket	180deg	30deg	120deg

After you have your limits set up, the joints should solve themselves properly so your character's knees and elbows won't bend backward. Still, the computer tries to move each joint equally to solve the rotations. Moving the right wrist, for example, may spread upward through the shoulders and to the spine, throwing the entire body out of whack. To correct this problem, many software vendors have devised weighting and damping systems to prevent movement in one part of the body from influencing the entire body.

Each of these systems is unique, so check your own software's owner's manual at this point.

Creating Seamless Characters

So far, you have looked at the construction of characters made from individual segments. People, however, are not made of segments; they're covered with a single piece of seamless skin. Your characters will look more realistic and professional if you find a way to eliminate those nasty seams. There are many ways to create seamless characters, and the following sections introduce a few of the most popular methods.

Skinning Between Segments

If you want to create a segmented character without telltale seams, some software packages, such as Animation Master, enable you to create a flexible skin between two segments. The skin automatically bends and flexes with the segments, giving you a smooth, seamless joint. Typically, this software works by generating a surface between each vertex on the ends of the segments. Each segment has to have the same number of vertices at both ends or else the software has trouble determining which surfaces to join. One easy way to ensure an equal number of vertices at both ends is to build your character as a single, solid object and then slice him into segments you can animate, using the skinning routine to stitch his skin back together.

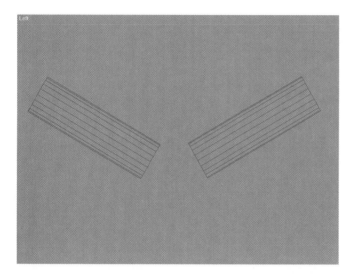

If your software supports it, you can automatically place skin between two segments so that it appears seamless. Here are two cylinders.

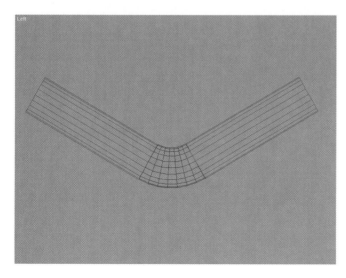

The skinning routine automatically generates a smooth surface (the skin) between the segments.

When it's shaded, the two cylinders and the skin appear as one smooth surface.

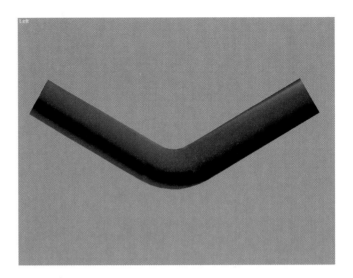

Using Metaballs to Create Seamless Characters

Metaballs are a great way to create a seamless character. In their simplest form, metaballs are spheres that blob together when rendered. Metaballs are a technology that 3D animators use to easily create round, blobby objects. As these objects move closer together, they seem to melt together. The "balls" in metaballs derive their name from simple spheres, which are the building blocks of metaball objects. By assigning each sphere a weight and a sphere of influence, the metaballs modeler fuses many spheres into a single blob. How much the spheres fuse really depends on the weights, influences, and the distances between the spheres.

Consider this simple example. Two spheres of equal size have a sphere of influence surrounding each of the spheres like a shell. Any other sphere coming within range tries to fuse with the balls. The weight of the spheres determines exactly how much fusion actually occurs. In the next figure are two balls of equal size. They'll fuse together at the intersection of their spheres of influence. The amount that they fuse depends on their weights. As weights and the spheres of influence change, you get different effects. A higher sphere of influence makes an object softer, blobbier, and more willing to fuse with another. On the other hand, if one sphere is given more weight than another, it appears more stable and solid.

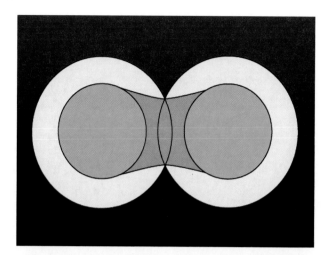

This diagram shows how each metaball (blue) has its own sphere of influence. Where these two spheres of influence cross determines how the two objects fuse.

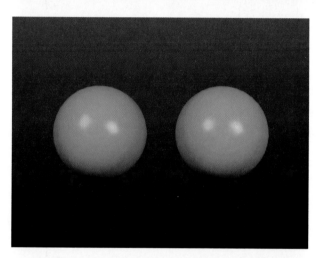

These two shots illustrate how metaballs can affect an ordinary pair of spheres and turn them into a blob. With metaballs turned off, they are discrete spheres.

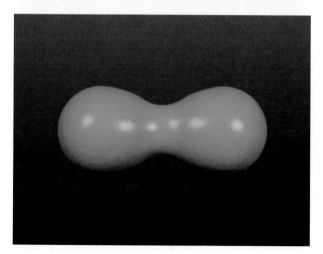

When they become metaballs, they blob together.

If you use a lot of spheres, you can make them fuse together like digital putty and build entire bodies. It's simply a matter of creating a group of spheres that are the shape of a body and adjusting the weights. It's a very good method for creating realistic humans.

A collection of metaballs...

...can be used to create a simple smooth body.

Not all metaballs implementations are restricted to spheres. Packages such as Softimage's Meta Clay and Digimation's Clay Studio for 3D Studio MAX include nonspherical objects. REM-Infografica's MetaReyes plug-in for 3D Studio MAX goes one step further and actually shapes its objects like muscles to give you some stunningly real effects. The technology is changing quickly.

Some metaballs modelers, such as Softimage's Meta Clay can use nonspherical objects, reducing considerably the number of primitives needed to construct a body. This body is made with only 10 ellipsoids.

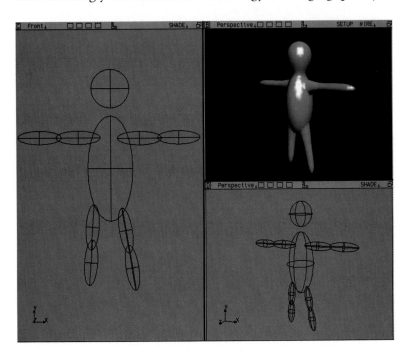

REM-Infografica's MetaReyes plug-in for 3D Studio MAX enables you to create MetaMuscles, or meta-balls shaped like muscles.

Exercise #2: Building a Body from Metaballs

This exercise demonstrates a simple way of building a character from metaballs. It uses only spheres so that it will be compatible with all metaballs implementations.

1. First, make a sphere.

2. Copy this sphere six to ten times. Resize and reposition the spheres so that you have a torso shaped a bit like a pear.

continues

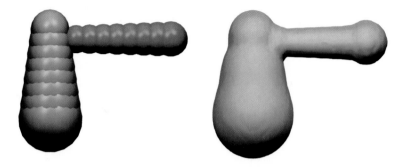

3. To make a simple arm, create a line of smaller spheres that go horizontally out from the body.

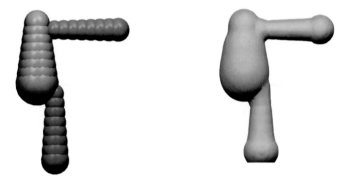

4. Create a line of spheres down from the body to make a leg.

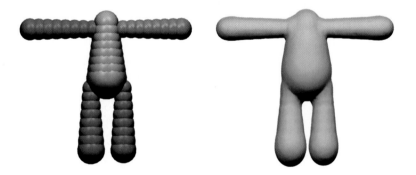

5. Duplicate the arm and leg on the other side.

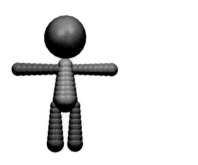

If you want, you can hang on to this model. If your metaballs modeler also supports animation, keep reading for some advice on how to manipulate your creation.

6. If you want, you can add a sphere for the head. (Head construction is covered in detail in Chapter 4, "Modeling Heads for Animation.")

Animating a Metaballs-Based Character

Many metaballs implementations also enable you to animate the balls directly. By manipulating the balls themselves, you can change the shape of your character and still keep him completely smooth. You may run into a problem with joints that get close together. The fingers are a good example. The blobbiness of the metaballs may tend to web your character's fingers into a solid blob. There are ways to prevent this from happening—most metaballs modelers enable you to group the balls. Each finger in the hand becomes a separate group. The grouping allows only fingers to blob together within the finger joint, not across joints to other fingers. Much of this is covered in the next chapter, when we build a hand with metaballs.

If you have a metaballs package that enables animation, you can simply animate the balls themselves.

By moving the balls of the arm down, the metaballs surface moves, but remains smooth.

If you have a large number of metaballs in your model, animating them individually can prove tedious, to say the least. In this case, you might want to create a skeleton to control the metaballs in groups. Simply create some cylinders that rest inside the metaballs structure and attach the balls to the cylinders using a hierarchy. You can then use the cylinders as a skeleton with which to manipulate the metaballs. Moving one cylinder moves all the metaballs associated with it. The skeleton itself can be manipulated with forward or inverse kinematics, similar to the segmented characters you constructed earlier.

The red cylinders that can be used to manipulate the spheres hidden underneath the skin of this metaballs character act as a skeleton.

By moving the skeleton, you move the spheres that make up the character's skin.

Using Polygons to Create Seamless Characters

Polygons can make a seamless character quite easily. The modeling methods are straightforward, and you can make a character out of primitives such as spheres and cylinders and use Boolean operations, bends, tapers, lattices, or other tools you have at your disposal. As you've seen previously, metaballs make a good modeling tool. The metaballs character you just made can be frozen into a solid polygonal mesh, on which you could then use tools such as bones (discussed later in the chapter) to deform the solid mesh.

The big issue with polygonal bodies, and bodies in general, is that they need to have the detail in the right places so that they deform and bend without crimping. Because polygonal models already require far more detail than an equivalent spline model, you should try to control the number of vertices in your model. Dish out the detail where it is needed—good advice no matter how you model.

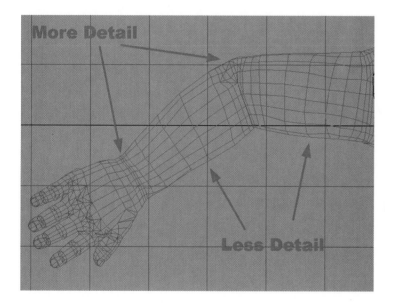

This arm has more detail at the wrist and elbow, where it bends and flexes the most. More detail in these critical areas helps avoid crimping when the mesh is deformed by a skeleton.

Areas around the elbow, shoulder, knee, hip, and wrist are typically problem areas, so it is best to model your character so that these spots have the greatest amount of flexibility from the start. To get this flexibility, build your character with its limbs as far apart as possible, with the arms and legs spread-eagle. If your character has fingers, you can model them far apart as well. As we'll see a bit later, bones can then be placed in the skeleton easily, and they will not affect unwanted areas of the body.

When using bones, build your characters with the palms down and the arms outstretched.

Exercise #3: Modeling a Simple Character from Polygons

In this exercise, you construct a simple cartoonish character from polygons. Although this little character is simple, its construction demonstrates a number of tools you can use to help the modeling process along. It also shows you how to make a character that can be animated using bones.

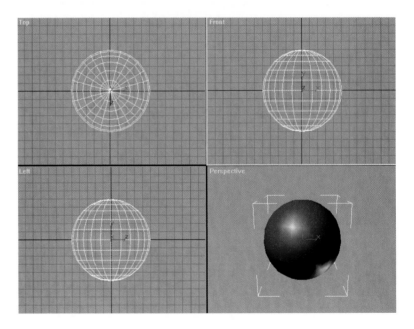

A simple character you can build from polygons.

1. Start with a sphere, which will become the torso.

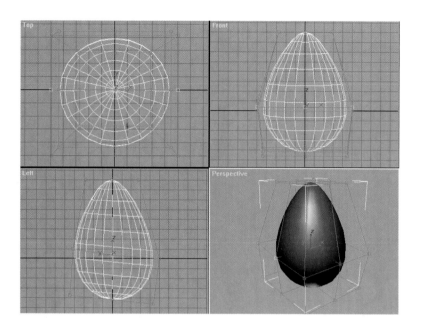

2. Reshape the sphere to make it egg-shaped. I used a lattice deformation tool to do this, but you can use whatever tools are at your disposal. A taper tool also works, or you can manually select and scale the sphere's vertices.

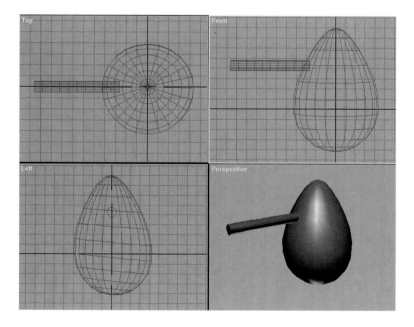

3. Next, create a cylinder, which will become an arm. Make sure that this cylinder has at least a dozen segments lengthwise so that you can add detail to the joints.

continues

Exercise #3: continued

4. Select the vertices near the end of the cylinder (the end near the torso) and resize them so that the cylinder's end flares out like a funnel.

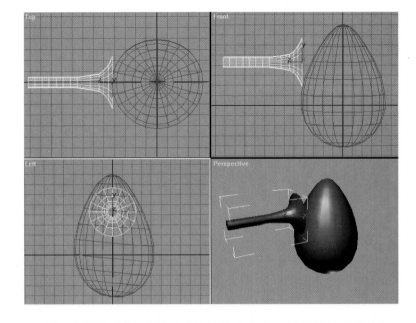

5. Continue to manipulate the funnel shape, fitting it to the egg-shaped body. From the front, you can see how the four cross sections near the shoulder go from vertical to slightly slanted at the shoulder. This extra detail gives you a smoother bend in the shoulder.

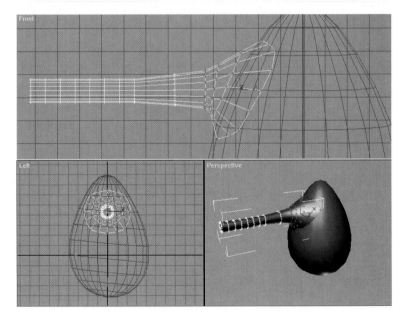

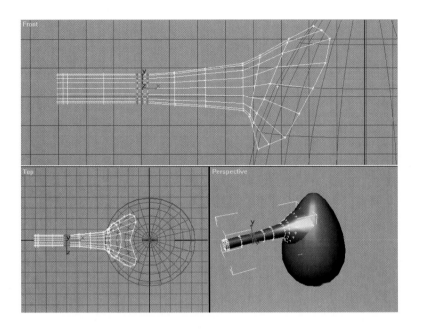

6. Select some more cross sections and slide them together near the elbow for extra detail on that joint.

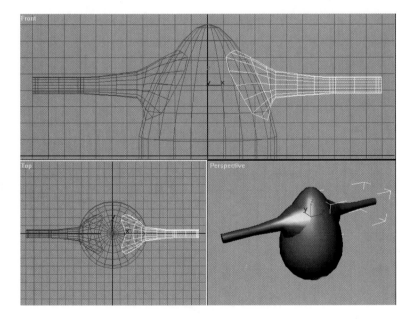

7. Copy this arm, rotate it, and position it on the other side of the body.

continues

Exercise #3: continued

8. Making a leg is almost the same process as making an arm. Create a cylinder with about a dozen subdivisions.

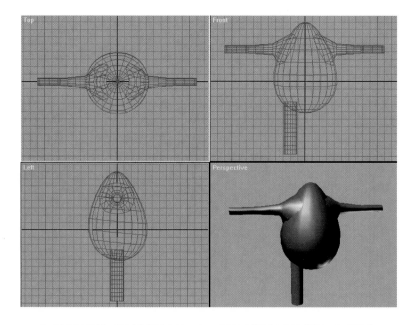

9. Then make a funnel along the top part and fit it to the body to form a hip. Add detail at the knee (as you did earlier, at the elbow). Duplicate and rotate this shape to make the other leg.

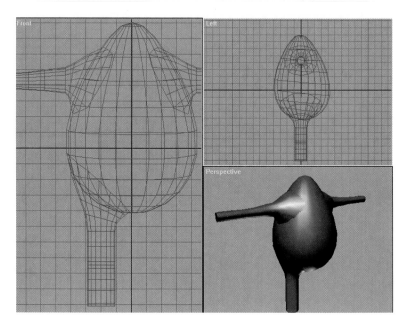

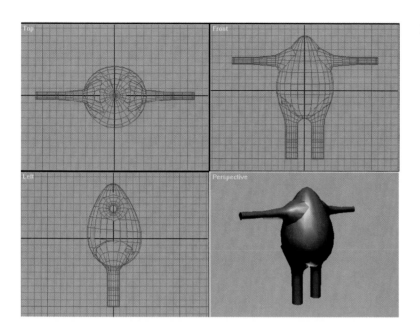

10. Using a Boolean union, weld the arms and legs to the body so that it is one solid object.

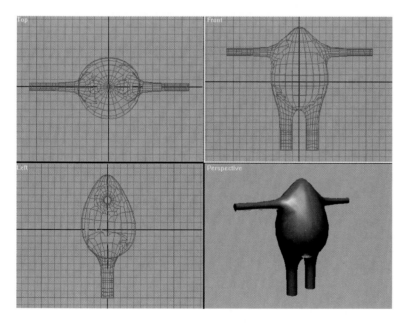

11. You might want to apply a rounding or smoothing operation to this figure to make it look even smoother. Digimation's Blend, LightWave's Metaform, Softimage's Rounding, and 3D Studio MAX's Relax are all tools that can do this.

continues

Exercise #3: continued

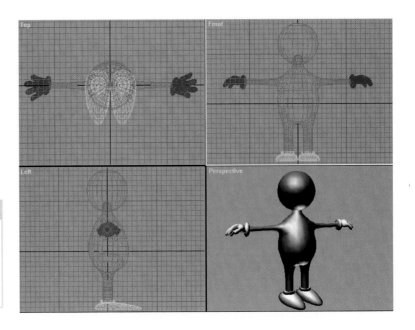

  On the CD

On the CD is a copy of this model, along with his head, hands, and shoes. His name is JAMABOY.DXF or JAM-ABOY.3DS.

12. You can then add a head, hands, and feet, which can be connected as segments, or you can use a Boolean operation to make them a seamless part of the mesh. The next two chapters tell you how to build heads and hands. Save this body so you can add a head and hands to it. The next exercise shows you a quick way to create simple shoes for a character like this one.

Exercise #4: Making Cartoon Shoes

This exercise shows you an easy way to make simple shoes to put on your character's feet. This method works for just about any modeler and applies equally to both spline and polygonal modelers.

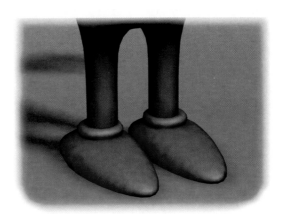

Cartoon shoes are a snap to make.

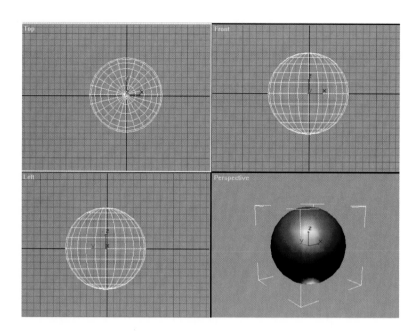

1. Start with a sphere.

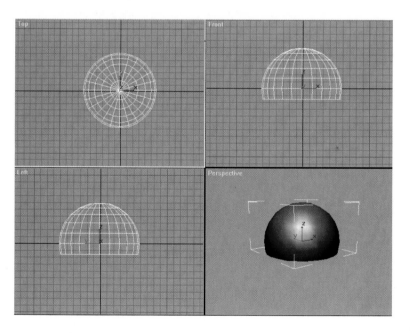

2. Cut off the bottom of the sphere, a little below the halfway point.

Exercise #4: continued

3. Squash the sphere down vertically and along the length of the foot.

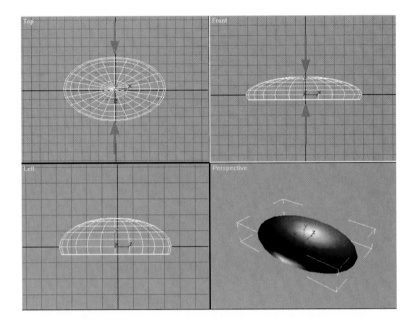

4. Pull the vertices along the top half of the shoe back so that the shoe angles down slightly from the ankle to the toe.

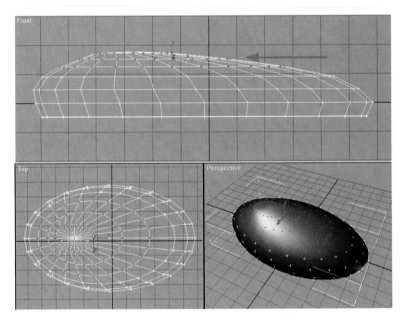

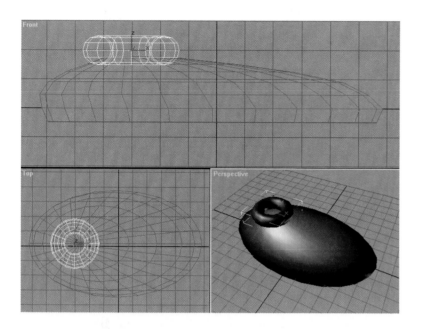

5. If you want, you can add a torus where the leg hits the shoe. Not only does the torus hide the seam where the leg fits in the shoe, it also gives the shoe that classic 1930s cartoon look.

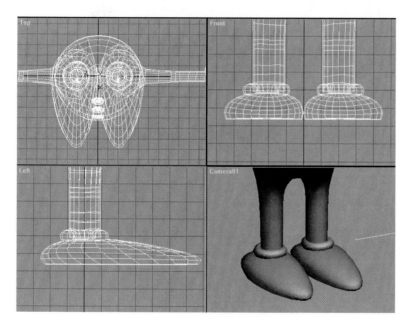

6. Finally, place the shoe on the end of your character's leg and resize it to fit. Shoes can be welded in place by using a Boolean union operation, or a you can keep them segmented and connect them by using a hierarchy or a constraint.

Creating Seamless Characters from Splines

Splines are probably the best way to create digital flesh. Splines are curves, so they're more organic. They can define a large area with fewer vertices than polygons, so spline models animate more easily. Splines also stay smooth, so you can move a spline body through a wide range of motion without much fear of unwanted cracks or creases.

Topologies for Building Spline-Based Characters

Because many packages limit you to patches that are flat, cylindrical, or spherical, you can run into topology problems when creating a four-limbed character. Most of the ways to get around this limitation involve segmenting the character in a few places and then stitching it back together with any number of seam-hiding tricks. As you've seen previously, skinning between segmented joints is one trick that many packages use, but you can take this a step further. Instead of creating an arm out of two separate segments, you can make the arm a single object that connects at the shoulder. That way, you have fewer seams to worry about. Here are a few of the more popular topologies you can use when building a character out of spline patches.

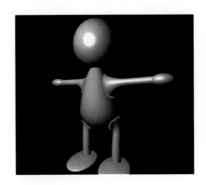

Separate Arms and Legs

This method has five separate objects. The arms are seamed at the shoulders, and the legs at the hips. Typically, you should keep the seams as far away from the main area of motion as you can. For the arms, you should place the seam along the chest, over the shoulders, and down the back. The legs should connect well into the hip and crotch area.

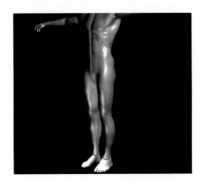

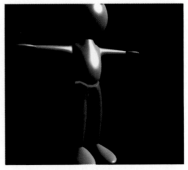

Separate Upper and Lower Body

This method keeps the upper body and the lower body separate, with a single seam at the waist. This seam can be hidden quite easily with a belt, shirt, or other piece of clothing. One of the big advantages of this topology is that it makes it very easy to bend over the character at the waist; the seam-hiding belt or shirt simply moves with the bend.

Seam Up the Middle

You can also model your character in two halves, with the seam running along the inside of the leg, joining at the crotch and continuing up the middle of the torso to the neck. The seam hides quite easily because the inside of the leg is not usually visible. The torso is also a good place for a seam because it doesn't flex and bend nearly as much as the shoulders and hips, thus minimizing the possibility of a seam popping open.

Exercise #5: Building a Simple Character from Splines

This simple character can be created in nearly any spline-based modeler, using spheres as its basic shapes.

In this exercise you create a flexible character with a single seam at the waist. The character is constructed from two simple spheres and can be made in almost any spline modeling package. He can be animated quite easily using skeletal deformations, as described later in this chapter.

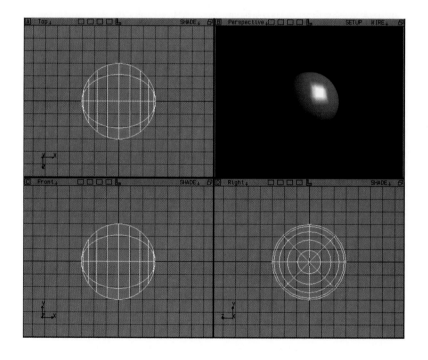

1. Model the legs first. Create a sphere and then orient the sphere so that the poles lie along the horizontal axis.

continues

2. Scale the sphere along the horizontal axis so that it is shaped like a foot-long hot dog.

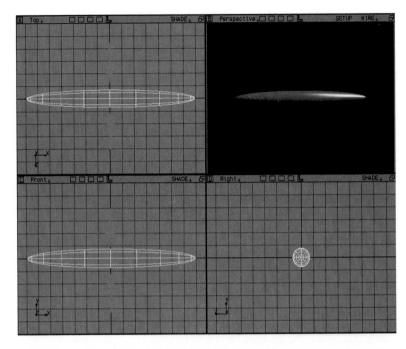

3. Bend the ends of the shape down, making a horseshoe shape. Be sure to keep detail in the hip and crotch area.

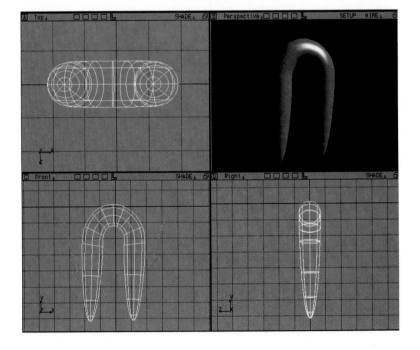

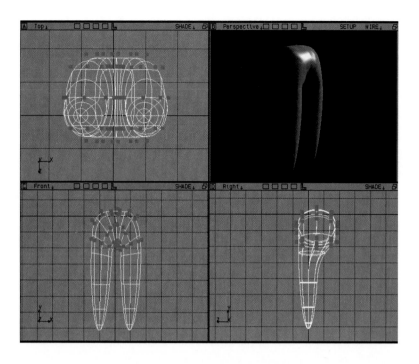

4. Adjust the vertices around the hips and crotch, lowering the crotch area a bit and adding some volume to the rear end.

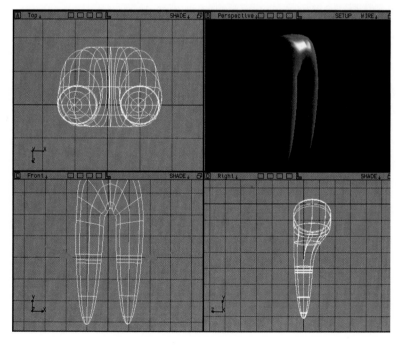

5. These are the legs, so add a bit of detail at the knees so that they will bend properly.

continues

6. Put the legs aside for a moment while you create the upper body. Create another sphere aligned along the horizontal axis.

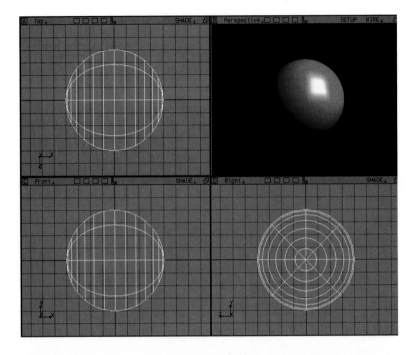

7. Push the poles of the sphere up. These vertices will become the arms.

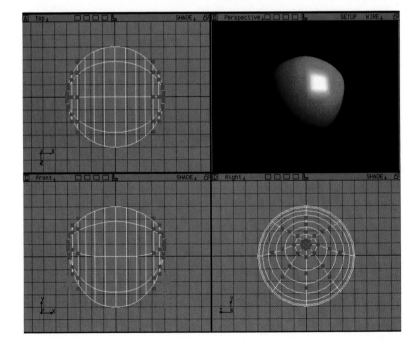

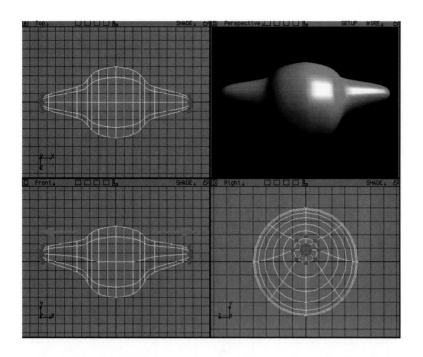

8. Select the vertices at the poles and pull them horizontally away from the body to create the arms.

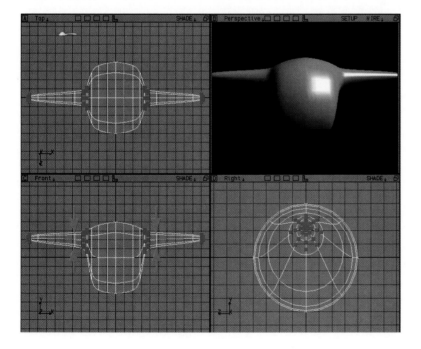

9. Reshape the arms to give them a cylindrical outline and push them up a bit more to help define the shoulders.

continues

10. As with the legs, be sure to add extra detail where the arms flex—at the shoulders and the elbows.

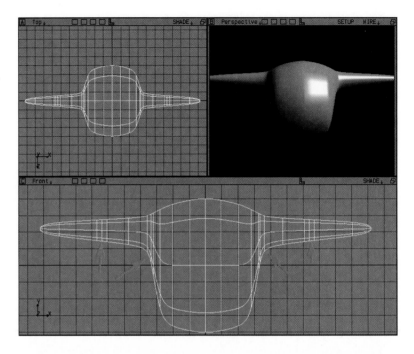

11. If you want, you can reshape the upper body a bit to give the character a big chest or a big belly. You can also pull the vertices at the top of the torso up to create a neck stub.

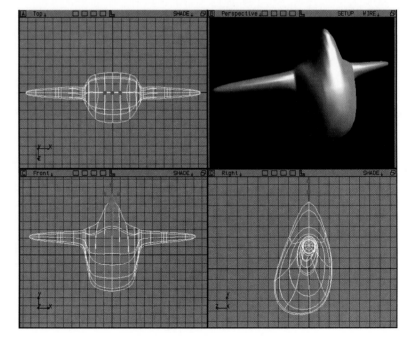

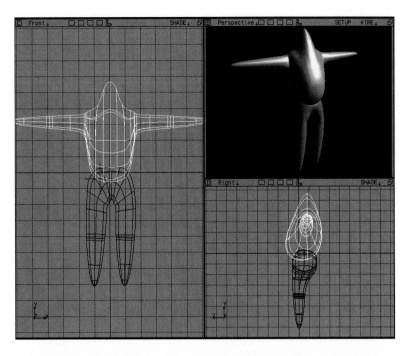

12. Add the legs to the body. Position the legs so they intersect the torso at the waist. This character's belly hides the seam, but if your character is more svelte, you can use a belt or some other article of clothing to help hide the seam.

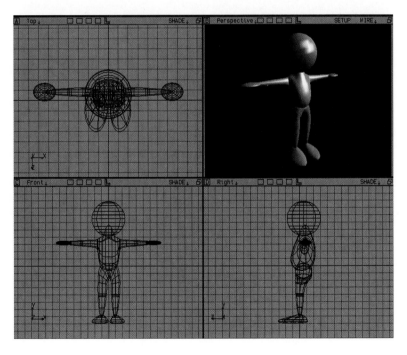

13. Add shoes, hands, and a head, which can be attached using a hierarchy or constraints. If you want, hang on to this model for use later.

Advanced Seaming Techniques for Spline Modelers

If you want to create a completely smooth character by using a NURBS or other spline modeler, you need to use some more advanced techniques found in packages such as Softimage and Alias.

Surface Deformations

One way to lock an arm or a leg to your character is to use a surface deformation. First, create a circular patch out of a flattened sphere. You can then use a surface deformation and deform this patch to your character's body, skinning the limb to the patch. Softimage's Zip Surfaces function does this task very well.

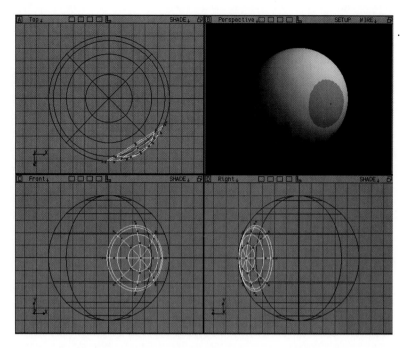

A circular patch deformed to a sphere. The patch conforms perfectly to the surface of the sphere.

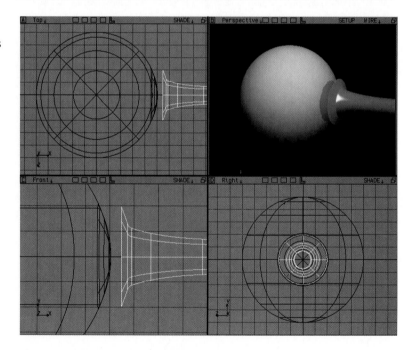

Place a cylinder directly above the patch...

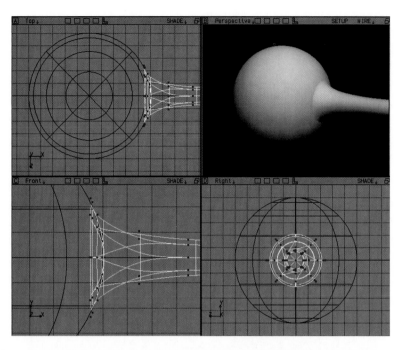

...and using Softimage's Zip surfaces command, skin the two together seamlessly. This sphere could have easily been a torso and the cylinder an arm or a leg.

Blends, NURBS Trims, and Projected NURBS

Blends, NURBS Trims, and projected NURBS are other tools for locking down curves to surfaces. A Blend automatically connects and blends two spline surfaces. Projected NURBS places a curve on a NURBS surface, while NURBS Trims projects a curve and also cuts a hole in the surface. Using both NURBS Trims and projected NURBS, it is possible to extract the curve and use it as a skin for creating a seamless surface between two objects.

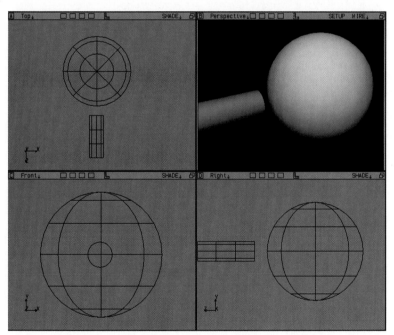

The same example as before, but this time with projected NURBS.

64

First, project a curve on the sphere (shown in red). After the curve is projected on the surface, it remains locked to the sphere.

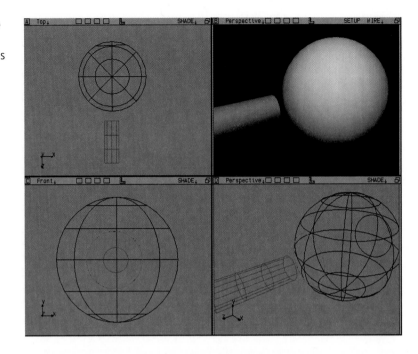

Next, extract the curve and copy it a few times (shown in orange).

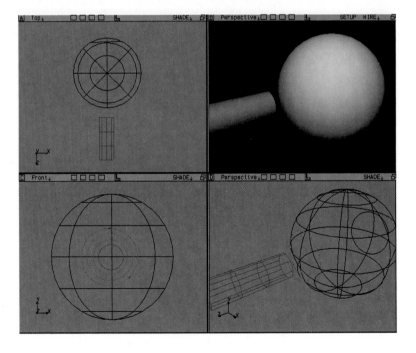

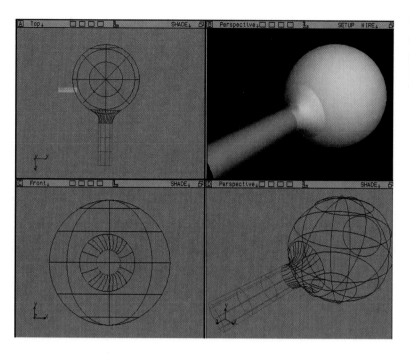

Then use these curves as a bridge to generate a skin between the sphere and the cylinder. Again, you have a seamless bridge between the two.

These techniques can be used to seamlessly connect arms and legs to bodies as well. It's simply a matter of seaming the limbs to the bodies using whatever tool suits your fancy.

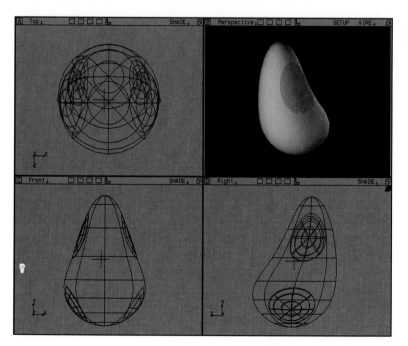

A primitive torso with a circular patch deformed to its surface.

Simply place some cylinders above the patches and skin them all together.

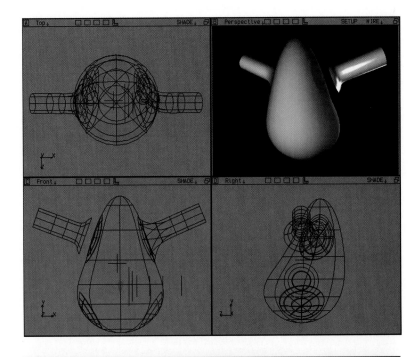

You can do the same with projected NURBS for the legs. You can then manipulate the seamlessly attached cylinders into arms and legs.

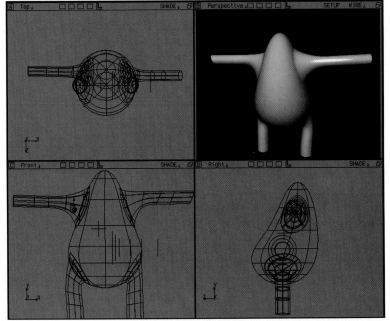

When creating seams using a spline modeler, you should still try to keep the seams away from the flexible areas of the joint itself. If your seams are where the character bends and flexes the most, you're asking for trouble. Seams are best placed away from areas of activity, so that they don't pop up. Anchor a hand in the middle of a forearm rather than the wrist; attach the arm along the chest and back rather than at the shoulder.

Other Techniques for Hiding Seams

Finally, consider using some of these devious little tricks to hide seams.

- **Wrinkles, bumps, and other complexion problems.** If your character is old and wrinkled, an elephant, a burn victim, or a kid with acne problems, you can hide seams with bumps, wrinkles, scars, or other types of skin blemishes. Usually, you use a simple displacement map to create the blemishes. The seams appear to be wrinkles or bumps themselves and effectively disappear.

- **Clothing.** A well-placed wristwatch, belt, shoulder pad, or other article of clothing can help hide a seam. All good characters need to accessorize!

- **Hair.** The hair on a furry creature effectively hides any seam, no matter how huge. Of course, hair can be difficult to create if your software doesn't support it.

- **Fading Textures.** A very easy way to hide a seam is to fade the texture of one object so it is transparent where it meets the other; the seam becomes transparent as well.

Creating Skeletal Deformations

You now have several characters without seams. Your characters, however, will look like rigid statues unless you find a way to deform the characters' mesh. In real life, skin is very flexible, and the actions of muscles and bones beneath the skin are all that are needed to bend and flex the skin. In the digital world, a number of tools do exactly the same thing. They are known as skeletal deformation tools, or simply *bones*.

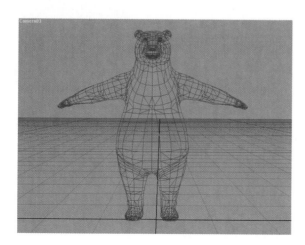

This bear is formed from a solid polygonal mesh.

As such, he has no seams. Because he's a solid object, however, you don't have segments to animate. You must deform the mesh directly.

A skeleton of bones—represented by these boxes—helps to deform the mesh. Each box deforms the vertices closest to it.

If you move the bones, the mesh follows.

And by hiding the bones before rendering, the mesh looks smooth. No seams!

All skeletal deformation packages perform the same basic task— deform the vertices in a solid mesh so that it moves and flexes like skin. Bones work for any type of geometry—polygons or splines. Some packages use boxes or other solid geometry as bones, others use a custom object, typically tetrahedral in shape, that performs the same function. If your package uses boxes as bones, such as Kinetix's Biped or Digimation's Bones Pro, you must remember that the bones are objects that will show up at rendering time. You'll have to hide these objects or make them transparent before rendering.

Bones don't have to be boxes. Many packages, such as Softimage, use this standard tetrahedral shape to represent a bone. No matter what the shape, all bones are designed to deform your meshes smoothly.

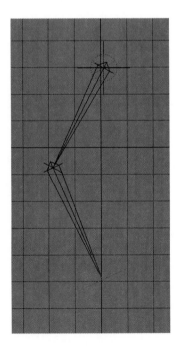

Bones, too, can be set up in hierarchies, just like with a segmented character. You simply animate the bones like segments, and the mesh follows. After they're set up in a hierarchy, the bones look much like the bones in a human skeleton. If you want to use IK on the bones, you can set up joint constraints as with a segmented character. You can also design generic skeletons that can be resized and fitted to almost any character.

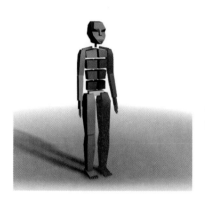

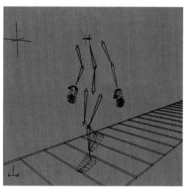

Kinetix's Biped plug-in for 3D Studio MAX creates its own generic skeletons made of boxlike objects. You can then apply this skeleton to any two-legged character's mesh.

You can also make your own skeletons. When viewed without the mesh, they look similar to a real skeleton, with leg bones, arm bones, and a spinal column.

Getting Bones to Behave

While bones make deforming a character look easy, getting your mesh to deform smoothly can sometimes be a real problem. Many times, your joints crimp, bulge, tear, or flatten at the wrong places, making your character look worse than when you started. You can use several techniques, however, to help your bones behave.

- **Build Your Character Properly.** First and foremost, the best way to avoid problems is to build your character correctly in the first place. Build your characters with arms outstretched and with extra detail at the bends.

- **Know Your Influences.** Most packages have a way of defining exactly how much a bone influences the mesh. Known as an influence or an envelope, it is typically defined by a pill-shaped volume that surrounds the bone. Only vertices that fall within this volume are affected by the bone. A finger bone has a much smaller influence than a thigh bone, for instance. Make sure the bones influence only the area directly surrounding the joint.

■ **Get Down to the Vertex.** Many packages take the process one step further by enabling you to assign specific vertices to specific bones, which is great when fields of influence overlap slightly and a vertex gets caught in the middle. It gives you one more tool in your arsenal for tweaking the way the skeleton deforms your character.

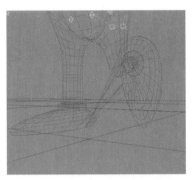

In this situation you might need to get down to the vertex level when setting up your bones. The bone in the right shoe is accidentally affecting three vertices in the left shoe. These vertices stick to the right shoe and cause the mesh to tear when the left foot is moved.

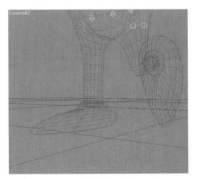

Simply by reassigning the three offending vertices to the bones in the left foot, the problem is solved.

Exercise #6: Boning a Body

In this exercise you create a skeleton for a two-legged character's body, concentrating on only the arms, legs, and body. The hands and the head can also be manipulated using bones, but that is covered in the next two chapters. For this exercise, you need a software package that supports bones for skeletal deformations. It doesn't matter if your bones are shaped like tetrahedrons or boxes; the principles apply equally.

A simple character, with bones.

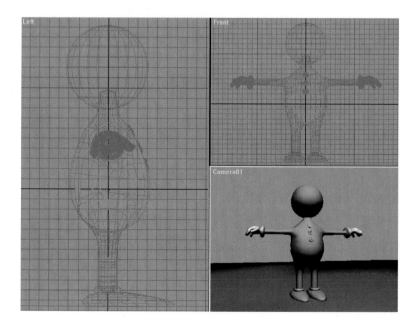

1. Load your favorite two-legged character. It can be made of splines, or polygons. If you want, you can use one of the models on the CD, or you can use a model that you've built yourself.

continues

2. Start with one of the legs. Create a thigh bone and a shin bone. Link them together hierarchically so that the thigh bone parents the shin bone. (Some packages, such as Softimage, do this automatically.) If you want, you can make the knee slightly bent because it helps guide some Inverse Kinematics systems in bending the leg properly.

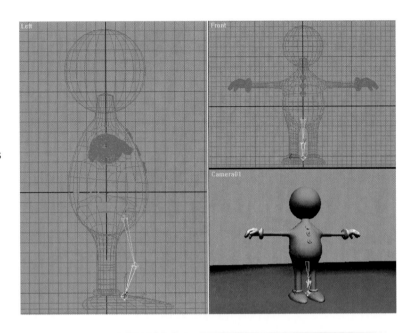

3. Align these two bones so that they lie entirely within the leg and so that the knee joint is centered in the knee. If you modeled your character properly, there should be some extra detail in the knee area to help guide you. Align the top of the thigh bone at the hip, and the bottom of the shin bone at the ankle.

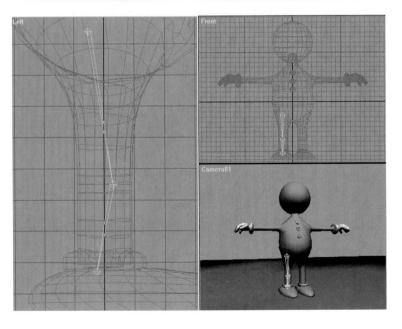

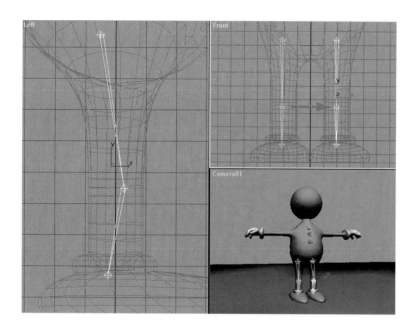

4. Duplicate the first two bones for the other leg. Center and align these bones as well.

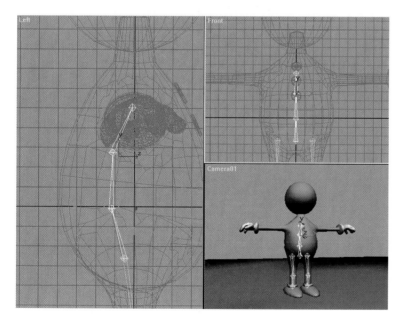

5. Now create a spine, simply a chain of three or four bones that runs from the hips to the collarbone. The parent of this chain needs to be at the bottom, near the hips.

continues

digital character animation

6. Next, create two arm bones. Center the bones along the length of the arm and center the elbow joint. Again, if the character is modeled correctly, there should be some extra detail in the elbow area to help guide you. You can bend the bones at the elbow slightly to help your Inverse Kinematics system, if you want. Copy these two bones and place them in the other arm.

7. Add a heel bone and a toe bone to the foot. If your character is barefoot, you may want to model individual bones for each of the toes. Toes are similar to fingers, so use the guidelines for boning a hand set forth in the next chapter. Link the heel bone to the bottom of the shin bone, at the ankle. Repeat these steps for the other foot.

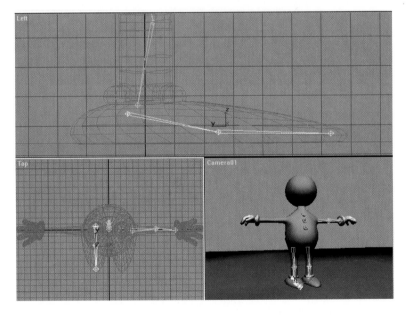

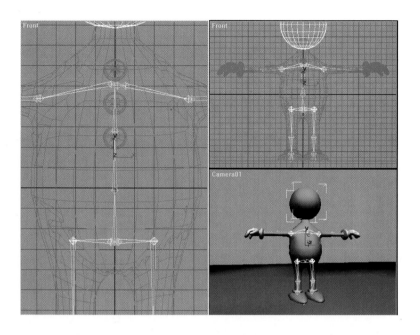

8. Create two bones for the hips and two for the shoulders. The shoulders should link the arms to the top of the spine, and the hips should link the legs to the base of the spine. If you've built your character properly and aligned your bones, half your work is done. Assign the skeleton to the mesh.

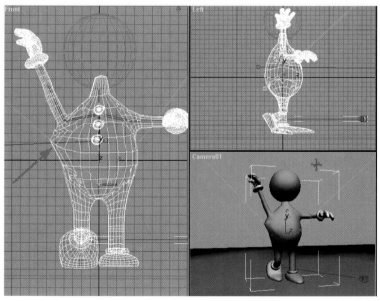

9. After the skeleton is assigned, test your character over a wide range of motions. Bend his legs and arms, raise his hands above his head, bend him at the waist, and flex the feet. You will probably notice stray vertices or bulging and crimping. A common situation is when the biceps affect the area under the arm, causing a huge bulge, which can be fixed.

continues

10. This is more like it. The problem was fixed by reducing the influence of the arm and reassigning some errant vertices to the spine. You should adjust the influences of your bones first and then resort to vertex reassignment last. Influences should have a bit of overlap on neighboring joints. Both the thigh and the shin should influence the knee vertices, for example.

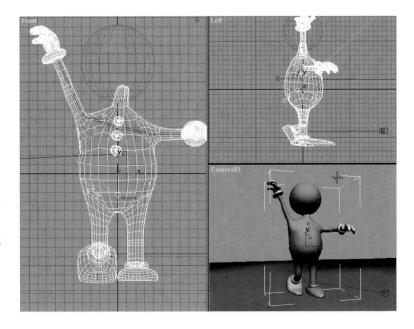

Getting your mesh to deform properly over a wide range of motion may give you some headaches, but if you're diligent and test every conceivable body position, you should have a rock-solid character. Hopefully, you'll only have to set up the skeleton once. After it's set up, however, you'll have a character that you can use again and again. Even if it takes a day or two to set up the skeleton properly, it's worth it, because the time you spend tweaking the skeleton pales in comparison to the time you'll spend animating your character. Also, having to go back and fix things is never pleasant, so test thoroughly.

Using Bones to Create Bulging Muscles

Some of the more advanced skeletal deformation systems enable you to make your character's muscles flex and bulge as if they were on steroids. While this gimmick is great for animators working on the latest superhero project, it also is great for anyone working with characters. The same tools used to create flexing and bulging muscles also can accurately control unwanted bulges and crimps in your character's arms. Your characters remain the same shape over a wide range of motion without unsightly flattening of the joints. Packages in this category include Alias/Wavefront's Kinemation and 3D Studio MAX's Physique.

An arm with lots of muscles.

When the arm bends, the biceps
bulge like a real muscle.

How does this work? In nature, the arm bends at the elbow
because the biceps are pulling it. The angle of the joint determines exactly how much the biceps are pulling. If the arm is flat,
the bicep is flat. If the arm is bent, the bicep expands. In the
computer, the angle of the joint determines the amount of bulge,
simulating nature very well. The way you tie the angle of the
joint to the amount of bulge does depend on the individual
package.

One good example is Kinetix's Physique for 3D Studio. It enables
you to animate the cross sections of your character's joints. In the
bicep example, the cross sections of the bicep grow and shrink as
the arm changes angle, causing the mesh of the bicep itself to
grow and shrink. Cross sections can also be applied to areas of the
body such as the hand to get realistic crimping of the finger
joints.

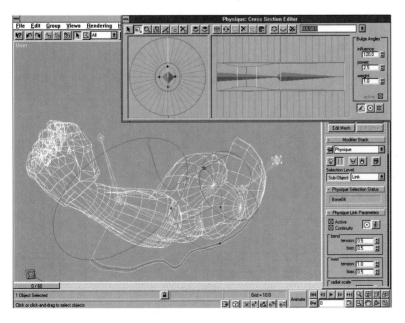

In Kinetix's Physique for 3D
Studio MAX, the biceps are
broken up into cross sections.
One of these is shown in red.
The Cross Section Editor
enables you to animate the
outline of the biceps as they
change angles.

78

When the arm bends, the cross sections animate, causing the biceps to flex. Notice how the profile of the arm in the Cross Section Editor has changed to a bulge.

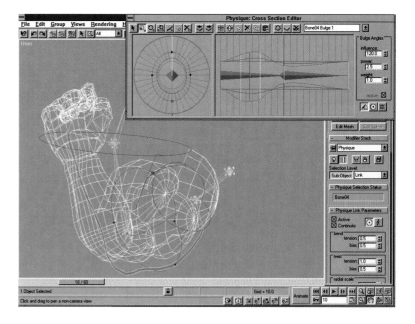

If you don't have sophisticated software such as this, you're not out of luck. With a bit of ingenuity, you can get almost any bones package to flex muscles. The arm is a good example. Simply add a second bone in the biceps where the muscle would bulge. When the arm flexes, move the second bone up, so that it pulls the vertices of the biceps into a nice, muscular bulge.

Another way to get this same effect is to simply add a bone specifically to bulge the muscle.

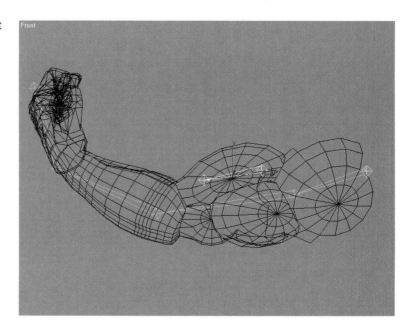

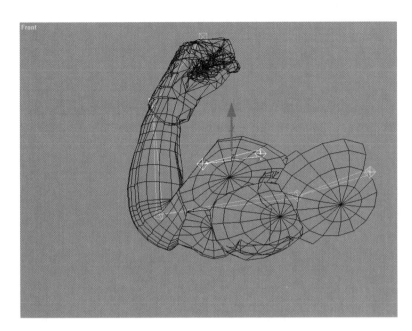

When the arm bends, the muscle bone moves up, dragging the biceps into a nice bulge.

Some packages, such as Softimage's Expressions feature, enable you to apply mathematical formulas to objects so that they can move procedurally. In the case of Softimage's Expressions feature, you use the sine of the elbow's angle to derive a height for the muscle bone. Now, I don't want to end this chapter with a mathematical formula, so you can also use your trained artist's eye and animate the muscle bones manually.

CHAPTER 3

Modeling Hands for Animation

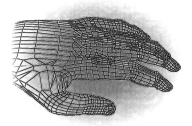

Next to faces, hands can be one of the more expressive parts of the human body. If you've ever watched anyone who gestures a lot, you know that hands can be a very important part of communication. In addition to helping with communication, hands also give humans the facility to manipulate and build things.

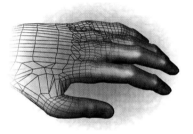

When animating, hands can be particularly tricky. Like the person who's thrust upon a stage without preparation, many animators don't know what to do with their hands—or, at least, the hands of their characters.

The hand is a very complex structure, with dozens of bones, muscles, and tendons all covered by pliable skin. Modeling the hand is a challenging task, and preparing it for animation can prove frustrating as well. Like many complex tasks, however, modeling a hand can be broken down into simple steps that make the job easier.

Examining the Hand's Structure

Although hands are complex structures, they can be thought of as a collection of simple shapes. When you look at your own hand, you see that the palm is basically a rectangular box, with the fingers as cylinders attached along the top edge. The thumb is a stubbier cylinder attached at about a 45-degree angle in the bottom corner. Depending on your character, you may need to create anything from long, skinny hands to short, stubby hands. Whatever the proportions, the basic shapes are essentially the same.

The palm is basically rectangular, and the fingers are basically cylindrical.

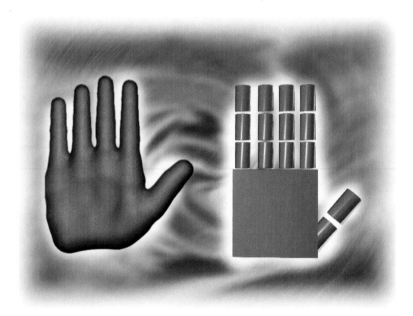

These basic shapes can be hierarchically linked, giving you a stylized but serviceable segmented hand. If you want a different look, expand and enhance these basic shapes with other, more sophisticated modeling tools. You can use almost any technology at your disposal. Polygons and metaballs can make good hands. A good spline modeler with skinning capabilities does a good job, as well.

Another issue is the number of fingers to use. For some unexplained reason, most cartoon characters have only three fingers. Stylistically, a three-fingered hand gives you a more cartoony look, and it's also one less finger to worry about in animation. But even if your character has four, five, or 20 fingers, the same principles apply.

You can animate hands in a number of ways. If you build your hand out of segments, they can be joined in a hierarchy and manipulated directly. Hands built from metaballs can also be joined in the same manner and manipulated directly. Solid mesh or spline-based hands are usually best animated with bones.

When building a hand to be animated with bones, it's always best to construct the hand with the fingers fully extended and as far apart as possible, the same as when building bodies. Keeping the fingers as far apart as possible prevents problems with the bones affecting vertices in the wrong fingers and also will give your hand more flexibility when it deforms.

Flexibility of the Hand and Fingers

However you animate your character's hands, you should make sure that the hand is flexible enough to move like a real hand does. Part of this flexibility comes from the construction of the hand and part from how it's manipulated. A hand manipulated with bones will probably be more flexible than one made of hard segments because the skin on the hand changes shape constantly as the hand flexes. Flex your hand and observe how it changes shape as it moves. Here are a few pointers to help you understand the hand and how it moves.

The Fingers

If you look at your own hand, the motion of the fingers is pretty obvious. Compare your own hand to the following illustrations.

They angle out a bit when the hand spreads.

They can also curl toward the palm.

The skin creases and folds as the fingers bend (arrow).

That last effect (the folding and creasing of the skin) is a tough one. One way to mimic it digitally is with a bones system that enables you to bulge and crimp the mesh according to the angle of the joint. Softimage, Alias/Wavefront's Kinemation, and Kinetix's Physique are a few that support this type of deformation.

The Thumb

The thumb is a bit more complex than the other fingers. Its three joints give it a much higher degree of motion than the three joints of a finger. Again, look at your own thumb and notice how it compares to the following illustrations.

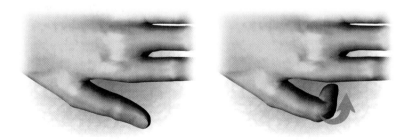

The top joint of the thumb bends toward the palm.

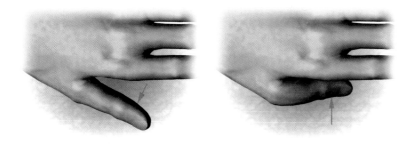

The second joint pulls the entire thumb toward and away from the palm.

There is actually a third joint in the thumb, forming the base of the palm, hidden inside the skin. This joint enables the thumb to move below the plane of the hand.

This flexibility enables the thumb to reach over and touch all of the fingers. This one bone is what gives humans the "opposable thumbs" that separate humans from the rest of the animal kingdom.

This last type of motion also causes the skin in the palm to crease. Again, a bones system that enables you to define bulging and crimping is necessary for this movement to look correct in your modeled hands.

Modeling Methods for Hands

As is possible with bodies, you can model hands out of segments, metaballs, polygons or splines, depending on your software. Each method can produce good hands. In these exercises, construction of hands from a number of different methods will be discussed. Hopefully, one of these will work for you. Also, in each exercise, only one hand is modeled; it is simply a matter of mirroring your newly created hand to make its counterpart.

Modeling Hands from Polygons

Polygons are a good choice of tool to use to create hands. The complex structure of a hand makes it a good candidate for polygons, and there is a plethora of modeling methods. As with most polygon-based modeling tasks, it's best to build up the hand's structure from primitives. You can also use techniques such as metaballs that ultimately resolve to polygons. Whatever method you use, make sure that you model just enough detail so the hand deforms smoothly, but not so much that you have too many polygons.

One of the more popular forms of hands is the traditional three-fingered cartoon glove as worn by Bugs Bunny, Mickey Mouse, and Screwy Squirrel, among others. The following exercise shows you how to model one of these cartoon gloves using polygons. This type of hand affords a fair range of flexibility and, because it's a glove, seams at the joints are not much of a problem. To accomplish this modeling task, you need a good polygonal modeler that supports Boolean operations and a smoothing function, such as LightWave's Metaform, Softimage's Rounding, 3D Studio MAX's Relax, or Digimation's Blend.

The three-fingered cartoon glove is a favorite old standby of animators because of its simplicity and flexibility. This glove was constructed from polygons.

Exercise #1: Making Cartoon Gloves from Polygons

1. Start with a sphere, which is going to be the palm. Flatten and reshape the sphere so it is shaped like a square hamburger patty.

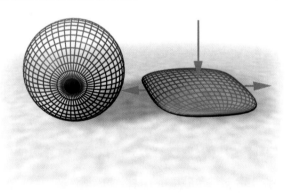

2. Create a cylinder and another sphere. They should both be the same diameter and share the same number of segments. The cylinder should be about twice the length of the palm, with the diameter about a fourth of the palm's width (a four fingered hand would have slightly smaller fingers). Position the two so that the sphere is aligned perfectly with the top of the cylinder. Using a Boolean addition, join the sphere to the cylinder. You now have a hot dog shape that will become a finger.

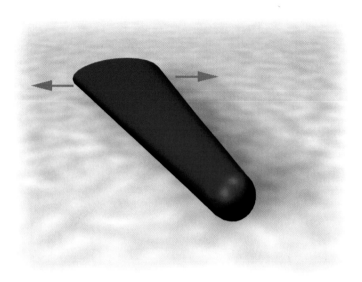

3. Taper the open end of this shape so that it is slightly wider at the base.

4. Duplicate this structure twice to create the other two fingers.

5. Duplicate the shape once again to create the thumb. Scale this copy down vertically by about a third and rotate it about 45 degrees. Now you're ready to attach the fingers and thumb to the palm.

6. Position all these elements near the palm.

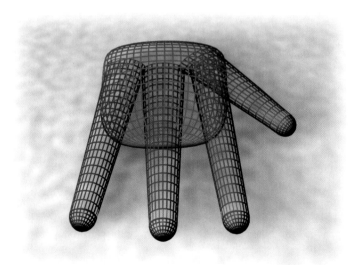

continues

Exercise #1: continued

7. Again, using Boolean addition, combine the palm, the three fingers, and the thumb into one object to form the basic hand. If you want to, you can use it as is, but it looks better if it is modified a bit more.

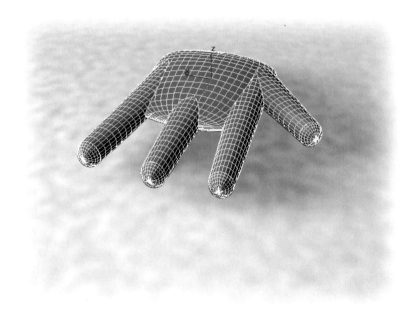

8. Apply a smoothing operation to blend the joints and smooth the hand's surface.

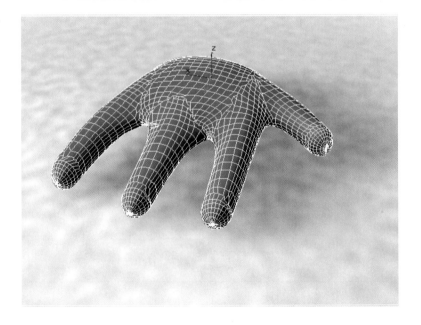

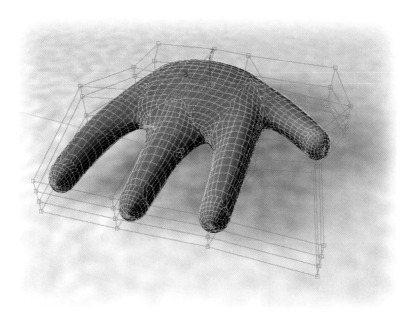

9. This hand is still pretty flat so give the back of the hand an arch and make the palm concave. A lattice deformation is one trick, but any other type of global deformation can do the job.

   You can add knuckles, but you can also animate them using a skeletal deformation system that supports the bulging and flexing of muscles. (The angle of the base of the finger to the palm determines the bulge of the knuckle.)

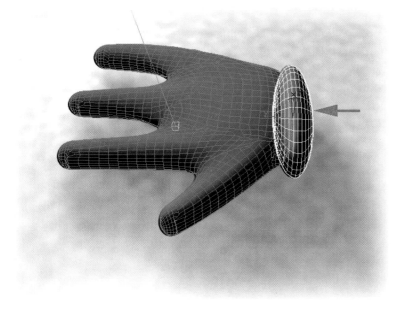

10. Finally, model a squashed sphere that's slightly wider than the base of the palm. Position it at the base of the palm; it will become the base of the glove (the rolled-up part, at the wrist). Using Boolean addition combine the two so they appear as one. I did this last because I like to have a bit of a crease at the base of the glove. If you want to avoid this crease, attach the base earlier in the procedure, before you smooth it, or not at all for an ungloved hand.

continues

Exercise #1: continued

11. The finished hand is ready to be textured and animated with bones. A matte white texture gives it the classic "cartoon" look, but any other texture is possible.

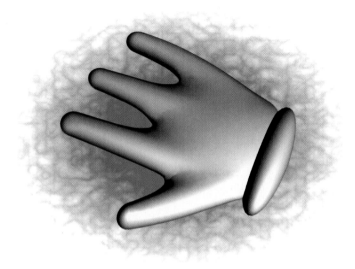

Shaping Hands from Metaballs

Metaballs offer a good method for creating and animating hands. They make a nice, smooth surface that can be deformed very easily. All you need to do is to animate the metaballs directly, and the hand remains smooth and pliable, resolving automatically to polygons at rendering time, and creating few problems with creases or bulges.

The problem with metaballs is that animating them directly can make texture mapping a bit hard to control and can prove troublesome for ultra-realistic hands. Metaballs can also be used strictly for modeling, as you can always extract a mesh from the metaballs system to get a nice polygonal hand that can be animated with bones and textured quite nicely.

Exercise #2: Making a Realistic Hand from Metaballs

In the following exercise, you learn a hand-modeling method that uses spherical objects, so it is compatible with all metaballs implementations. If you can use nonspherical objects, you should probably do so, because it significantly reduces the number of elements you have to animate.

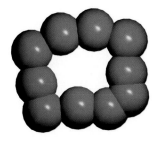 

1. Start creating the palm by using nine or ten equal sized spheres, and form a ring as shown. The most important part of this step is to have four spheres along the top side of the palm, where you'll attach the four fingers later (subtract one of these spheres for a three-fingered hand).

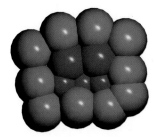 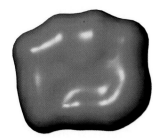

2. Next, fill in the center of the ring with five slightly smaller spheres, positioned to keep the back part of the hand flat and the inside of the palm slightly concave.

3. Now you're ready to create the first finger. Create six spheres and place them in a neat line.

continues

4. Duplicate this first finger three times, to create a total of four fingers.

5. Now, create a thumb by copying four of the six spheres in one of the fingers, and attach it to the hand. The hand is almost finished.

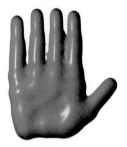

Well, not quite, because the fingers will tend to blob together.

6. To avoid of the blobbing problem, you need to assign each finger to its own group of metaballs. That way, adjacent fingers (those in different groups) won't affect each other adversely. Create one group for the palm and one for each finger (colored areas). To maintain smoothing, overlap the finger groups and the palm by one metaball each (stripes).

7. The final result is a smooth hand. If your metaballs program supports animation, read on. Otherwise, create a mesh out of this structure and animate the result with bones.

8. To animate the hand, hierarchically link the balls in the fingers together and manipulate them in groups of two (if you used elliptical or nonspherical metaballs, you can probably get away with one ellipsoid shaped metaball per joint.) Manipulating the balls directly enables you to deform and animate the hand. The hand always smoothes itself out at render time, eliminating crimping or bulging problems.

9. Animating so many individual objects, however, can get a bit unwieldy. One way to simplify animating a blobby hand such as this would be to attach each joint's metaballs to an invisible box and animate the boxes. The figure shows a skeleton of simple boxes, each attached to their overlapping metaballs. Manipulating the boxes manipulates the hand as a whole.

Building a Hand with Splines

Because hands are so complex, they can be a real challenge for a spline modeler. If you have a full-featured modeler that supports the skinning of animated blends, however, hand modeling should not be much of a problem.

Exercise #3: Making a Realistic Hand from Splines

1. First, make the index finger. Take a sphere and turn it into a hemisphere by slicing it off latitudinally at the equator. Stretch this hemisphere lengthwise to form a rough finger.

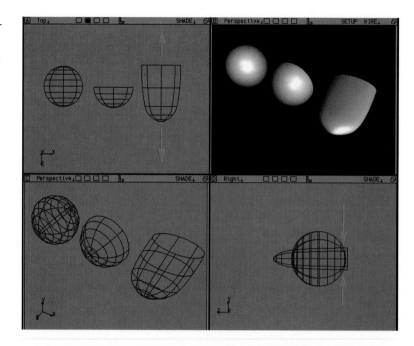

2. Continue to sculpt and reshape the finger. Be sure to model detail around the joints, so that the finger bends properly when animated.

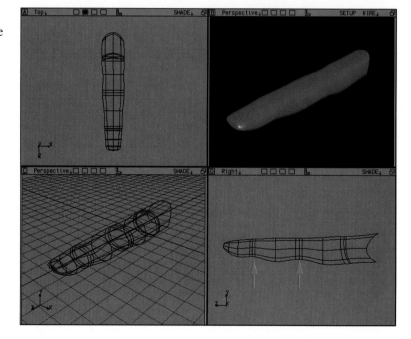

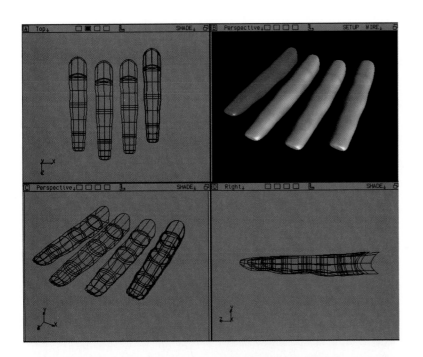

3. Duplicate the index finger to make the other three fingers. Scale them appropriately, with the middle finger the longest, the index and ring fingers the same size and the pinkie smaller than the rest.

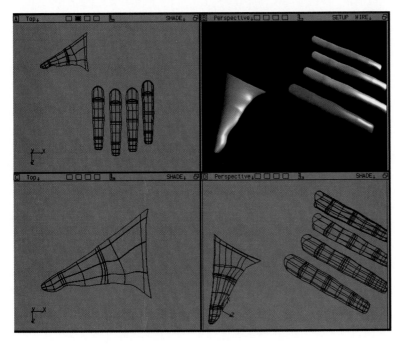

4. Copy the index finger once again to make the thumb. Rotate this object as shown in the figure. Expand the lowest joint to make a triangular base for the point where the thumb anchors to the palm.

continues

5. Now it's time to make the palm. Make another sphere with 16 segments, but this time slice it longitudinally. Reshape this object into a rounded pizza box shape.

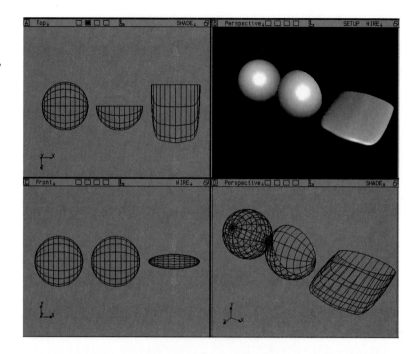

6. Keep shaping the hand until it resembles the next figure. Pull up the splines that run along the top of the hand, so you have a bit of a knuckle shape for each finger (arrows).

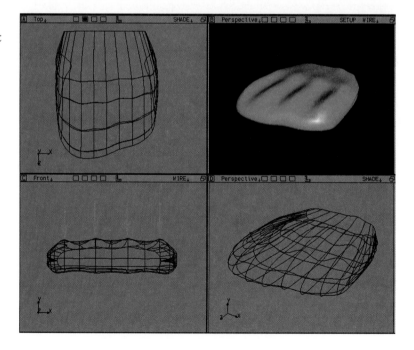

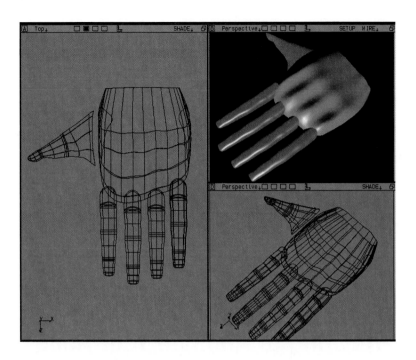

7. Move the fingers and thumb into position, but not yet touching the palm.

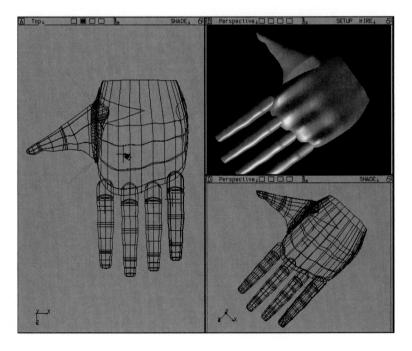

8. Using NURBS trim and skinning, or a blend tool, attach the thumb to the palm.

continues

digital character animation

98 Exercise #3: continued

9. Repeat the preceding
step for each of the fin-
gers. Your hand should
now be complete.

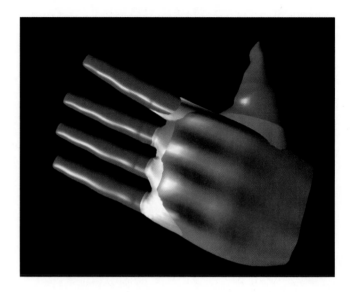

Preparing to Animate Your Hand

How you build your digital hands dictates the way you animate
them. As mentioned already, a metaball-based hand can be animated simply by manipulating the balls that make up the hand.
Similarly, a hand constructed of individual segments can be linked
into a hierarchy and manipulated directly. If your hand is constructed of a single polygonal mesh, or is made of spline patches,
then you need to use bones to animate it.

Boning a Hand

Adding bones to a hand is simply a task of following the guidelines set forth by mother nature. Each finger has three bones, and
the thumb has two. The thumb has a third joint hidden in the
mass of the palm, and similarly, each finger has a fourth bone that
connects it to the wrist.

The biggest problem with bones in many implementations is the
tendency for the mesh or patch to flatten out unrealistically when
bending. The flattening is caused by the bones program affecting
only the vertices of the mesh or patch.

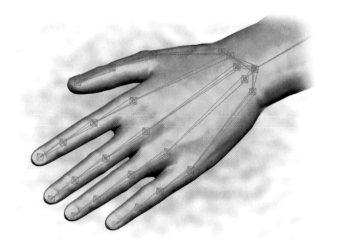

To add bones to your digital hand, simply imitate the bones of a real hand.

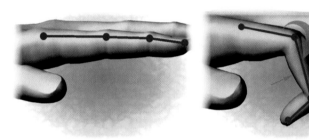

Flattening of a joint is common in many bones programs.

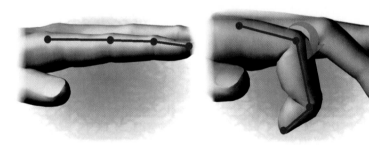

More advanced programs enable you to define bulges based on the angles of the joints, which results in a much more realistic crimping of the skin around the joints. The theory is identical to the bicep discussed in the previous chapter. A good skeletal deformation system can also effectively simulate bulging knuckles and the web between the thumb and the index finger.

If you don't have this feature, the same effect can be created by adding another bone (blue) in the offending joint to help maintain the volume.

Connecting the Hands to the Body

After you have the character's hands built, you need to attach them to the body. Depending on your character, you can connect them in several ways. One concern is the way you constructed the hands. If you made the hands from metaballs and have a spline body, then the connection scheme will be quite different than if the whole thing were made from polygons.

As when attaching any other body part, you need to concern yourself with seams. If you don't want them, try to make your character one object. If you can't keep it one object due to topology or other limitations, keep the seams away from the joints. For the hands, that usually means placing the seam halfway up the forearm. Because a seam can pop open if flexed, anchoring it to the forearm, which is stable, will keep the seam hidden. The simplest way to attach the hands is to attach them hierarchically to the wrists. This method, however, can produce visible seams.

With a simple character, seams aren't really a problem.

Even a slightly more complex character can have a few seams, enabling you to keep the hands as separate objects.

If your hand and body are a solid polygonal mesh, then simply use a Boolean operation to make the hand part of the mesh. With this method, there are no seams, and a good skeleton along with a bones program can deform the entire mesh smoothly.

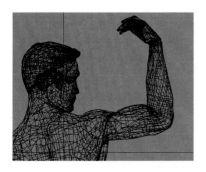

If both your character and the hand are polygonal, joining them into one mesh makes your character seamless…

…even after rendering.

Spline hands generally need to be attached a bit differently. The best way is to extrude the palm of the hand out at the wrist, and join it to the arm halfway up the forearm. With the seam away from the joint, the bend at the wrist will be smooth. Finally, you can also hide the seam with clothing. A hand and partial wrist hides quite nicely under a long sleeve shirt, for instance.

CHAPTER 4

Modeling Heads for Animation

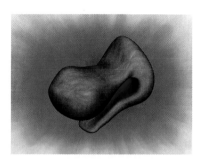

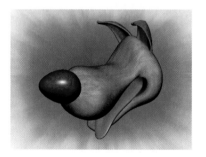

The head and face comprise a very complex structure that is difficult to model, let alone animate. Sculptors spend years learning how to create convincing heads and faces, and modeling a convincing head on the computer takes just as much practice. Added to this task is the need to easily animate your digital faces. Modeling a face is one thing; modeling one that animates well is another. The human face can express a wide variety of emotions through the subtlest changes in shape. Your digital heads must not only look good, they must be also be pliable enough to change shape easily.

Don't despair. The goal of creating a totally convincing face within the computer is something that eludes even the best animators. With a few tricks up your sleeve, however, you can construct heads and faces that work well in the context of your film.

This chapter covers the construction and modeling of heads that animate well. The subject of facial animation, expressions, and lip sync are covered in Chapter 9, "Facial Animation," after you have more animation experience under your belt.

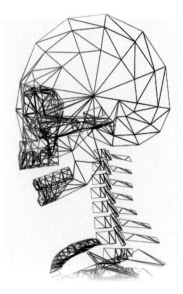

The head consists of two large masses: the skull and the jaw.

Understanding the Structure of the Head and Face

Before you can build believable digital heads and faces, you need to understand the underlying anatomy of the human head and face. The face is by far the most important part of the equation because this is where the majority of the movement takes place. The head typically acts as a solid frame for the face to live in. Outside of the facial area, the head doesn't move much, other than the occasional ear wiggle.

The head is basically made from two large bones: the skull and the jaw. The skull is really a collection of many smaller bones that are stitched together by cartilage. You can think of the skull as a single mass balanced on the top of the spine, with the jaw as a second mass hanging from the skull. The skull is solid, whereas the jaw rotates, and its movement affects the shape of the lower part of the face. When the mouth opens wide, the rotating jaw does all the work. Although we don't see the skull and jaw, their influence affects the structure and movement of the face and muscles that cover it.

The Muscles of the Face

The face is a complex collection of muscles that pull and stretch the skin in a variety of ways. Let's take a look at these muscle groups, which are roughly depicted in the following illustration and described in Table 4.1.

Understanding how the muscles of the face move will help you understand how to build a digital face that moves well.

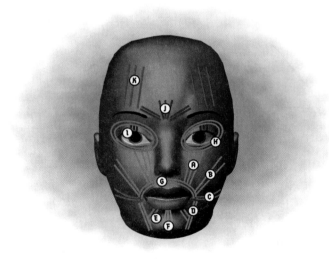

Table 4.1
Major Muscle Groups of the Human Face

Location	Muscle Group	Muscle Action on Figure
A	Levator labii superioris	Starts at the base of the nose and connects to the middle of the top lip. Used alone, the muscle pulls the top lip up into a sneer.
B	Zygomatic major	Lays across the cheek and connects to the corner of the mouth. Used alone, the muscle pulls the mouth into a smile.
C	Risorius	Stretches over the jaw and attaches at the corner of the mouth. Used alone, the muscle pulls the mouth to the side and down, as when crying.
D	Triangularis	Stretches over the lower side of the jaw and pulls the corner of the mouth down. Used when frowning or scowling.
E	Depressor labii inferioris	Connects the lower lip to the chin. Pulls the lower lip straight down, as when speaking.
F	Mentalis	Connects to the skin of the chin. When contracted, this muscle pulls the chin up, forcing the lower lip into a pout.
G	Orbicularis oris	Attaches to the corners of the mouth. Purses or tightens the lips.
H	Orbicularis oculi	Connects the cheek to the inner eye area. Contraction of this muscle results in squinting.
I	Levator palpebrae	Attaches to the upper eyelid and raises it when surprised.
J	Corrugator	Runs from the bridge of the nose to the middle of the eyebrow. Pulls the eyebrows down and in, as when frowning or concerned.
K	Frontalis	Runs across the forehead and con nects to the eyebrows. Pulls the eyebrows up.

All this anatomy is great, but how does it affect the way a digital model is created and animated? The trick is to understand how these muscles pull and shape the face to create expressions. Really, the groups of muscles fall into two categories: lower face muscles that control the mouth and jaw and upper face muscles that control the eyes and brows.

The muscles of the lower face are responsible for three major types of movements. First, the muscles that lie across the cheeks and jaw pull the lips outward radially from eight major anchor points. Second, the muscles surrounding the lips contract to purse the lips, forcing them together and forward. Finally, the jaw can drop.

The muscles on the upper face are responsible for three major movements. First, the muscles surrounding the eyes open, close, and squint the eyelids. Second, the Frontalis muscles on the brow raise and lower the eyebrows. Third, the Currugator pulls the eyebrows in toward the bridge of the nose, furrowing the brow.

If we can create a digital model that moves easily along the same lines that these muscles are pulling, we have a much better chance at animating the face convincingly.

Basic Head-Modeling Methods

When designing a digital head, you should take a good inventory of your animation tools before you start. You can easily back yourself into a corner by designing a head that cannot be easily animated. There is a plethora of ways to create and animate a face, so it is up to your imagination and creativity to think up new and innovative ways to accomplish this task. New tools are always being incorporated into software packages as well, so the methods described in this chapter cover general categories of construction rather than specific features.

Paste-On Features

The method of using paste-on features is probably the easiest way to model and has many of its roots in clay and puppet animation. Think of Gumby or Mr. Potato Head. These characters have a simple shape for the head, and the features are simply tacked on.

The Rankin-Bass Christmas specials of the 1960s (*Rudolph the Red-Nosed Reindeer*, *Santa Claus is Coming to Town*, and others) used this method effectively with puppets, using simple objects such as cardboard mouths and sewing beads for eyes. The same principles apply to digital animation.

With paste-on features, most or all of the character's features are separate objects, freeing the animator from complex modeling and shape animation.

You can create paste-on features from the simplest of objects. The nose and eyes can be simple spheres, for example, and the mouth can easily be constructed from a torus. Most software packages make it easy to animate such simple shapes. Another approach you can take is to paint the facial features on the head by using animated texture maps. This approach makes the modeling task downright easy because the head can be as simple as a sphere; the maps contain all the detail. The maps can be drawn and animated by hand or in a 2D paint or animation package. Bump and displacement maps can add a degree of dimension. This technique can prove cumbersome, however, because matching the 2D animation of the face to the 3D animation of the body usually requires flipping between several packages.

Paste-on features also provide a lot of flexibility. There is no law that says you need to make the entire face out of these objects. You can combine paste-on features with any of the other methods described later in this chapter. A typical example is a face with a flexible, built-in mouth, but with a paste-on clown nose.

Characters with paste-on features are easy to model and animate.

Faces with Flexible Skin

For realistic and quasi-realistic faces, you need to construct a head and face with skin that moves and flexes. This task requires more complex modeling and animation methods, found in packages such as Alias, Softimage, 3D Studio MAX, LightWave, and Animation Master. All of these packages have tools that can model and animate the many different expressions and poses the head and face will make.

This face is a simple texture map but still maintains a lot of character.

Polygonal Faces

Polygonal modelers can certainly create realistic heads and faces. The advantages to constructing a face with polygons is that you

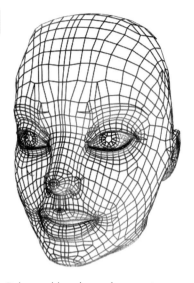

Polygonal heads can be easy to model, but because they have more detail, they are difficult to animate.

have much more control in defining the face's surface. You'll find it much easier to cut holes for eye sockets and nasal passages with polygonal methods because you are not limited by topology, as you are in many spline modelers. Modeling techniques such as metaballs can also give you a very organic and fleshy look that can be difficult to achieve with other methods.

Polygons are, however, inherently less flexible and harder to animate than splines. The extra vertices and detail needed to make a smooth surface out of polygons adds tremendously to the amount of detail that needs to be animated. This extra detail can be hard to control and many times results in unwanted crimping or bulging of the facial surface.

Still, with care and attention to detail, you'll be able to animate faces quite effectively with a good polygonal animation package. Typically, the face is animated with methods that can control groups of vertices, such as bones or lattices.

Exercise #1: Modeling a Simple Face

In this exercise, we'll create a basic polygonal head by using metaballs as the modeling technique. This is only one of many techniques you can use to create a polygonal head. Metaballs are a good choice because they create very smooth organic surfaces. This exercise can be done with just about any metaballs program.

This face is a simple texture map but still maintains a lot of character.

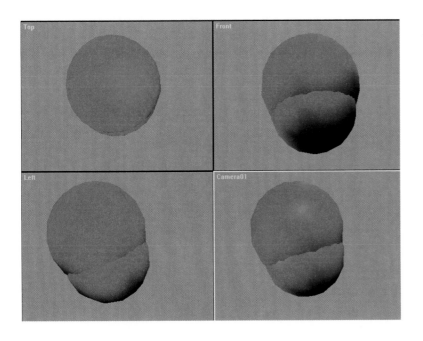

1. First, create two balls; these will serve as the base of the skull.

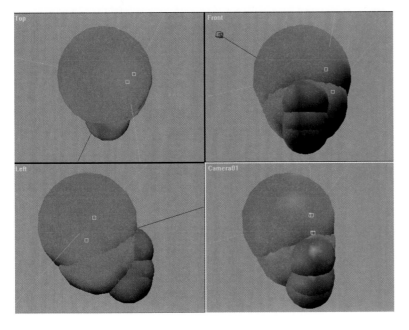

2. Create three more balls and place them along the front side of the face. These balls will form the face and chin.

continues

Exercise #1: continued

3. Three more balls on each side of the face will create cheeks. This character's cheeks will be exaggerated, and you can use smaller balls for a less exaggerated look.

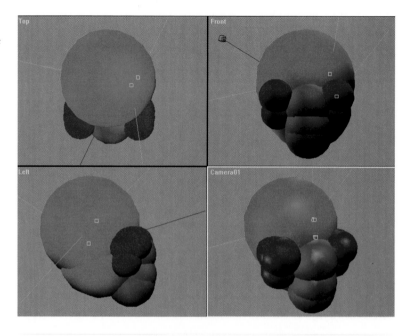

4. The nose can be made with three simple balls. If you want a nose that's less bulbous, you can add, resize, and reposition the balls to get the nose you want.

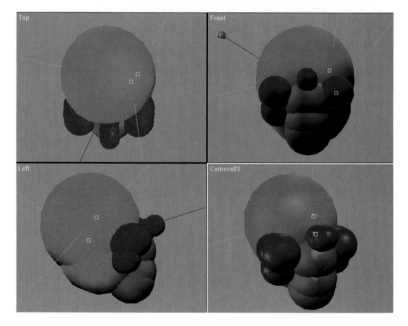

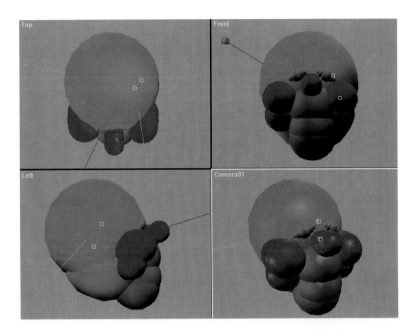

5. These red balls have a negative weight, meaning they will subtract from the final model, carving out eye sockets in the face. If your metaballs package does not support negative weights, you can get the same effect by using Boolean subtraction to create eye sockets.

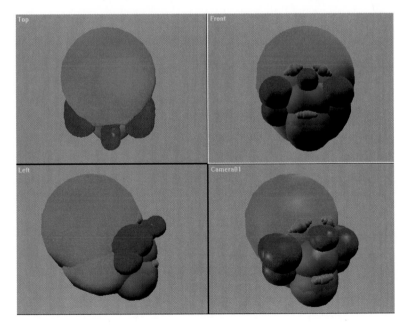

6. The mouth is constructed in much the same way, using balls with a negative weight. This is the last set of metaballs we need to add.

continues

Exercise #1: continued

7. Finalize the head by converting it into polygons. The raw head is now ready for additional features.

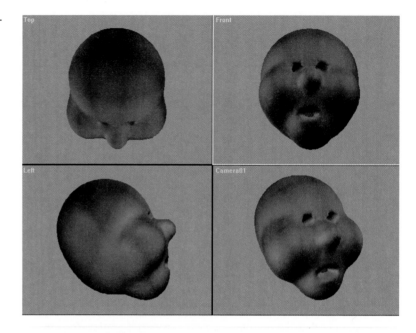

Eyes are simply spheres set behind the eye sockets. Detailed construction of these will be discussed later in the chapter. Eyebrows are deformed cylinders and the teeth are made from simple boxes. The cap is more complex to build, so I won't go into details, but it tops off the character nicely.

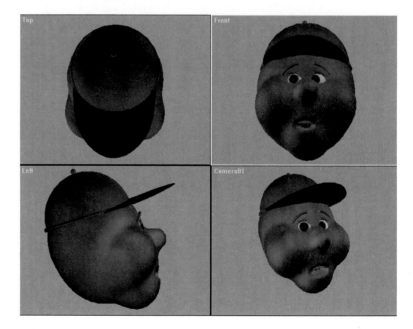

Splines

Splines are the preferred way to create digital flesh. Modeling a head with splines enables you to create faces that closely simulate the real thing. Because splines define a smooth surface with far fewer vertices than polygonal methods, it is much easier to control the shape of the face and maintain a smooth surface.

Modeling with splines is an exercise in Bauhausian simplicity: less is more, simple is elegant, form follows function. Keeping your models light is the key. The simpler the structure of your digital head, the easier it is to animate. Every time you add a control point, vertex, or extra spline, you should consider exactly what its function will be. If you don't need it, don't put it in your model. The lighter and simpler your models, the better.

Some spline modelers, however, are topologically challenged in that they restrict you to surfaces without holes or breaks. To get around this limitation, you need a NURBS-based modeler with trims, such as Softimage or Alias. Animation Master is unique in that it allows for holes without resorting to trims. You can also use many of the seaming and blending techniques discussed in Chapter 2 to attach seamless paste-on noses, mouths, eyes, and ears to your characters. Attached properly, these features can look quite realistic. Whatever your particular modeler's capabilities, spline heads can be constructed by using a number of different methods and topologies.

Spherical Heads

Topologically, a head can be thought of as a deformed sphere. You can place the sphere so that its "north pole" is at the top of the head, the front of the head or at the sides. How the sphere is oriented when modeling begins affects how the model will be constructed and animated.

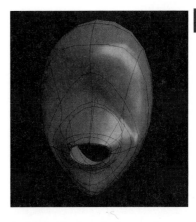

A simple head made from splines.

The same head made with polygons. Notice how much more data is needed with polygons to get the same smooth surface.

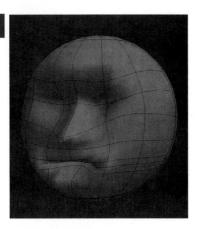

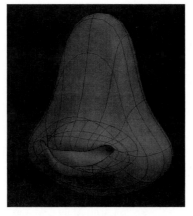

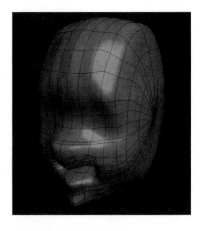

Pole at the Top of the Head

This topology is probably the first that comes to mind for most modelers. Unfortunately, this method orients the splines so that they don't flow along the same lines as the muscles of the face. This may make animation difficult.

Pole at the Mouth

This method is extremely effective and probably makes the best mouths. By placing the pole at the mouth, the splines naturally flow along the same radial lines as the muscles of the face, making animation of the mouth smooth and easy. This method, however, may limit you when it comes to modeling internal eye sockets because the orientation of the splines can be off.

Pole at the Ears

The pole at the ears methods is popular as well and lends itself to skinning methods of modeling. In this method, the directions of the splines have a better orientation for eye sockets and the nose, but they don't run parallel to the muscles of the mouth. Still, effective animation is possible.

Exercise #2: Modeling a Simple Face

In this exercise, we'll create a basic head with a mouth that animates well. To do this exercise, you need a spline modeler. Softimage and Alias are good choices, but the geometry of this head is so simple, it can be modeled in any decent spline-based package.

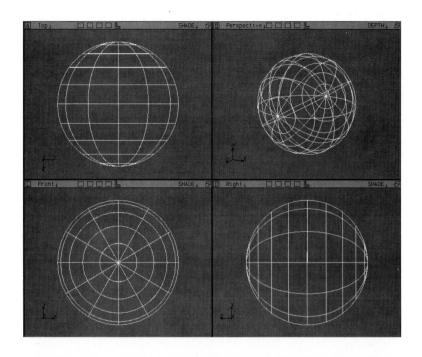

1. Start by creating a simple spline sphere. This particular surface is a NURBS primitive, but any spline surface should work. Orient the sphere so that the pole is facing forward.

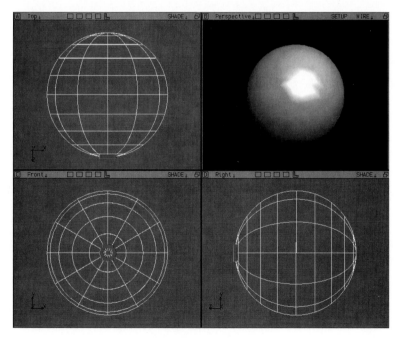

2. Select the control points on the front part of the sphere.

continues

Exercise #2: continued

3. Drag these points straight back, creating a hollow mouth cavity inside the head. The control points are now located at the back of the mouth.

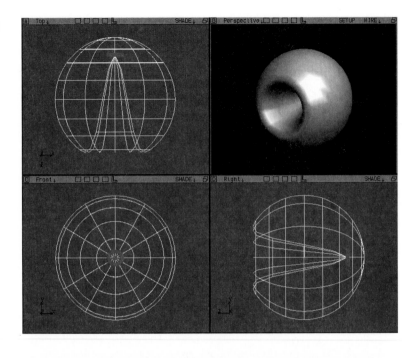

Tip

Another way you can create this simple model is to draw a simple spline and revolve or lathe it to get the rough outline of the head and mouth.

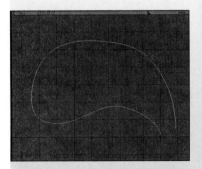

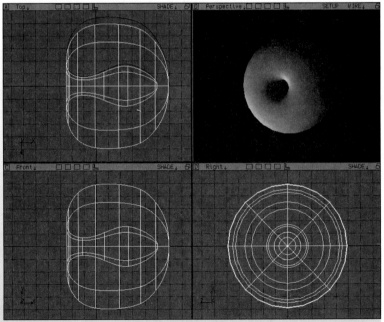

You can also build the head by creating a simple spline profile...

...and lathing it along a 360-degree path to form the head and mouth cavity.

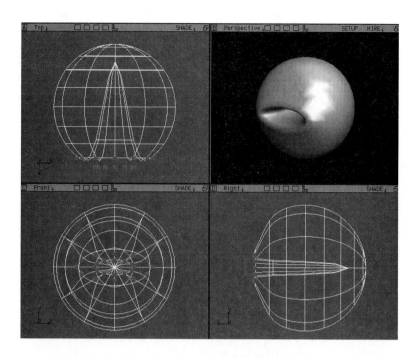

4. Select the vertices around the lips and scale or move them down vertically. You now have the beginnings of a mouth.

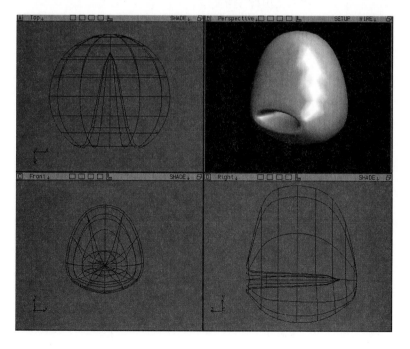

5. Reshape the head by using whatever method you desire. In this example, I used a lattice deformation, but any method would work fine.

continues

6. Continue reshaping the head, adding detail only where necessary.

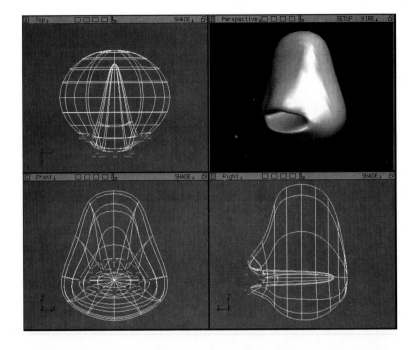

The preceding figure shows the basic shape of the head, which is now ready to have some features pasted onto it. If your modeler supports trims and blends, you can add these features to create a more realistic look. If you don't have this luxury, a clown nose and cartoon eyes will suffice.

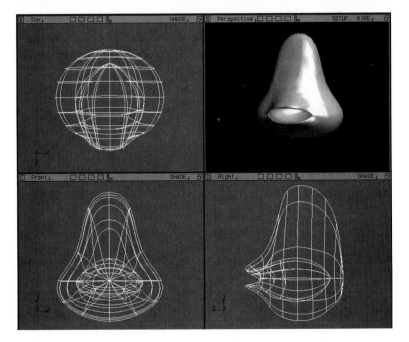

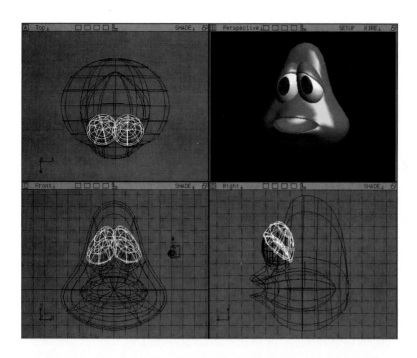

7. Add eyes that you built
   later in the chapter…

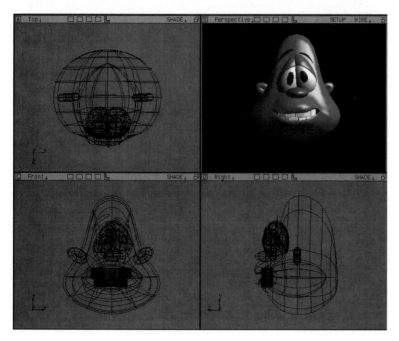

8. Add a nose, teeth, and
   some ears. These features
   can be realistic or stylized, and I'll go over
   construction of them
   in a bit.

Other Methods for Creating Heads

Deforming a sphere isn't the only method you can use for creating a head. You can take plenty of other approaches. Some people prefer to use skinning methods to make the head, sculpting the face from of a series of outlines. Others prefer to use flat patches, shaping them into a face and fitting them to a faceless skull much like a Halloween mask, hiding the seams under the hair or behind the ears, where the head doesn't flex.

Skinning

Some people like to build heads by skinning or lofting multiple outlines. Many packages force you to skin surfaces with outlines that contain the same number of control points. In this case, the methods are really just a topological extension of the spherical and cylindrical primitives mentioned previously. If your topology is a sphere with the poles at the ears, this method will enable you to model half the face and then mirror it to provide the other side, thereby cutting your modeling time in half.

These outlines can be skinned to create a face.

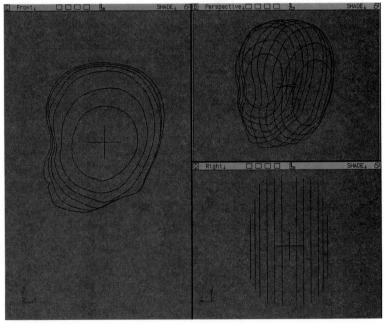

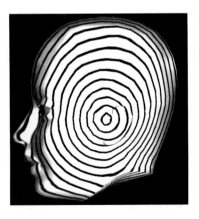

This head shows the contours of the head and face. These contours can be used as a guide to create outlines for a realistic skinned head.

For packages that support the skinning of outlines with disparate numbers of points, the method can be used to create more unique types of surface topologies, such as objects with holes.

Exercise #3: Modeling a Simple Skinned Head

In this exercise, we'll create a cartoon dog head by skinning together some circular shapes. This operation works particularly well with a NURBS-based modeler, but other spline modeling methods can do a good job as well.

An example of a character's head, created by skinning a series of circular profiles.

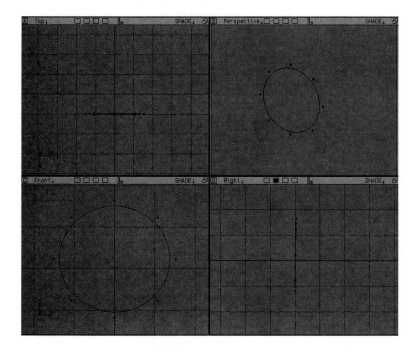

1. Create a circle with eight vertices. You'll want to keep the model simple and light, so eight is plenty. Scale the circle along the vertical axis to give it a slight oval shape.

continues

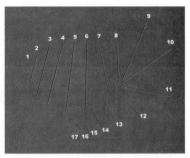

2. You need to copy this circle 16 times and then rotate and scale the copies to create a rough outline of the head.

3. The following illustration is a template of the head's outline. Create 16 copies of the original curve and fit them to this template by scaling the curve along the X and Y axes and rotating around the X. The shapes are numbered for reference.

Table 4.2 shows how each shape should be scaled and rotated before being fitted to the template.

Table 4.2

Setting Up the Head Template

Curve	SCALE X	SCALE Y	ROTATION (degrees)
1	0.1	0.05	-15.0
2	0.6	0.35	-15.0
3	0.8	0.85	-15.0
4	1.2	1.0	-15.0
5	1.2	1.0	-7.5
6	1.0	1.0	-1.25
7	0.9	0.8	12.0

Curve	SCALE X	SCALE Y	ROTATION (degrees)
8	1.0	0.6	2.75
9	1.1	1.1	-24.0
10	1.45	1.0	-56.0
11	1.45	0.8	-100.0
12	0.8	0.5	-133.0
13	0.7	0.35	-154.0
14	0.7	0.25	-146.0
15	0.6	0.2	-146.0
16	0.4	0.1	-138.0
17	0.2	0.05	-138.0

After you have the curves in place, they should look something like the ones shown in the following illustration.

4. Skin the shapes together. If everything is in place, the result should look something like this.

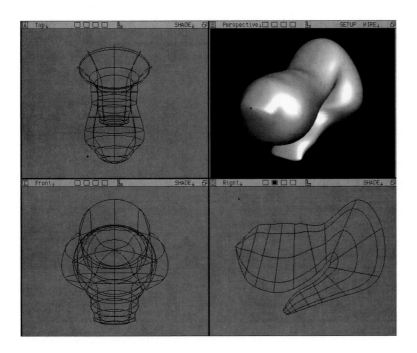

continues

Exercise #3: continued

5. Now that you have the rough head shape, you can sculpt it a bit further. First, select the vertices running along the bottom of the mouth.

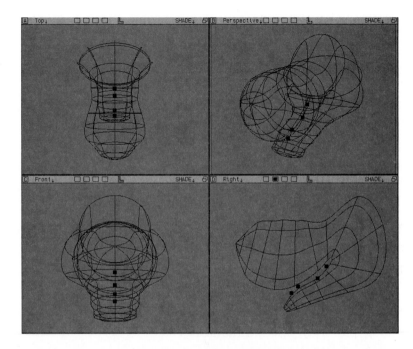

6. Drag these vertices downward a bit to create a nice concave surface along the bottom of the mouth cavity.

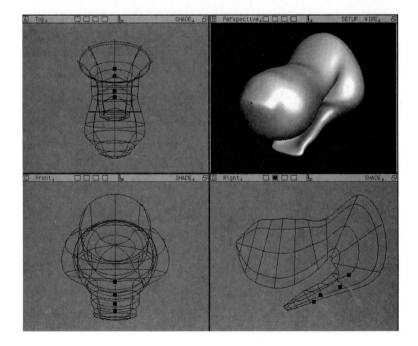

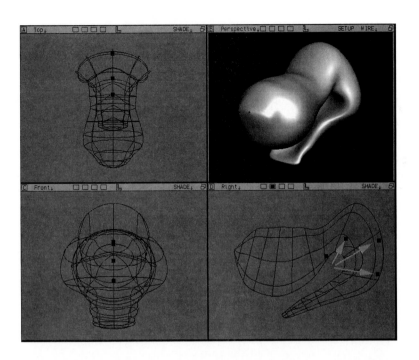

7. At the back of the mouth, pull the center vertices back to create a bit of a throat.

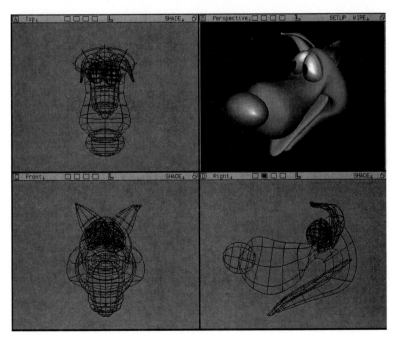

8. Go through the rest of the model and reshape as desired, removing any dents or bulges. You may want to make the nose longer or thicker or stubbier. You may want to make the forehead lower or higher. Do whatever suits your fancy at this point.

9. After the head is complete, you can add paste-on features such as eyes, a nose, and a tongue. Construction of these will be detailed later in this chapter.

Patches

Another way to model a head is to use one or more flat patches for the face and another spherical object for the head, seaming it all together. Think of the patches as a mask pasted onto a blank head. The flat patches should extend well beyond the movable surface of the face to the sides and top of the head so that the seams remain stable. You can hide the seems by using any number of techniques. Hair or a hat can hide most of the seams, or if your seams are on bare skin, a fading texture may do the trick.

Scanned Heads

If you have access to a 3D digitizer or laser scanner, you may want to scan or digitize a real person's head or a sculpture of a head. Sculpting a head out of clay is a very good way to visualize your character and some people simply create better looking models when working in a physical medium. A physical model must be digitized, however, and 3D digitizers are expensive to own. When digitizing a sculpture of a head, you need to be aware of how the face will be modeled and animated so that you can scan in the sculpture with the splines properly positioned. Most people draw these lines directly on the sculpture before digitizing. Some companies, such as Viewpoint, offer 3D digitizing as a service, and an expert's assistance can be a good alternative to scanning a model yourself.

Laser-scanned heads can be problematic when it comes to animation. Typically, a laser-scanned head has a pole at the top, with the polygons fairly dense throughout and in a strict grid arrangement. It's best to do quite a bit of polygon reduction on these before you animate them. If you're using splines, you need to fit your curves to the surface of the model, using it as a template for rebuilding the model with splines, ultimately doing away with the original polygonal scan.

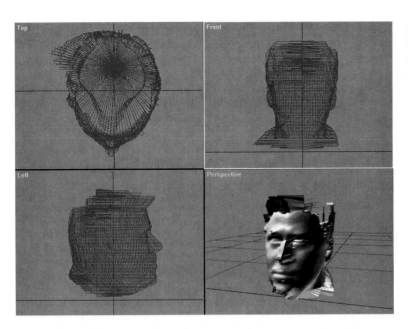

A Cyberscan of the author's head. Notice the tremendous amount of detail. This detail needs to be eliminated before animating.

Modeling Other Elements of the Face and Head

After you've constructed a basic head shape, you need to flesh it out with a few other tiny details such as eyes, a nose, teeth, and a tongue. These are equally as important, and how you build these depends a lot on your character. The possibilities are vast, but here's a handful of ways to build these important features.

Noses

A nose can be anything from a simple bump on the character's face to a clownlike ball nose to an ultra-realistic nose. Simple noses made of simple geometry are easy to construct and can be fashioned easily out of spheres or cylinders. It's also a trivial matter to pull a few vertices on the face to create a little bulge.

You can create a simple bump nose by pulling some vertices away from the face.

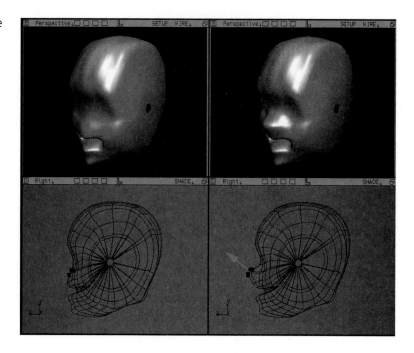

Realistic noses, however, are much more difficult to create. First, noses are complex in structure and thus require quite a bit of geometry to get them right. Building a nose that is integral to the face's skin can add an inordinate number of splines to an otherwise simple face, particularly if you want to add details such as nostrils.

If you want to create a more realistic nose by using a spline-based modeler...

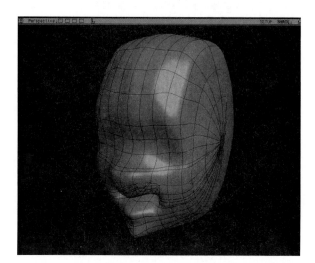

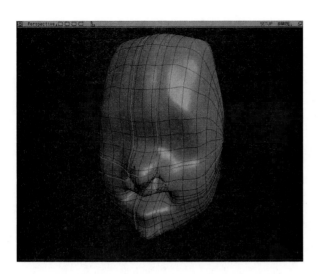

...the extra detail required for the nose and nostrils means extra detail throughout the face and in the animation.

The fact that the nose doesn't move makes building it into the face an even less attractive proposition because those extra splines will go to waste at animation time. You may find it advantageous to create the nose as a separate object and then attach it to the face by blending or skinning—if your package supports these methods.

Exercise #4: Modeling a Realistic Nose

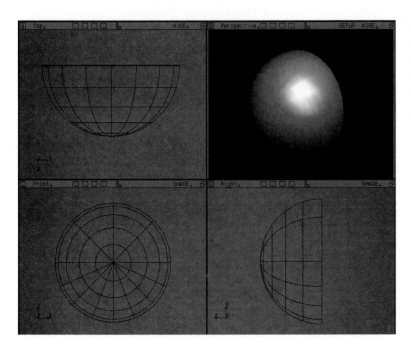

Here is a good method for creating a separate nose that you can later blend into a face. This nose was modeled with NURBS, but any decent spline modeler should do the job.

1. Create a simple hemisphere, with six latitudinal subdivisions and 12 longitudinal subdivisions, with four splines on the top of the hemisphere, eight on the bottom. We'll need the extra detail on the underside of the nose for the nostrils. If your modeler is incapable of this, use a hemisphere with 16 equal longitudinal subdivisions.

continues

Exercise #4: continued

2. Squash the hemisphere
   from the sides, as shown
   in the following illustration, to give it a nice oval
   outline.

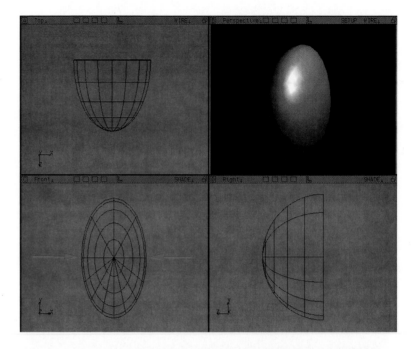

3. Select the forward vertices and scale them
   down along the vertical
   axis.

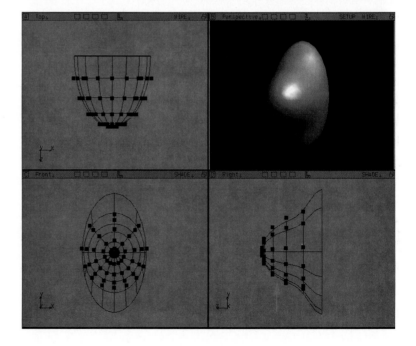

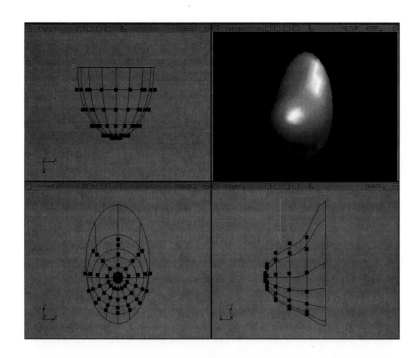

4. Move these same vertices downward to create the ball of the nose.

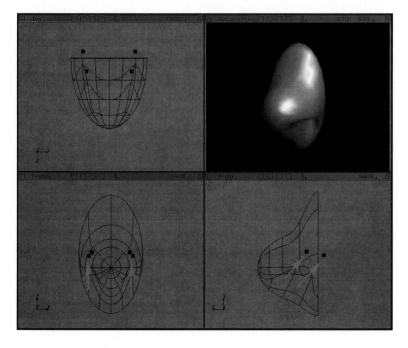

5. Select the four vertices that represent the nostrils and pull them up and back.

continues

You now have a basic nose. Work with the shape until you are satisfied with it. Here, I stretched it out to create a hook nose.

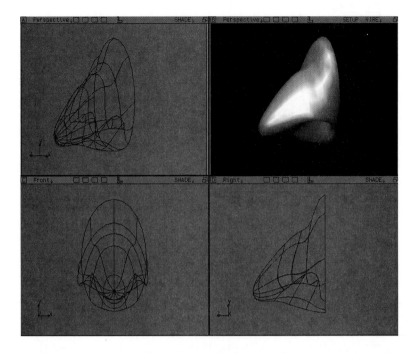

The great thing about this simple nose is that you can sculpt it into a wide variety of shapes and use it for many types of characters.

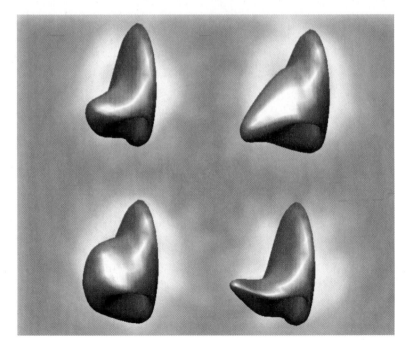

Blending a Nose into a Face

One trick you can use to simplify the geometry of a face and maintain realism is to use a NURBS trim to cut a hole in the surface and use blending to attach a feature such as a nose or eyes. If you don't have a trim feature in your modeler, another technique would be to attach the features with any one of the seam-hiding methods mentioned in Chapter 3. The face is so flexible, however, that many times even the best seam hiders throw their hands up in frustration. I never said this stuff was easy.

Let's continue our exercise by attaching the nose to a face. Here's a simple way to do it seamlessly. To do this properly, you need a NURBS modeler that supports trims and blends or projected NURBS.

1. Take your basic nose and a noseless face. Scale the nose up by about 10 percent. (You'll scale it back down later.) Reshape the vertices at the base of the nose so that they roughly follow the curvature of the face. Extract the curve at the base of the nose (red).

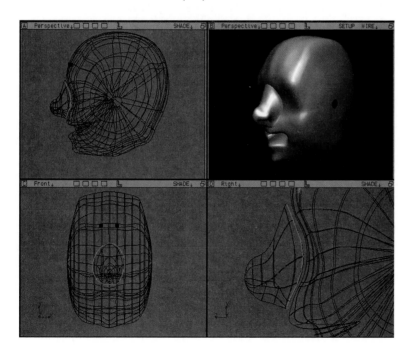

2. Use the extracted curve
   to generate a trim on the
   surface of the face. The
   trim should extend out
   along the face but stop
   short of the top lip.

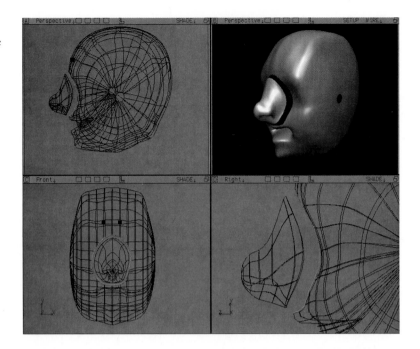

3. Scale the nose down and
   blend the base of the
   nose to the surface of the
   face. In some packages,
   you may need to project
   a second curve on the
   face and use this curve
   as an outline to skin the
   curves on the face to
   the nose.

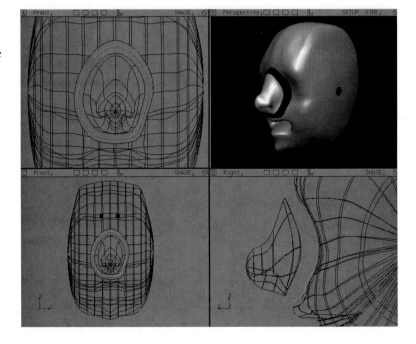

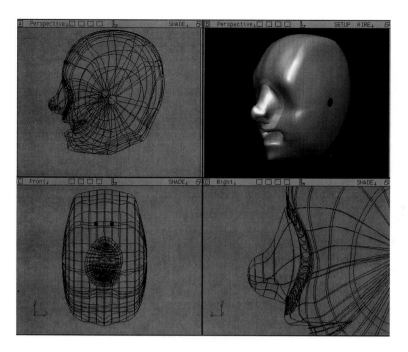

Most packages that support blends support animated blends, so the blended surface should move with the face as well, providing a seamless fit.

You can use this technique for more than noses, however. You can use it for just about anything, including eyes, ears, and mouths. This technique is a great way to make realistic heads because you can use the geometry needed for each feature without having to worry about the rest of the head's geometry.

Eyes

Eyes are one of the most expressive areas of the face, so it's essential to have eyes that are controllable in every respect. Eyes tend to fall into two broad categories: internal and external.

Internal Eyes

Internal eyes are akin to realistic eyes. The eyelids are part of the facial surface, with the eyeball inside the skull. If your character design dictates internal eyes, you need to plan for this by model-

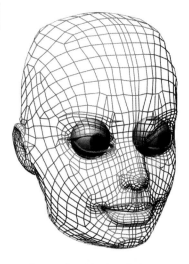

Eyes internal to the head give a realistic look when rendered. An eyeball is really just a simple sphere or hemisphere.

If you use bones to move the lid, pivot the bones on the center of the eyeball. That way, they will move along the eyeball's surface.

Eyes external to the head have a cartoony look.

ing eye sockets when constructing the head. One way to do this is to simply carve out a hole in your face by using a Boolean operator or a NURBS trim. Another way is to blend the eyelid's surface to the surface of the face. If you don't want to cut holes, another way is to create a little pouch for the eyeball to sit in. This operation, however, can add a lot of detail that may come back to haunt you at animation time.

The eyeball itself can be either a sphere or a hemisphere because only the front part of the eye shows through the skin. You can create the pupil from a simple texture map or from a second hemisphere sitting on the first.

The big problem with internal eyes is that you need to keep the eyeballs locked in the socket while the head moves. This is usually accomplished with a hierarchy—the head being the parent of the eyes.

Another issue to consider when modeling internal eyes is the movement of the eyelids, which must move along an arc that has the same radius as the eyes. One way to keep the eyelid moving along the surface of the eye is to place a bone or similar effector on the eyelid to close it. To make sure that the skin of the lid follows the arc of the eyeball, place the pivot point of the bone at the center of the eyeball. That way, rotating the bone automatically makes it track the surface of the eye.

Another way to make a realistic eye closure without using bones is to create a second lid that animates and remains hidden until the eyes blink, the lid on the model being just for show. For fast eye closures, such as blinks, this method can be fine, but if the lid is closed too long, the audience may pick up the seam where the second lid pokes through the skin.

External Eyes

External eyes have a more cartoonlike appearance and are easier to control than internal eyes. These eyes are separate objects that are created from spheres or cylinders that sit on the surface of the face. Because they don't have to line up exactly with the eye sockets on the face, you have greater control over how they're placed. They're great for Tex Avery-style eye popping and afford the animator a variety of stylistic choices.

Exercise #5: Modeling Eyes

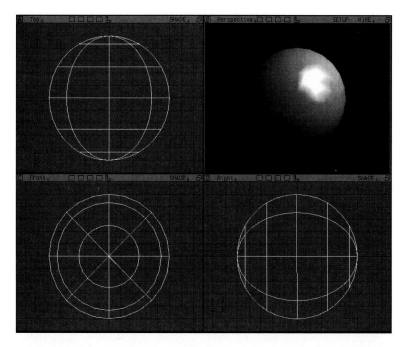

External eyes are easy to make and can be fashioned just as easily from splines as from polygons. You can also attach these to the heads we created earlier.

1. Model a simple sphere. This sphere will be the eyeball.

2. Duplicate the sphere and rescale the duplicate so that it is slightly larger than the original. Cut the second sphere in half to create a hemisphere—the eyelid.

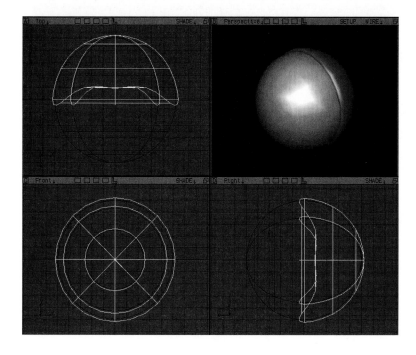

3. As a design choice, some people prefer to also model a lower eyelid, which is really just a duplicate of the first and shares the same center. The lower eyelid can help with certain types of expressions, such as shiftiness and deviousness.

continues

Exercise #5: continued

4. To make the pupil, you can simply texture map it onto the eyeball. Here's a simple texture map you can use.

On the CD

You can find a texture called PUPIL.TGA, which you can use for the pupil, on the accompanying CD.

Tip

Another way to create the pupil is to model a squashed sphere, making it protrude slightly through the eyeball. If the sphere protrudes too much, it will pop through the lid when the eye blinks. Resize the lid or the pupil accordingly so this doesn't happen. A similar way to create the pupil is to create a hemisphere instead of a sphere. The hemisphere should be the same size as the eyeball and should be placed like a contact lens on the eyeball's surface.

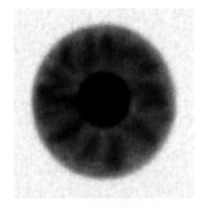

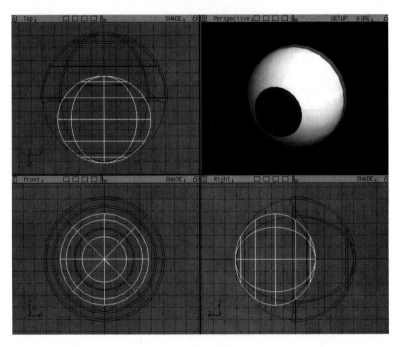

5. After you model these pieces, place the objects so that they all pivot around the same center. Hierarchically link the lid and pupil to the eyeball.

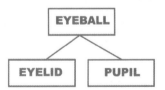

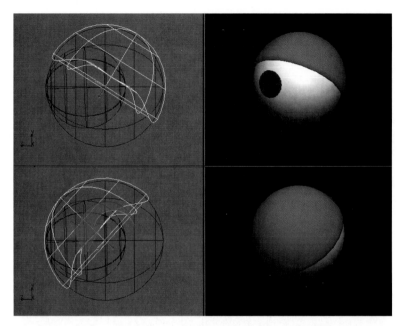

Because the objects all rotate around the same center, eye rotation is as simple as rotating the pupil, and blinking is as simple as rotating the lid.

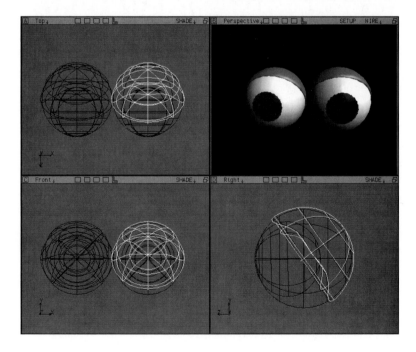

6. Duplicate this hierarchy to make a second eyeball.

This method produces spherical eyeballs. Sometimes, it's nice to break from this to get oblong or asymmetrical eyes. Many packages, such as 3D Studio MAX and LightWave, enable you to rescale the entire hierarchy to make oblong eyes. Because the pupil and lid's deformation are parented to the eyeball, they will continue to move along the surface, even though the eyeball is nonspherical.

When modeled correctly, oblong or asymmetrical eyes can behave just as logically as normal, spherical eyes.

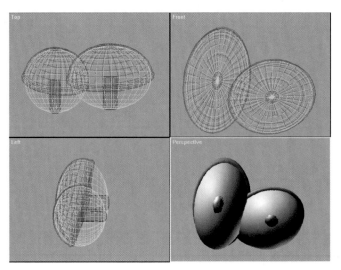

Softimage's Lattice Deformation enables you to take this concept one step further. Applying a lattice (yellow) to the eyeball hierarchy enables you to reshape the eyes in a variety of ways, while still keeping the lid and pupil moving along the surface of the eyeball. Furthermore, the lattice can be animated, allowing for some very cartoony effects.

Constructing cartoony eyeballs with a lattice deformation.

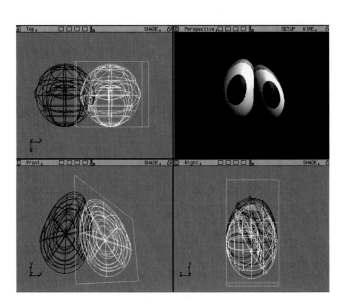

Eyebrows

Depending on the design of your face, the eyebrows can be on the surface of the face or separate. Eyebrows go a long way toward indicating emotion, so be sure to plan for them when designing your characters. If the eyebrows are on the surface of the face, they can be painted on as a texture. For a more complex effect, you can use a displacement or bump map to further define the illusion of hair. Moving these eyebrows requires moving and animating the surface of the face.

Eyebrows separate from the face are less realistic but can take a wider variety of shapes and positions. These eyeballs can be constructed from a variety of shapes and can float free or ride along the surface of the forehead. You can animate the eyebrows by rotating them or by changing the shape of the eyebrows themselves through bones, lattices, splines, or any other form of shape animation. The eyebrows are attached to the head by adding them to the hierarchy of the head.

These eyebrows are painted on the character's face. Moving them requires moving the underlying geometry.

Tongues

The tongue is particularly important when animating speech. The tongue is an incredibly flexible object and needs to be animated with bones, spline deformations, or some other form of shape animation. The tongue is invariably a separate object that simply floats in the mouth cavity. Because we rarely fly our digital camera down our character's throat, the back of the tongue is rarely seen.

The easiest way to build a tongue is to squash a sphere and put a dent down its length. You can also use texture and bump maps to make a more detailed surface. If you choose to use a texture, you should fade this texture to black at the back of the tongue so that the back of the tongue remains hidden.

This dog's eyebrows are separate objects that float above his head but are still attached through a hierarchy. The eyebrows can be moved much more easily than those embedded in the skin, but are more stylized.

Typically, the tongue is a separate object that floats inside the mouth cavity and is hierarchically attached to the head.

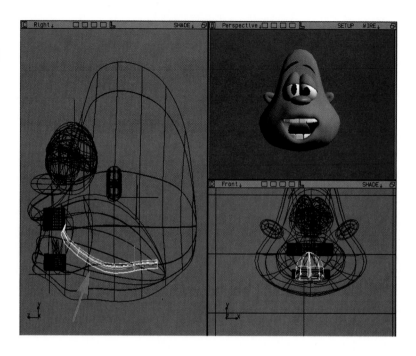

Exercise #6: Modeling a Tongue

1. A sphere is a good place to start when modeling a tongue. Create a sphere with eight lateral and eight longitudinal subdivisions.

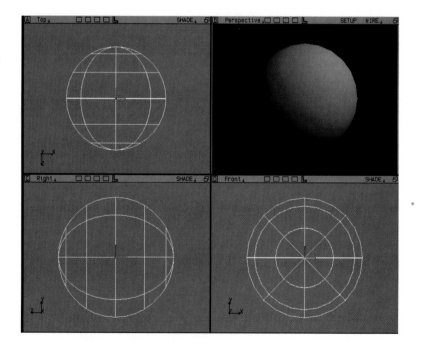

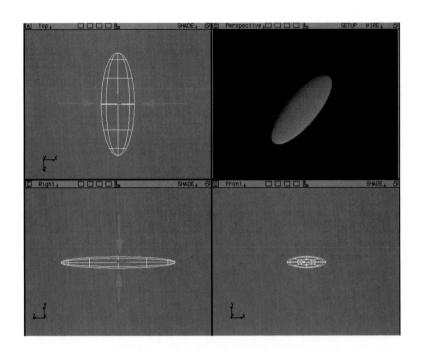

2. Squash the sphere so that it is almost flat and slightly elongated.

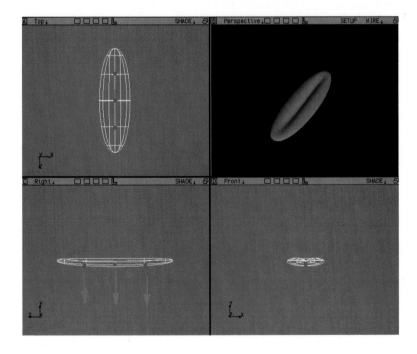

3. Select the middle row of vertices along the top of the tongue and pull these downward. This should give the tongue a nice crease.

Teeth

Because teeth are rigid objects, they are fairly easy to construct out of either polygons or splines. Basically, teeth are rectangular in shape, slightly rounded at the corners. Teeth can be constructed individually and then grouped together in a hierarchy, or they can be constructed as one solid object.

For that movie star look, you can model all the teeth as one solid object, ensuring that they always remain straight and solid.

Modeling the teeth individually can give you quite a different effect.

Teeth are usually placed in the head behind the lips. Because we usually don't model a skull or a jaw, the teeth are the audience's only clue for this underlying structure. To maintain believability, you should move the teeth the same way they're moved in real life.

In real life, top teeth are attached to the skull and do not move in relation to the head as a whole. To get this effect digitally, use the head as a parent and don't move the top teeth. Bottom teeth are attached to the jaw and rotate along with it when the mouth opens. One way to ensure this rotation is to make the bottom teeth pivot around the same axis that the jaw rotates. This axis is located slightly in front of and below the ear. The lower teeth then can give a good impression of a true jaw.

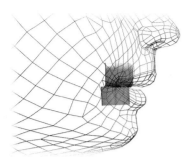

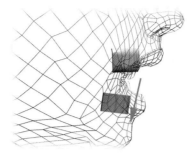

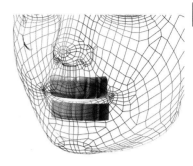

The top teeth remain stable with the skull.

The bottom teeth rotate with the jaw.

Teeth follow the inside of the skull and the jaw, making the teeth slightly curved.

Hair

At the time of this writing, hair is still a tough nut to crack. The complex geometry and motion required to create convincing hair is beyond many packages. The typical head contains tens of thousands of hairs. Modeling and animating these tens of thousands of hairs individually requires hardware and memory resources beyond the budgets of most productions. This situation will probably change as systems inevitably get faster.

The surface texture of the hair and how it behaves in light is particularly vexing. With thousands of hairs—all moving, and all scattering and reflecting light—shading becomes difficult. The edges of the hair pose particular problems when texturing because the light coming through shows the individual hairs and their movement quite honestly, making it difficult to cheat.

Longer hairstyles pose additional problems because they have to flow and move realistically. Short hairstyles, such as crewcuts, are easier to create because they don't move much.

Some vendors, such as Alias, offer custom software specifically geared toward this problem. Alias's hair algorithm is based on a particle system and provides a number of hair types and styles that behave well with light and move realistically. Other high-end software vendors, such as Softimage, are starting to offer hair shaders as well.

If you are fortunate enough to have a package that can generate hair, creating a nice hairdo is a straightforward task. Most hair shaders give you a plethora of options to use in defining the hair's characteristics. These options span the gamut from the color of the hair, to its length, diameter, and stiffness. You can attach the hair directly to the character's head, or you can model a little wig to help position the hair accurately.

To create a wig, model a patch that fits the top of the head.

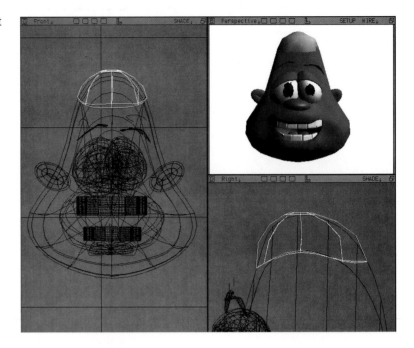

Next, add a hair shader to the patch. Different shaders will have different features, but most have controls for hair color, density length, and stiffness. These examples were created using Softimage's fur shader for Mental Ray.

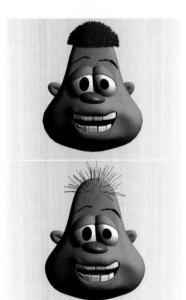

Another approach to modeling hair is with less geometry and a procedural shader to simulate many individual strands for each piece of geometry. Clever application of the shaders can reduce the geometry overhead to a few hundred—rather than several thousand—hairs, making it pragmatic for production purposes. You can then animate these strands by using a physics package with collision detection to yield a fairly realistic motion.

These little blue cones attached to the head can make a very simple type of hair.

Using a shader that blurs and softens the cones' edges makes them blur into a nice '70s-era hairstyle.

Connecting a Head to a Body

After you create the head, you need to create a neck and attach it to the body. You can choose from a couple of different approaches.

Neck on the Body

You can model a neck as a small protuberance from the body and place the head over it, to get a bit of a seam where the head connects.

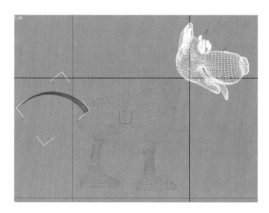

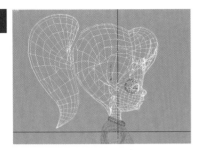

Neck on the Head

You can also extrude a neck from the head and attach it to the body at the shoulders. This is good approach because it leaves no seam on the open skin of the head and neck. The seam of the neck and body can be better hidden on the shoulders or under a piece of clothing.

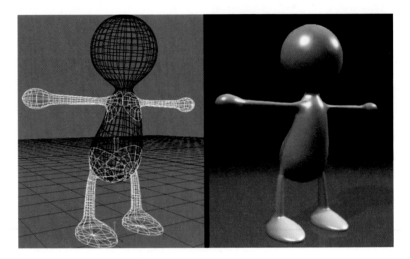

The head, neck, and body as one object.

If you can get the head so that the neck goes all the way to the shoulders, you can continue the extrude and form the entire body. This type of operation makes for a seamless character, although other branching areas, such as the arms and legs, may still need to be seamed.

Putting It All Together

You should have already created a body with a spherical head in the previous chapter. Take the head you have just constructed (or build a new head) and attach it to the body by using any of the methods outlined above and you have a completely animatable character.

CHAPTER 5

Posing Digital Characters

Having built a few characters, you can start reviewing some of the fundamentals of character animation. Before you actually move your characters, however, you need to understand where and how they will be moving; you need to understand how your characters are going to be *posed*—exactly how they will stand, sit, walk, or float in relation to the camera. The pose is a fundamental building block of animation and determines to a great extent how your audience perceives the characters and their emotions.

Intimately involved with posing is the concept of *staging,* which determines where your characters are in relation to the camera, their environment, and each other. Again, these relationships determine exactly how your animation plays to the audience.

Until you understand how to place your characters properly in front of the camera, it makes no sense to move them. With that premise in mind, let's take a look at the basics of posing your characters.

Methods for Animating Your Characters

Theater, dance, mime, and countless other performing arts involve posing to a great extent. Animation is another art form that relies heavily on clear poses to convey its message. A pose is simply the way a character presents itself to the camera. If the character is sad, happy, frightened, or brave, the audience should be able to see and understand it in his pose—by the way he stands, the positioning of his hands, the positioning of his head, and so on. Every part of the body plays a role in creating the pose.

In the golden age of animation, animators discovered two basic methods for animating a scene: pose-to-pose and straight-ahead. Each method uses posing in different ways and has its own unique place and advantages.

Pose-to-pose animation is the more controlled of the two. By using this method, you plan out your shot and block out the character's main poses within the shot. If your character is getting in a taxi, for example, the poses may be as follows:

1. Hailing the cab.

2. Opening the door.

3. Entering the cab.

The theory behind pose-to-pose animation is that every action can be broken down into a series of distinct poses. From there it's simply a matter of creating inbetweens (or letting the computer inbetween the poses for you) and tweaking these as necessary, of course. It is the best way to animate difficult and tightly choreographed shots. Pose-to-pose animation, however, may lack spontaneity.

Straight-ahead animation is pretty much what the name implies. In this method, you start on frame 1 and animate "straight-ahead." This method is more improvisational in nature and usually leads to some very spontaneous and complex motions. It's the method closest to "acting," a frame at a time. Still, this method can make well-defined and solid poses hard to achieve, sometimes making animation that is hard to "read" or comprehend. In straight-ahead animation, complex shots can be difficult to animate.

You can, however, combine the two methods and get the best of both. Computer animation gives you the bonus of being able to combine them rather easily. Most fast machines can play back an animation test almost instantly, making it easy for the animator to block out a series of poses and change them on the fly, adding new poses or changing them when necessary.

Animators who use other media don't have this flexibility. An animator who uses a pencil would have to inbetween the drawings leading up to that new pose—which can be daunting—and a single pose change ripples through the entire sequence. Clay animators don't even have the luxury of changing their poses. Because everything is photographed as it's posed, the medium dictates that they animate straight ahead. Computers really do provide much more flexibility in manipulating and changing your poses no matter how you decide to animate—by using the straight-ahead method, the pose-to-pose method, or both.

The question that still remains is how do you approach animating your scene? Do you plan your shot carefully (pose-to-pose) or do you improvise (straight-ahead)? These questions have no easy answers, and the best advice is to use your intuition and experience. Overplanning a shot may well sap the life out of it. Being more improvisational can add unexpected touches and details you would have never dreamed of. On the other hand, complex shots need to be planned out carefully, or they simply will not work. As you build experience as a character animator, you'll know which shots need strict planning and which can be handled more loosely.

Either way, the first concept you need to know in becoming an animator is how to stage and pose characters so the audience can read them quickly and effectively.

Posing Your Characters Naturally

Strong poses read well the instant they're viewed. If your poses are strong, the audience knows exactly what's happening and understands your character's actions. Also, strong poses are always balanced, giving your digital characters the distinct feeling of weight. In the computer, your digital characters have no mass. You must give them weight through proper posing.

This is an unnatural pose. Rarely does the body rest equally on both feet.

Placing the weight on one leg gives the hips a natural lean, but now the body looks like it's going to tip over!

This is much better. The spine and shoulders are turned in the opposite direction to maintain balance in the system.

Balance

The body is really a system of joints trying to stay in balance. Each bone acts as a tiny lever, distributing the weight of the body through the spine to the hips. In the human body, all balance starts with the hips. The spine and the upper body rest on the hips, and the hips rest on the legs. Any forces generated by the legs reach the upper body through the hips. The hips, then, are the center of gravity of the body and the center of most motions. Because everything stems from the hips, they're the best place to start when posing a character.

In a relaxed stance, the body usually rests on one leg, not both. If you've ever watched people waiting in a long line, you know what I mean. People constantly shift their weight from one foot to another as they wait. Rarely do they ever place their weight equally on both feet.

Symmetry

When a person rests on one leg, the action throws the whole system off center. When the weight is on one leg, the free leg pulls the hip down and out of balance, in turn curving the spine and forcing the shoulders in the opposite direction to maintain balance. If the body is about to move forward, the shoulder drops on the same side as the hip. Either way, the body's natural state of balance is asymmetrical.

You'll be tempted to place the body into symmetrical poses because it is so symmetrical. Not only is this dull and boring, but it is unnatural. People rarely place their weight equally on both feet. This stance happens only in odd circumstances, such as when a soldier stands at strict attention.

To keep your characters looking natural, you need to keep them asymmetrical in almost every way—from the positions of the eyes, hands, and feet to the motions and actions they perform. Symmetry has an odd habit of creeping in at the worst times. Even minor details in a pose, such as both feet pointing in the same direction, can make a character look strange.

Look at the poses on the next page and decide which is more natural.

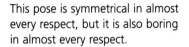

This pose is symmetrical in almost every respect, but it is also boring in almost every respect.

This pose breaks symmetry in a number of places...

...and so does this one. Both poses are more interesting than the first and look more natural.

One way to ensure that your characters are balanced is to look at them from several different directions. A character that seems well-balanced from the front may be totally off balance when viewed from the side. Because your characters are three-dimensional, you need to pose them in three dimensions. It's also nice to keep a strong shadow underneath your characters at all times. The shadow helps lock your characters to the ground and gives them a sense of weight.

The bear on the left has no shadow and looks as if he's floating somewhere near the ground. On the right, the bear's shadow helps lock his feet to the ground.

Exercise #1: Creating a Natural Pose

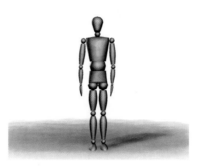

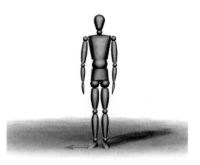

1. Load one of the charac-
    ters you built into your
    favorite 3D program. To
    help illustrate, I'll use a
    simple segmented charac-
    ter. This character is very
    stiff and symmetrical.

2. People rarely stand with
    their feet straight ahead.
    Rotate the right leg along
    its vertical axis about 30
    to 45 degrees so that the
    toes are pointed outward.

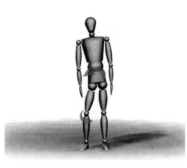

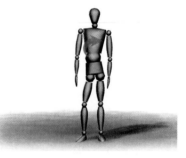

3. Give the hips a slight
    rotation so that the left
    leg is straight. Rotate the
    right leg at both the thigh
    and the knee so that the
    leg has a natural bend but
    still touches the ground.

4. Finally, twist the spine and
    shoulders so the pose
    looks balanced. Keep the
    head vertical.

You can create an infinite number of poses with your character.
For additional practice, continue this exercise on your own by
using the principles of balance and symmetry to pose your characters doing some simple actions. View these characters from several different angles to make sure they're actually balanced. You
may want to pose your characters doing the following:

- Reaching for something on a high shelf
- Climbing a wall
- Picking up a coin
- Dangling from a rope

Making Strong Silhouettes

Remember that your 3D animated creation is almost always going to be shown on a 2D screen. The screen is your stage, with the audience viewing everything through the camera. As such, your characters must present their actions clearly to the camera so that the audience can read and understand them well.

Probably the best way to pose characters for the camera is by studying methods pioneered over the centuries by magicians, mimes, and stage actors. One of the most important fundamentals is presenting a strong silhouette to the audience—in our case, the camera. The human eye first picks out the silhouette of an object and then fills in the rest of the detail. If the action is presented so that the outline is clear, the action will be clear, as well.

Think of a magician pulling a rabbit out of a hat. He always pulls the rabbit out to his right or his left and away from his body so that even the person in the back row can see what's going on. If the magician wants to hide something, he usually does it when his hands are passing in front of his body. The body, along with the motions, serve to conceal the action. The same principles apply to animation. Although animators usually don't have to worry about performing slight of hand, they are very concerned about making actions seen or read. The silhouette is the key.

When you eliminate all the detail and focus only on the silhouette, you can easily guess what this little guy is doing...

...he's about to pull something from his hat. If the silhouette reads, so does the pose.

Here's a little trick that most traditional animators learn in art school. This will help you determine whether your pose reads clearly. First, draw the pose. Next, take a piece of charcoal and blacken in everything, leaving only an outline. Finally, ask yourself, "What is this character doing?" If the silhouette is clear, the action and the pose will read well.

But what if you don't draw? Well, first I would say that all animators can use a life drawing class or two. Next, I would say that you can still do the same exercise digitally.

First, pose your 3D character to the camera in your favorite 3D package. Next, apply a matte black texture to the character and render the pose. You have nothing left but the silhouette. Either the pose reads or it doesn't. Another way to get a silhouette is to simply look at the alpha channel matte used to composite the character into the shot; the matte is always the silhouette.

A good example of silhouetting is this karate kick. This image reads well both as an image and in silhouette.

If the kick is into the camera, however, the exact same pose is destroyed. The angle from which you view your character is just as important as the pose itself.

Exercise #2: Silhouetting

Take one of the poses you created in the previous exercise and see how it looks in silhouette.

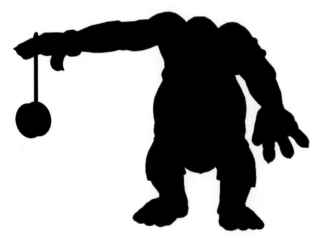

1. First, load one of the poses in your favorite 3D editor.

2. Apply a non-reflective, matte black texture to the character's body and any props he's using.

3. Render the image. The result is your character in silhouette. Now ask yourself, "What is this character doing?"

Creating a Line of Action

In addition to a strong silhouette, a good pose should also have a definite *line of action*—a strong line that you can follow from your character's feet to the tip of his fingers. A strong line not only makes your pose more effective, it also adds beauty to the pose. The human eye is naturally drawn to a good line.

For example, if your character is throwing a ball, arch the back and make his arm follow along the same arc. Getting all of the body parts to follow an arc not only strengthens the pose, it makes the pose much more pleasing to the eye. If you put the whole body into the throw, the movement looks more convincing.

If a character is in a tug-of-war, for example, he'll dig his heels into the ground and arch his back, putting every muscle he can into the effort. Even simple actions should follow a definite line. If a character is happy, he'll arch his back and throw out his chest. If he's sad, he'll slump over and have a completely different arc.

This first pose is weak because it has no discernible line of action.

Getting the character's whole body into the action makes it follow a stronger line, giving him a better pose.

This character, engaged in a tug of war, shows a great line of action.

Sadness causes the body to slump over and calls for a different line of action.

Staging Your Characters

Staging is important for anyone involved in film. *Staging* involves the placement of characters in relation to other characters, the camera, and the environment for maximum effect. Placing the character in just the right place at the right time is an art that every director needs to master.

The following is a simple but good example of proper staging. What if you have a character dangling from a rope over a deep crevasse?

If you shoot the character from the side, the audience will have many questions. How deep is this pit? Where's the danger? What's the point?

By shooting downward toward the character, the staging becomes much more convincing. This shot tells you everything you need to know—the character is in deep trouble.

Another important factor in staging is how the camera's position affects the audience's perception of the shot. When the camera is placed low and is shooting up at a character, he appears more menacing. Think of any 1950s sci-fi movie where the giant insect is menacing a major metropolis and you'll get the idea. Conversely, keeping the camera high makes a character seem helpless and insignificant, much like ants when viewed from above.

Placing the camera low makes the character look ominous and threatening.

Conversely, placing the camera high makes the character seem smaller and less threatening.

Staging Multiple Characters

Not only do you need to know where to place the characters in relation to the camera, but you also need to know where to place the characters in relation to one another. How do you make them interact and read properly?

The solution depends on a study of acting and interpersonal relationships. Characters who are friendly can be staged closer to one another than characters who are enemies. Every situation has its own demands. For example, a Marine drill sergeant intimidates a recruit by yelling at him a few slim inches from his face. Lovers who are angry at each other turn away and stand practically back to back.

You can stage two characters by simply placing them next to each other. These stagings might work for a simple conversation.

To get more depth, bring one character closer to the camera. This also gives more emphasis to one character, thereby creating a more dramatic effect.

When you have more than two characters in a scene, use the composition to direct the eye to what's important. Think of the characters as weights. If you put one character off to the side of the screen, you may need several toward the center of the shot to keep the scene balanced.

Working with the Camera

One advantage of computer animation is that it is extremely easy to move the camera. Computer animators probably move their cameras far more often than necessary. For spaceship fly-bys and architectural walk-throughs, moving the camera may be great, but for character animators it can spell instant disaster—especially when trying to present an action, feeling, or emotion to the camera. When the camera moves, the motion draws attention away from the actors and toward the movement. Also, because moving the camera effectively changes the pose, it also forces you to rethink your poses every single time the camera moves.

Still, moving the camera can be very effective when you do it at the right time and for the right reasons. Panning with a running character gives the feeling of motion. A rack focus will blur the background or foreground, giving strong emphasis to one part of the scene. You may want to move the camera in quickly in a moment of fear—letting the camera do the acting. These techniques are simple tricks that live-action directors have used for decades, and for 3D animation they work in much the same way.

This rack focus effect can give strong emphasis to one part of the scene or another by blurring the foreground or background elements.

In a digital environment, you can easily place several cameras in a shot to get the equivalent of the live-action, three-camera shoot. Use one lens for establishing the shot, one for the action, and one for the close-up. Even in 3D, different lenses have different effects. For example, many live-action directors prefer to shoot close-ups with a longer lens because it flattens the perspective and focuses attention on the actor. On a panoramic shot, the director might choose a shorter, wide-angle lens to get as much of the landscape into the shot as possible.

The same holds true in 3D. Instead of just pushing the same old camera in for the close-up, change the lens or create a new camera with the proper lens for the shot. For animators without stock lenses, the lens length is equivalent to the angle of the camera's field of view. The wider the angle, the shorter the lens. These values are shown in table 4.1.

Table 4.1		
Conversion between the lens length and the camera field of view.		
Lens	Field of view	Type of lens
15 mm	115.0 degrees	Ultra Wide Angle
20 mm	94.286 degrees	Very Wide Angle
28 mm	76.364 degrees	Wide Angle
35 mm	63.0 degrees	Medium Wide Angle
50 mm	46.0 degrees	Normal/Standard
85 mm	28.0 degrees	Medium Long
135 mm	18.0 degrees	Long/Telephoto
200 mm	12.0 degrees	Extra Long/Super

Although using a variety of lenses is important, it's also a good idea to reuse your lenses for the same types of shots. For continuity, most live-action directors use the same lenses for close-ups and the same ones for long shots throughout a film. Reusing the same lenses for the same types of shots will also give your 3D film a better sense of continuity.

Here's an example of how lens choice can affect the composition of a shot.

The exact same pose rendered through three different lenses: a 15 mm, a 50 mm, and a 135 mm. The longer the lens, the tighter the angle, so the further back you have to move the camera to frame the same shot.

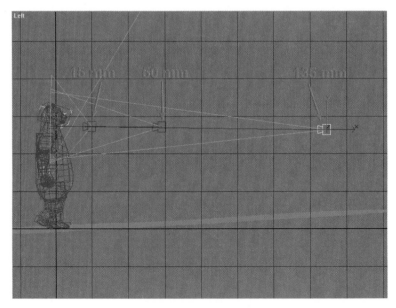

What the audience sees through a 15 mm ultrawide angle lens. Notice how it distorts the bear for a fish-eye effect. Also notice how a good portion of the sky and landscape is included in the shot. This lens is not intended for close-ups but works great on panoramic shots or staging multiple characters in depth.

This shot was taken through a standard 50 mm lens. Notice how the landscape recedes a bit and the fish-eye effect flattens out. The 50 mm is a good all-around lens.

166 This shot was taken through a 135 mm telephoto lens. This lens tends to flatten out a character even more and practically eliminates the background. The 135 mm lens is great for close-ups.

Conclusion

This chapter discussed various methods that you can use to help pose and focus your characters. The way you pose your characters can be the difference between realistic digital animations and unbelievable ones. Try to mimic the way humans and animals pose in real life.

CHAPTER 6

The Basics of Character Animation

You are now ready to begin animating some characters. As you have seen, animation is more than just moving things around. It involves proper construction of your characters, as well as proper staging (the ability to pose your characters naturally). It's time to delve into the nitty-gritty of motion and timing, the two concepts at the heart of animation.

Understanding motion is one component of the equation. Watching and observing the way people and animals move is something every animator needs to do. Watching reference materials—whether it's nature films, silent comedies, or classic cartoons—is one way to understand motion. It's important to familiarize yourself with basic animation concepts such as squash and stretch, anticipation, overshoot, follow-through, and many others.

In addition to learning basic animation concepts and observing the world around you, time is a precious quantity that must be used wisely. Timing is a raw material that actors, comedians, and musicians use constantly. Good comic timing means knowing exactly when to spring the punch line. Good animation timing means knowing exactly when your character should react, blink, or pull that huge mallet out from behind his back. Timing is the only thing that separates animation from illustration. With proper timing, your characters appear to live. Without it, they look like nothing more than poorly controlled puppets.

Understanding the Importance of Timing

Timing affects every aspect of a film on many levels. First, the film is a specific length—from a 30-second commercial to a two-hour feature. Second, the cutting of the scenes within this time constraint affects the mood and pace of the film. Third, the performing and timing of the character's actions influences how each individual scene plays.

Think of your film as music. Both mediums are totally reliant on time. The film is your entire work, much like the song is a musician's entire work. Your film's scenes can be seen as verses, choruses, or movements. The individual notes of the instruments are the same as the individual actions of your characters. Each action, as in each musical note, must occur in the right place and at the right time. As in music, bad timing in animation sticks out like a sore thumb.

One Thing at a Time

"One thing at a time" is the cardinal rule in animation timing. The audience perceives actions best if the actions are presented sequentially, so you should present your main actions that way— one at a time within a smooth sequence of motions. A character stubs his toe, recoils, and then reacts. If the reaction is too quick, the audience will not have time to read it, so the recoil acts as a bridge between the two main actions.

You must remember that the audience is usually seeing your film for the first time. As the animator, you need to guide viewers and give them clues as to exactly where to look at each point in the film. Think of a Roadrunner cartoon. When the Coyote steps out over the gorge, he takes a while to notice he's suspended in mid-air. He reacts typically and then looks directly at the camera with a pitiful expression. This one drawing can be held for almost a second. He may blink or his whiskers may twitch, but this is essentially a still pose. He then zips off the screen in a few frames. This is a great example of timing because in the short span that the pose is held, the audience comes to the same realization as the Coyote— he's doomed. It also draws the audience's full attention to the Coyote so that when he does fall off screen, the audience sees that clearly.

One of the most important lessons you can learn about timing is to draw attention to what is about to move before it moves. An action reads effectively only when the audience is fully focused on it. As the animator, you must guide the audience's eyes through the character's actions.

Developing Good Timing

Every animator needs to understand how things move with respect to time. A good sense of timing is something that animators develop through years of practice. The next section reviews some of the basic steps you can take to develop your own sense of timing.

Observing the world around you is the first step in this process. Breaking down these observations into their exact timing is the next. I've known many animators who have dissected classic animated and live-action films frame by frame to understand the timing. A VCR with a good freeze frame capability is an excellent investment for an animator.

Another essential tool for an animator is a stopwatch. Whenever I need to time a shot, the first thing I do is reach for my stopwatch and act out the scene, timing the approximate length of each action. I plug in these amounts for my rough pose timing and then tweak it in my 3D program. The stopwatch is one of the most important tools an animator can own. It enables you to physically act out your scene and get a fairly good idea of the timing. If you're shy, close the door and draw the blinds, but act out your shots, regardless. It's very important to understand how your characters will move in relation to time.

Computer animators have some extra advantages when it comes to tweaking and adjusting their timing. The highly interactive nature of digital animation makes it very easy to make interim tests. This instant feedback goes a long way. I remember when I was in animation school and had to film everything on Super 8 and wait days for pencil tests to come back. It was about as far from interactive as you could get, and learning which timings worked and which didn't, took forever. When I finally got some cheap animation software and could see my pencil tests instantly, my sense of timing improved immediately.

Automatic inbetweening can also be advantageous to the computer animator. Letting the computer calculate the frames in between the main poses gives you more flexibility in altering and changing poses and makes for some very smooth animation. Letting the computer do too much may make your animations look stale and generic. You must always be aware of exactly how the computer is calculating inbetweens; you can stay aware through a number of methods, the most important of which are motion graphs and paths.

Motion Graphs

Most good animation software can present you with a graphical representation—called a *motion graph*—of how your objects are moving. Motion graphs are an invaluable tool for the animator in diagnosing and fixing animation problems. Knowing how to read and manipulate motion graphs is an essential skill.

Every software package is different, but most motion graphs work in similar ways. Typically, the horizontal axis of the graph represents time whereas the vertical axis represents the parameter being changed—position, rotation, scaling, and so on. These parameters are plotted graphically to tell you exactly how an object moves.

For example, take a car driving through city streets. The car's motion can be represented as a graph. First, the car may be going a steady rate of 35 mph. The car encounters a stoplight and slows to a stop for a bit. When the light changes, the car accelerates again to a steady rate of speed.

A motion graph of a car in traffic.

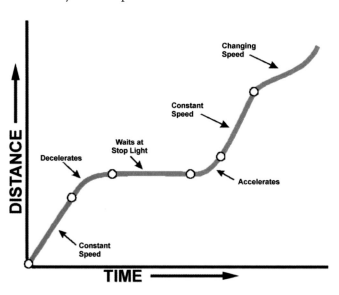

When the car is traveling at a steady rate of speed, the graph is linear—a straight, diagonal line. When the car is stopped, the change is zero, so the graph is flat. When the car is accelerating, decelerating, or changing its velocity in any way, the result is a curve. A curve that slopes toward vertical represents acceleration, but a curve that slopes toward horizontal represents deceleration.

In most software packages, you have three motion graphs for the object—one each for the x, y, and z axis, allowing you to manipulate each separately.

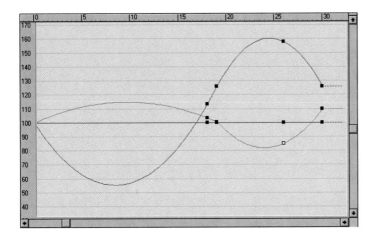

In this software graph, red represents the x axis, green represents the y axis, and blue is the z axis. Notice that the blue line is flat, indicating there is no motion along the z axis.

Motion graphs are also good for finding and fixing annoying glitches in your animation. Generally, animation problems show up as distinct spikes in a motion graph. The spikes may be places where a key has been altered or is in the wrong position. Another use for motion graphs is determining whether something is moving or not. If you want your character's feet to remain fixed to the floor, the foot's motion graph remains flat at the level of the floor.

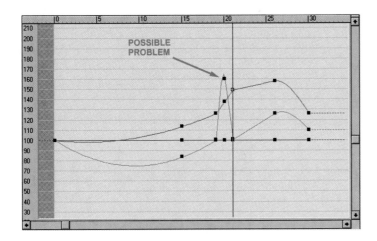

This spike in the motion graph indicates a sudden change that may cause problems in the final animation.

Motion Graphs by any other name...

Every package is different, and every package calls its features by
different names. In this book, I'm trying to present concepts
broadly, so you can apply them no matter what animation package
you choose. You may get confused because the terminology used
in this book may not match exactly what's in your manual.
Motion graphs are a good example of a concept that applies to
many packages; you only need to know what the feature is called
in your software.

In Softimage, a motion graph is
called an Fcurve and looks like this.

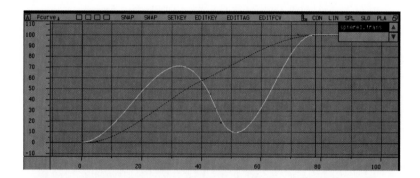

In LightWave, it is called a Motion
Graph and looks like this.

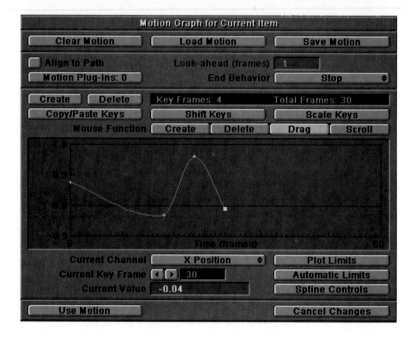

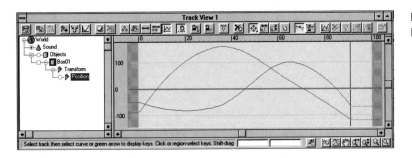

In 3D Studio MAX, it is called a Function Curve and looks like this.

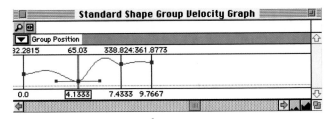

In ElectricImage, it is called a Velocity Graph and looks like this.

These dialog boxes span three platforms (Mac, PC, and UNIX), so they may look different, but they do exactly the same thing. That is, they all plot an animated parameter (translation, scaling, rotation, and so on) against time and enable you to edit the curves. These four packages are not the only ones that support this feature. As you can see, it doesn't matter what the feature is named, the concepts are identical regardless of the software you use.

Paths

Another way of looking at your animation is through the use of *paths*. Most packages can display the path that your object takes through space—a good way of determining exactly how an object is moving. By adjusting the shape and position of the path, you can alter the way an object or character moves through the scene.

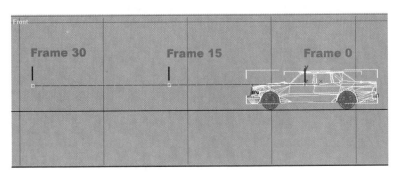

A car is moving through the scene. You can place keyframes at the beginning, middle, and end of the move (blue lines). Looking at the path, the keys are evenly spaced, meaning the car is traveling at a constant rate of speed.

If you move the key in the middle, the car travels much farther in the first half of the shot, appearing to move faster, and then it slows down in the second half. The distance between the keys along the path determines velocity.

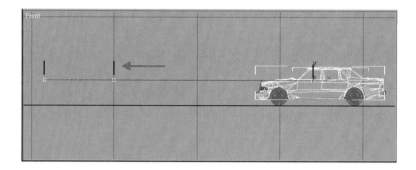

In addition to generating a path for keyframed motion, many packages also enable you to draw a spine and use that line as the path. For example, if you want your character to follow a straight line, the path will be straight as well.

The path shows how the objects are set to move through the scene. The first object moves along an arc whereas the second object moves along straight lines.

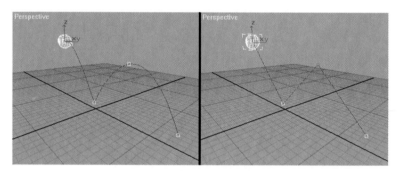

Using Timing to Suggest Weight

Unless your software calculates real-world physics, there is no way to indicate an object's weight. Think of a simple sphere sitting on the ground. Is it a bowling ball or a basketball? Until it moves, you have no idea whether the sphere is filled with air or lead. After the sphere is in motion some of its characteristics become apparent. A bowling ball is heavy. It moves slowly and a great deal of force is required to change its direction. A basketball, on the other hand, is relatively light. It moves fast, bounces easily, and very little force is needed to change its direction.

Which sphere is filled with air and which one is filled with lead? Until they move, there is no way of knowing.

Exercise #1: Creating the Illusion of Weight Through Motion

One of the best ways to develop your sense of timing is to do some experiments with simple objects, such as spheres and boxes. These shapes are great because they can be modeled and animated quickly in any 3D package. Also, by animating simple objects, you can limit your focus to pure motion and timing.

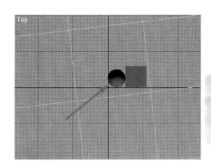

1. Model a sphere, a box, and a ground plane. Position the sphere and the box on the ground plane with some distance between them.

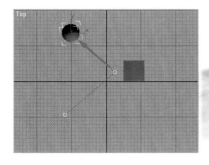

2. Animate the sphere so that it travels in a straight line toward one face of the box.

3. When the sphere touches the box, change the direction of the sphere so that it moves off in the opposite direction. Keep the box absolutely still. Render the shot.

   Looking at it, the final animation leads you to believe that the box is very heavy and that the ball is relatively light. Now reverse the process.

continues

Exercise #1: continued

4. Using the exact same setup as before, animate the sphere so that it travels in a straight line toward the box.

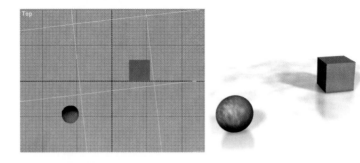

5. This time, when the ball strikes the box, keep the ball moving in a straight line. Next, animate the box by rotating it, as if it were pushed aside by the ball. Render the shot.

   This animation leads you to believe that the ball is much heavier than the box and knocks it out of its path.

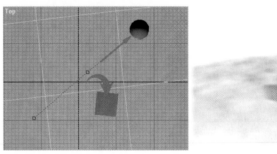

What does this example teach the animator? In both shots, the ball and the box are identical; the only thing that changes is their motions; in the first example, the ball appears light, in the second, it appears heavy. As you can see, motion and timing affect our perception of an object's weight.

On the CD

For reference, I've included my takes on these two exercises on the CD. View BOXBALL1.AVI and BOXBALL2.AVI (or BOXBALL1.MOV and BOXBALL2.MOV for Mac users) to see what I mean.

Understanding the Language of Movement

The animator must understand the language of movement. By that, I mean animation has a very specific vocabulary of motion from which animators can draw. This vocabulary includes such things as arcs, anticipation, overshoot, secondary motion, follow-through, overlap, and moving holds. These motions are the raw material; good timing is the glue that holds it all together.

Arcs

In real life, nearly every part of the human body moves in arcs, partly due to physics and the way muscles move, but also due to the fact that nearly every joint in the body rotates. The hand doesn't simply move forward; the shoulder and elbow rotate in combination to move the hand. This forces the hand to sweep out an arc through space, rather than a straight line.

The rotation of an arm's joints caus-es the hand to move along an arc.

Gravity is another important factor in causing objects to move along arcs. Falling objects and cartoon characters' bodies follow arcs. Gravity causes planets to follow elliptical orbits. It also causes a thrown ball to follow a parabolic trajectory. As you can see, arcs are everywhere in nature.

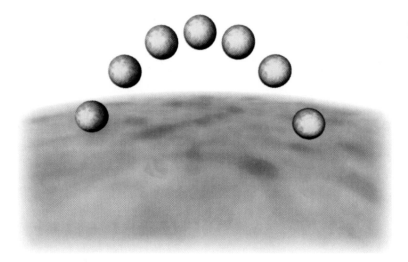

A ball thrown in the air also follows an arc.

Slow-Ins and Slow-Outs

Another fact about natural motions is that things don't simply start and stop suddenly. Rather, they accelerate from a start and decelerate to a stop. Force plays a role in every motion. Newtonian physics states that any object subjected to a force accelerates. Think of a ball thrown straight up. The force of gravity slows it to a stop and then accelerates the ball as it falls back to earth. In animation, this effect is known as a *slow-in and slow-out*.

Even the body's joints follow this principle; the muscle puts a constant force on the joint, accelerating the limb in one direction. Another muscle pulls it in the opposite direction, slowing it to a stop. Most software can automatically inbetween two poses and do the slow-ins and slow-outs for you.

There are many times when you might not want to do a slow-in or slow-out. If a character hits a brick wall, for instance, he stops dead in his tracks, without decelerating.

Any object subjected to a force accelerates. In animation, this is known as a slow-in.

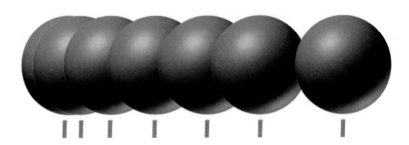

The motion graph for a slow-in and slow-out looks something like this. Notice how the curve slopes toward horizontal as the speed nears zero.

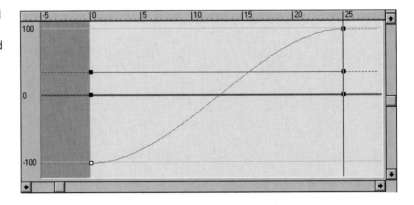

Exercise #2: Using Slow-In and Slow-Out

Let's raise a character's arm by using slow-in and slow-out. First, we'll do a straight inbetween that has no slow in and slow out; next we will add slow-in and slow-out to cushion the move. We can do this exercise using any character with an arm. If you want to use a character of your own, that's fine, or you can load a character off of the CD.

1. Position your character in front of the camera so that his arm falls limp at his side. Go to frame 15 and create a keyframe for this pose.

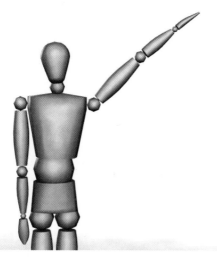

2. Go to frame 30. Move the character's arm so that his hand is above his head. Create another keyframe.

continues

3. Now load your motion graph editor (or whatever it's called in your software) and create a straight inbetween for the character. This is done by making the character's motion graph look like a straight line. Remember, a straight line means a straight inbetween. Render a test.

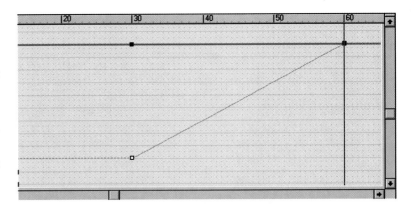

4. Next, using the same two keyframes, modify the motion graph so that it looks like this. The curve tells the computer to accelerate (or slow-in) to the move and decelerate (or slow-out) of the move. Render a test.

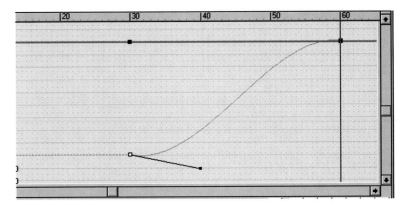

Now view both animations and ask yourself which one looks more natural. If you did the exercise right, it will be the second example.

Force and Drag

When animating, you also need to consider the effects of drag on an object. Force transmitted to an object does not affect all parts of the object equally. Imagine two sticks connected at a flexible joint. If you pulled one of the sticks straight down, the second stick would take a while to "get in line," so to speak. This effect is called *drag*.

Another point to consider is how a multijointed object moves. If an object has more than two joints, each joint drags behind the other. A third joint added to the stick drags behind the second joint.

Drag causes the second joint to take some time to follow the first. If you pull down on the first stick…

…the second stick must rotate to get into alignment with it.

Drag causes a delay in the two sticks' lining up.

Three sticks means more drag. The third stick drags behind the second, which drags behind the first.

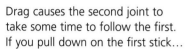

The same principles apply to the joints of your character. The spine is really just a collection of similar joints. Force transmitted to one end of the spine takes time to reach the other. Force applied to the arm takes time to reach the shoulder and even longer to reach the feet. Think of a dog's tail. The joints in the tail behave exactly like the joints in the stick example. The base of the tail rotates in a cycle, causing the outer parts of the tail to drag.

The body's skeleton is really just a collection of joints. Force applied to one part of the skeleton takes time to reach the others.

A dog's tail behaves exactly like the sticks; the end of the tail drags behind the base.

Squash and Stretch

On the CD

There is an animation called DOGTAIL.AVI or DOGTAIL.MOV on the accompanying CD-ROM. Watch this for reference.

Unless you're animating the Statue of Liberty, your characters are usually made of flesh. Flesh is very pliable and flexes and bends considerably when moving. Think of how many different shapes the human face can make. The same goes for just about any part of the body. This characteristic is known as squash and stretch.

The easiest way to illustrate this concept is with a bouncing ball. When a ball hits the ground, the force of impact makes it "squash" from a sphere into an oblong shape. As it recoils, you can see it "stretch" in the other direction. The same principles apply in character animation. When a character jumps in the air, he stretches as he takes off; when he lands, he squashes. The same goes for such things as muscles and limbs.

When a ball hits the ground, the force of impact squashes it. Upon recoil, it stretches.

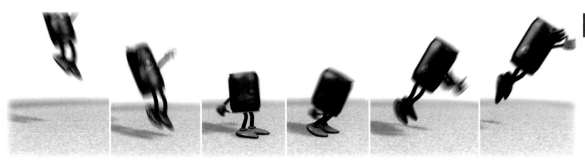

The same theory applies to characters.

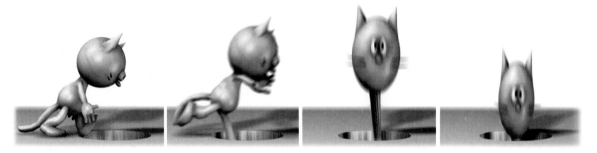

For an exaggerated, cartoony effect, a character falling down a hole can stretch quite a bit in a few frames.

When squashing and stretching, you must remember to maintain your character's volume. Consider a balloon filled with water. If you stretch it or squash it, the water in one part of the balloon moves to another area. The volume never changes. People are mostly water too, and the same principle applies. No matter how squashed or distended the character, his volume always remains the same. If the volume increases or decreases, it appears as though the character is growing or shrinking.

When you stretch a character, make sure you maintain his volume. The one in the middle is correctly stretched, but the one on the right has gained volume.

Exactly how you squash and stretch a character in a computer depends a great deal on how the character is built and how it animates. The following are some methods for squashing and stretching your characters.

Scaling

The easiest method for squashing and stretching is to scale all or part of your character along one axis. If your character is being squashed, reduce his size along the axis; increase the size to stretch him. To maintain volume you need to increase or reduce the volume along the other two axes.

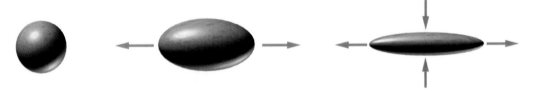

Scaling an object along one axis alone increases its volume. You must compensate by scaling back along the other axes as well.

Bones

Bones enable you to squash and stretch your characters easily. Most packages that support bones enable you to scale and resize each bone. The affected vertices of your character's mesh will scale accordingly. If you want to stretch the arm, for example, stretch the bones in the arm. Most of the same principles of scaling apply here; if you stretch the bone in one direction, shrink it along the others to maintain volume.

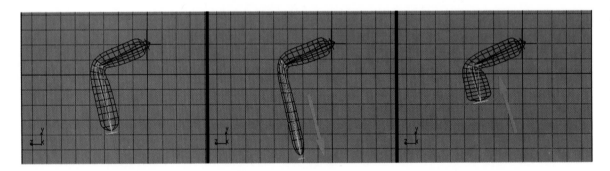

Scaling the bone itself causes its assigned vertices to squash and stretch.

Lattices and Other Deformations

Lattice deformations and global deformations that enable you to bend, taper, or otherwise modify the shape of your object are great for creating squash and stretch. You can apply these to the character as a whole, or to part of a character, if your software enables it.

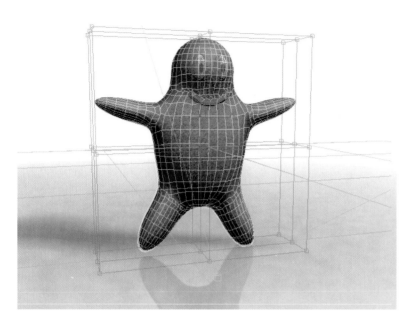

Another way to squash or stretch all or part of a character is with a deformation tool such as this lattice.

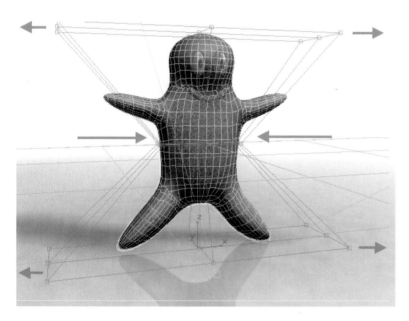

Manipulating the lattice causes the character to stretch.

Automatic Stretching

Another method is to let the computer do the stretching for you. Softimage has a feature called Quick Stretch that automatically stretches and squashes objects according to their velocity and acceleration. Other packages do this through plug-ins. This type of feature is great for creating drag in such things as floppy ears and hair because you can let the computer figure out the keys for you.

Exercise #3: Squashing and Stretching a Ball

This simple ball bounce exercise illustrates how to do squash and stretch simply by resizing the object.

1. Model a sphere and ground plane.

2. Make the ball bounce on the ground. The ball should slow in on a parabolic arc as it accelerates toward the ground. When it hits, it will reverse its direction immediately when it bounces and follow the opposite arc, slowing out. The timing should take 15 frames for the ball to fall to the ground and 15 after the bounce.

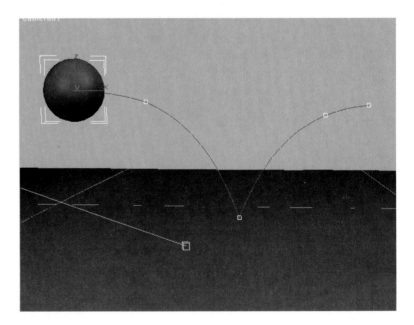

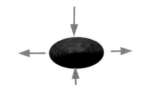

3. Now add a bit of squash and stretch. On frame 13, before the ball hits, scale the ball so that it is elongated along the path it is falling. This will make the ball appear to stretch as it falls, giving it a rubbery motion.

4. On frame 15, when the ball hits the ground, squash the ball by scaling it down vertically and out horizontally. Be sure to maintain the volume of the ball. If squashing makes the ball lose contact with the ground, adjust the ball so that it makes firm contact.

5. On frame 18, elongate the ball along the path once more, stretching it, and on frame 30, when the ball hits the top of the trajectory, return the ball to normal size. Render a test.

 On the CD

A rendered version of the animation is on the CD. It is called BOUNCE.AVI or BOUNCE.MOV.

Anticipation

Anticipation is the body's natural way of gaining momentum before an action begins. Think of a man jumping. He swings his arms behind him, bends his knees, and actually moves down slightly to get momentum before jumping up. A baseball batter moves the bat back before swinging it forward. You lean back before getting out of a chair. It's kind of like getting a head start on the action.

Anticipation can also be used to control the audience and get its members looking where you want them to. The human eye works somewhat automatically. It is naturally drawn to things that move. By moving an object in the opposite direction, you draw attention to it before it moves. When it does move, the audience is already watching, so the motion can be much faster. Anticipation is a perfectly natural part of motion, and by exaggerating it you can keep the audience's attention and achieve crisper timing.

Many times, you may need to animate a very fast action, such as a zip out. The most important point to remember is that when animating a fast action, your audience needs to be fully aware of the action before it occurs. The anticipation of the action is very important. When animating a very fast action, it's best to add motion blur to the shot so that the animation looks smooth.

I cannot overstate the importance of anticipating your character's motions when animating, because it's the way the body naturally moves. An anticipation does not have to be a big motion or a giant pause in the action. It can be as short and subtle as one or two frames for a small action.

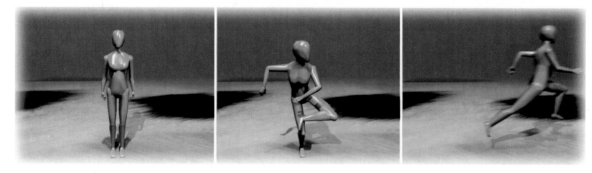

Anticipation means moving left before you move right, moving down before moving up. Before this character zips off, she cocks her body in anticipation of the move.

Before this character puts his hand in the hat, he anticipates the move by flipping his wrist back before moving it down.

Exercise #4: Anticipation

Simply by making a character leap out of frame, you can see how anticipation works. Before you do the following exercise, stand up and do a small jump. Pay attention to how your knees bend and your arms anticipate the jump by moving back before swinging forward when you jump. If you want, use a stopwatch as you jump to get a rough idea of the timing.

1. Place your character in front of the camera in a simple, relaxed pose.

2. Rotate the arms back and bend the knees in anticipation of the leap. To maintain balance, the body should tilt forward and down at the hips in anticipation of the leap. This motion should take about a quarter to a half second past the first pose.

3. Make your character leap. Straighten out the body and swing the arms forward. Straighten out the legs as they push against the ground and send the character forward. This action should take only a few frames to complete.

4. Render a test and adjust the poses and timing until you are satisfied.

This leap can be expanded with other little details. First, when leaping, the arms lead the action by a frame or two. The feet do not have to leave the ground at the same time, dragging one foot by a frame or two behind the other makes the leap more natural. Finally, remember that the path your character follows is the beginning of a parabola. As he leaps out, make him follow an arc.

Overshoot

As you've seen, anticipation is used to make the start of an action more lifelike. At the tail end, *overshoot* makes the completion of an action more realistic. Many times, the body does not come to a slow and perfect stop. Instead, it overshoots the stopping point for a few frames and settles into the pose. Like anticipation, it is a natural part of motion and can be exaggerated to the animator's advantage.

Think of a character throwing out his arm to point his finger. Before the action starts, the arm anticipates the move. If the motion is quick, the character's arm naturally overshoots the pose so that the arm is absolutely straight. After a few frames, the arm settles into a more natural, relaxed pose. Overshoot can be used to give your character's actions more snap. If you're animating pose-to-pose, you can overshoot a pose for a few frames and then settle in.

When this character throws out his arm, he overshoots the final pose and settles in. The overshoot and settle in usually happen in just a few frames but give the action more snap.

Secondary Action

Although this discussion has been concentrating on the primary motions of the body, there are many secondary parts of the body that move. This type of movement is known to animators as *secondary action*. This broad category of actions includes the little tweaks, gestures, and added touches that bring life and personality to your character. It could be as simple as a character tilting his hat before storming off or a baby in a high chair wiggling her toes while she eats. The primary action is eating, but the secondary action—wiggling the toes—adds personality and life to the character.

Secondary action is best animated as a layer on the primary action. First animate the main motion. When this is correct, add the secondary actions. They should be little extra touches that do not detract from the main point of the shot. Secondary actions are usually bracketed around the main action but do not interfere. Remember, the cardinal rule in animation is to do one thing at a time. The secondary actions serve as a nice, subtle bridge between the main actions. If they get too wild or noticeable, they will become primary actions themselves and detract from the shot.

Follow-Through and Overlap

When a character comes to a stop, not every part of his body stops on the same frame. Momentum carries some parts of the body past the stopping point. When some parts of the body continue moving, it is called *follow-through*. Think of a running dog with big, floppy ears. The ears continue to follow-through after the dog has stopped and behave much like a pendulum. Drag also plays a big part in this.

Overlap is almost identical to follow-through in that it involves secondary motion of the body. The body itself has many parts that don't all move at once—a fat person's belly bounces up and down during a walk, overlapping the action by several frames.

The same goes for the limbs of a body. The hips usually start an action, with the spine and arms dragging by a few frames. Think of an athlete completing a broad jump. His feet may hit the ground, but it may take many frames for the arms to swing forward and come to a complete stop. Again, they act a bit like pendulums.

The dog doesn't stop all at once.

His front feet stop first...

...and then his ears, collar, and tail all follow-through...

...and come to rest a few frames later.

It's important to have overlap in the actions of the scene. Things do not move all at once. Think of the situation where many characters are walking through the scene. If you started all the walks on frame 1, the characters would appear to march in unison. Instead, the best choice is to overlap the motions of the walk, offsetting some of the characters.

This herd of noodles all have the same motion and look like they're marching.

By simply overlapping the cycles, they can be made to look random.

Exercise #5: Using Overshoot, Overlap, and Follow-Through

In this exercise you complete the other half of that leap you created by making your character land to illustrate how different parts of the body follow-through, overlap, and overshoot poses as a character moves.

Again, before animating this shot, act out the action. Stand up and take a short hop. Notice how, as you land, your knees bend to absorb the shock, and your arms naturally swing forward.

1. The character should come in from the leap in a few frames. As the character is about to land, his knees should be slightly bent, hips forward, arms and shoulders back.

2. Two frames later, the character touches the ground, the feet hit heel first, stop and lock to the ground. The rest of the body is nowhere near stopping.

3. Two frames later, momentum of the body is still downward and forward, forcing the knees to bend and the body to bend forward at the waist to absorb the shock. The arms are still back.

4. Three frames later, the body has recoiled and is beginning to stand up. The spine is straightening out—one vertebrae at a time due to drag—and the knees are straightening out. The arms swing forward and start following-through.

5. Four frames later, the body is overshooting the final pose. The spine and legs are almost straight, and the arms are coming to a stop above the head and beginning to move back down again.

6. Six frames later is the final pose. The spine and legs bend a bit for a nice relaxed stance; the arms hang loose.

7. Render a test and adjust the poses and timing until you are happy with the shot. For additional practice, you can hook up this landing with the leap from the previous exercise. Remember that your character's center of mass follows a smooth parabola during the leap.

Animating in Cycles

One way to save time when animating is to animate in *cycles*. A cycle is the same sequence of keyframes repeated over and over. Think of somebody riding a bicycle. The feet on the pedals undergo a regular, cyclical motion. After you've animated one rotation of the pedals, you can copy the keys to create as many repetitions as you want.

Riding a bicycle is a good example of the repetitive motions that can be handled by cycles.

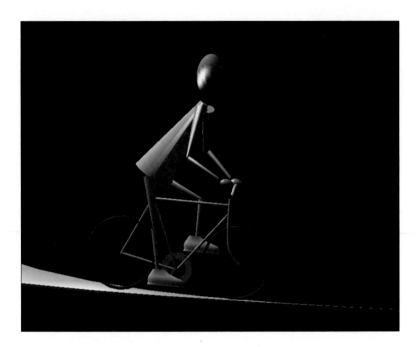

In cel animation, the process is a matter of repeating your drawings. In 3D animation, you need to copy the keyframes to other places on the timeline. One problem with copying the keyframes is that you need to remember that the last keys of the first cycle need to flow into the first key of the next cycle. Many programs have a function that aligns your keys automatically for a smooth transition, and it repeats the cycle for as many times as you want.

If you don't have such a feature, the best way to repeat cycles is manually. You copy the first frame of the cycle to the first frame of the next cycle before you begin animating. Basically, you want the cycles to match up exactly, so you designate the first frame as the place where everything "syncs up"—where it's all in the same place. Copy this frame to the start of the next cycle, and all of your motions in the middle of the cycle will hit this target. Because these two frames are identical, all the motions within the cycle should sync up.

Another problem with cycles is that they are repetitive motions and can get stale and boring quickly. One tack you can take to avoid the monotony is to cycle part of a character's motions. Suppose the character is walking. You can cycle the feet and legs, but change the animation in the upper body to give the shot more variation.

Exercise #6: Using Cycles to Dribble a Basketball

Bouncing a ball is a nice cyclical motion that can be done easily. The trick for getting a cycle right is copying the keys to the right places. This cycle will be 24 frames long.

1. Load a character into your favorite 3D package. Model a simple sphere to represent the basketball. Pose the character so that one arm is out to dribble the ball.

2. Create a keyframe of this pose at frame one and copy it to frame 25, one frame past the end of the cycle. The first frame is where everything syncs up, and the cycle begins anew. By placing these keys at the start of the next cycle, the motions in the middle should match up perfectly.

   Go to frame 12, the middle of the animation. Place the ball on the floor. If you want, you can add a bit of squash to it. Move the character's arm down.

continues

3. Now you actually have an animation that will cycle. Still, you need to add a few more keys to make it look more realistic. Go to frame 5 and key the character's hand as he lets go of the ball.

4. Go to frame 20 and key the character's hand meeting the ball as it comes up. Render a test and tweak as needed.

Moving Holds

Many times your character may need to hold a pose or be still anywhere from a few frames to a few seconds. This pose is known as a *hold*. In cel animation, the hold is typically done by keeping a single drawing on the screen for the duration of the hold. In computer animation, the hold is the kiss of death. For some unexplained reason (maybe because of the realistic nature of the medium), a digital character held in a single position for more than a few frames completely dies. It looks as though you hit the freeze frame button on the VCR.

A character on hold looks like you hit the freeze frame.

Move the character slightly over the duration of the hold. Here, the character has shifted his weight to his left slightly. Be sure to overlap these motions.

To avoid an on-screen death, you need to keep your character moving, even slightly. One of the many tricks for keeping your character alive is to create *moving holds*. If the hold is for a handful of frames, you can create two slightly different variations of the same pose and have the computer inbetween these over the course of the hold.

If the hold is in the range of seconds, you have to take another tack. Secondary actions help a lot, but you need to overlap many subtle actions in the hold to keep the character from looking too mechanical. You may want to shift the character's weight from one foot to another. Move the arm slightly. Tilt the head. Add some blinks. Be sure to overlap these subtle motions. It's really a matter of keeping the character still, but still alive.

A good exercise is to go stand in the corner for a minute or two and try to remain still. If you pay attention to your body, you soon realize that it's constantly moving. Your weight may shift from foot to foot, you're constantly breathing, you're blinking, and so on. These are the same actions you can use to keep your character looking alive.

Exercise #7: Putting It All Together

This last exercise uses most of the techniques you've learned so far. By making a character stand up from a seated position, you use anticipation, drag, overlap, follow-through, and overshoot.

Before going any further, I want you to get up from your chair several times. Notice exactly how your body moves; you lean back to anticipate the move and then you lean forward and stand up. You now have a guideline for the motion of your character. What about the timing? If you have a stopwatch, time yourself standing up and use that to block in your timing; otherwise, use the timing I give you and adjust it to your needs.

Load a character into your 3D program. Next, model a box for the character to sit on. If you want to create a chair or a sofa for the character to sit on, that's fine, but not essential.

1. Seat your character in a relaxed position—your first pose.

2. For your character to stand up, it needs to anticipate the move to help it get some momentum. Rotate the upper body back at the hips. As in the jump exercise, the arms should go back slightly. Place this keyframe—your second pose—approximately a quarter to a half second after the first.

3. As the body gets out of the chair, it leans forward quite a bit. The momentum of the upper body pulls the rear end out of the chair as the weight transfers to the feet. Rotate the upper body forward and rotate the knees so that the rear end is slightly out of the chair. Swing the arms forward to maintain balance, but drag them behind the body by a few frames. A quarter to a half second is a good general timing.

4. Create a standing pose. Keep the feet firmly on the ground as the character stands—lock them in place with IK or by watching and manipulating the keys. The timing should take from a half second to a second after the previous key. The arms also do a bit of follow-through and come to a stop a few frames after the body is standing.

continues

5. Now, let the computer calculate the inbetweens. If your computer is fast enough, press play; otherwise, render a test to see how you did. Go back and rework the timing and poses until you are happy with the shot.

Conclusion

This chapter taught the basic character animation concepts. It also tried to instill an understanding of the subtleties of movement—timing, anticipation, and overshoot. Observe how you move, and how other people around you move. Try to imitate these movements in your animations—even if you are working with a cartoon and need to exaggerate movements. Combining timing, anticipation, overshoot, and your observations will give you the most realistic animations possible.

CHAPTER 7

Walking and Locomotion

Now that you've had a bit of practice animating the human figure, it's time to start moving your characters around. By this, I mean walking and running. Walking requires tons of balance and coordination; I'm amazed at how easy people make it look.

Walking conveys a great deal about a character's personality. The next time you're in a crowded place, notice the different types of walks that people have. Some people waddle, others saunter, and some drag their feet. It's amazing how almost everyone you see has a unique walk. Mae West, Groucho Marx, John Wayne, and Charlie Chaplin are all characters who have very distinctive walks. If you want to know who a character is, figure out how he walks.

Computer animators have a number of tools available for animating walks. It seems as though software vendors have focused a considerable amount of effort on technology for animating walks, and quite a few new and innovative tools are available for automating all or part of the walking process. These sophisticated tools can be both good and bad. As the animator, you should still understand exactly how characters walk and how you want your characters to walk. If a piece of software helps you to get this done in half the time, that's fantastic. Just be sure that you, not a piece of software, controls the animation process.

The walk usually starts with the feet at the "extended position," in which the feet are farthest apart and the character's weight shifts to the forward foot.

As the weight of the body is transferred to the forward foot, the forward knee bends to absorb the shock. This position is called the "recoil position," and is the lowest point in the walk.

Understanding the Mechanics of Walking

Walking has been described as "controlled falling". Every time you take a step, you lean forward and fall slightly, and are caught by your outstretched foot. If you failed to put your foot forward, you would fall flat on your face. After your foot touches the ground, your body's weight is transferred to it and your knee bends to absorb the shock. The front leg then lifts the body and propels it forward as the rear leg swings up to catch you again, and the cycle repeats.

Before you read any further, get up and walk around the room for a bit. Pay attention to how each part of your body moves. You'll soon notice that every part of your body, from your feet to your arms to your head, has its own unique set of motions. As you walk around, notice how you lean forward into the walk, and how your legs neatly catch your body to prevent it from falling. If you purposely hold your foot back on a step, you'll fall flat on your face.

The process of walking is very complex. Not only do the feet have to move across the ground, but the hips, spine, arms, shoulders, and head all move in sync to keep the system in balance. Although these movements are complex, if you break them down joint by joint, the mechanics of walking becomes clear.

The following sections break down a basic walk, step by step. For clarity, I've animated a simple skeleton so you can see how each joint moves.

The Feet and Legs

The feet and legs propel the body forward. To keep your character looking natural, you should always keep the joints bent slightly, even at full leg extension.

The Hips, Spine, and Shoulders

The body's center of gravity is at the hips; all balance starts there, as does the rest of the body's motion. During a walk, it's best to think of the hips' motion as two separate, overlapping rotations. First, the hips rotate along the axis of the spine, forward and back with the legs. If the right leg is forward, the right hip is rotated forward. Second, at the passing position, the free leg pulls the hip out of center, forcing the hips to rock from side to side. These two motions are then transmitted through the spine to the shoulders, which mirror the hips to maintain balance.

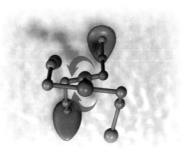

When the feet are fully extended, the hips must rotate along the axis of the spine. To keep balance, the shoulders swing in the opposite direction. From the front, the spine is relatively straight, but from the top, you can see how the hips and shoulders twist in opposite directions to maintain balance.

At the passing position, the front view shows the hip being pulled out of center by the weight of the free leg, causing a counter-rotation in the shoulders. From the top, the hips and shoulders are at nearly equal angles.

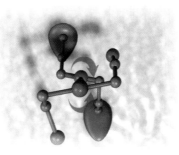

At the extension of the second leg, the hips and shoulders are again flat when viewed from the front. From the top, you can see the completed rotation of the hips and shoulders.

This figure illustrates the point halfway through the first step. As the character moves forward, the forward knee straightens and lifts the body to its highest point. This position is called the "passing position" because the free foot passes the supporting leg at this point.

As the character moves forward, the weight-bearing foot lifts off the ground at the heel, transmitting the force to the ball of the foot. The body starts to fall forward. The free foot swings forward like a pendulum to meet the ground and catch the body's weight.

The free leg makes contact with the ground, completing half of the cycle. The second half is an exact mirror of the first. If it differs, the character may appear to limp.

Because walking is kind of like falling forward, the body should be angled forward slightly at the hips for most walks. The spine arches up slightly to keep the chest and head over the hips. However, this line of action can change with the character's attitude.

For example, if a character is terribly sad he tends to hunch forward and hang his head low. This posture forces the hips to rotate in the opposite direction, giving the body a different attitude. He'll most likely drag his feet as well.

The Arms

Unless the character is holding something or gesturing, its arms hang loose at the sides. When walking, they act like pendulums, dragging a few frames behind the motion of the hips and shoulders. Even at full extension the arms should be slightly bent at the elbows, to make them look natural.

The Head and Spine from the Side

If you look at a character's spine from the side, you can see its general posture, which may be very stiff or slouched over, depending on the character's attitude. The spine also absorbs some of the shock transmitted to the hips from the legs, making it flex from front to back a bit.

In a standard walk, the head tries to stay level, with the eyes pointing in the direction of the walk, but it bobs around slightly to stay balanced. If a character is excited, this bobbing is more pronounced. The head may hang low for a sad character, or look around if the scene requires it.

The Differences Between Walking and Running

A run is a fast viewing running as a state of and highly exaggerated walk. Instead of continuous falling, it's best to view a run as continuous leaping, with the body tending to lean forward a lot more. In a walk, one foot is always on the ground; in a run, there are times when both feet are airborne. The stride length also increases, making this distance longer than the feet could normally reach in a walk.

The timing of a run is faster than a walk, and there are sometimes only a few frames per step. If you're animating an extremely fast run, motion blur is absolutely required to keep the feet and legs from strobing. Of course, any fast action requires motion blur to make it look realistic.

Take a look at a running character to see the differences between a walk and a run.

This figure illustrates the "contact position." Notice that the body leans forward and the legs are farther apart than they are during a walk.

After contact is made, the forward leg absorbs the shock of the body at the "recoil position." As is the case in walking, this point is the lowest position in the cycle. Because the body is moving faster, momentum is increased, causing the bent leg to be even more exaggerated.

This figure illustrates a position similar to the "passing position" because it is halfway through the step. At this point in the cycle, the grounded foot pushes the body upward.

On the CD

On the CD are four animations that will show you this runing sequence from four different views. These files are called RUN1.AVI through RUN4.AVI (Mac users should load RUN1.MOV through RUN4.MOV.) Watch these animations for reference.

At the highest point in the cycle, the body is airborne.

The body lands and the next step starts. As in the walk, the second half of the cycle should be a mirror of the first.

Animating a Walk

Now that you understand the underlying mechanics of walking, you can attempt to animate a walk. Using traditional animation techniques, a walk cycle is tough create; it can be just as tricky on a computer.

Timing the Walk

The first thing you need to concern yourself with is the timing of the walk. How many frames does it take? That's not an easy question to answer. Is your character large and lumbering, or small and scrappy? Is your character running or walking? Happy or sad? All these factors determine the amount of time it takes your character to take a step.

At a normal walking gait, a step takes anywhere from one-third to two-thirds of a second, (8 to 16 frames at 24 fps, or 10 to 20 frames at 30 fps) with a half second per step being about average. A full cycle (both right and left steps) takes about a second per cycle. Larger characters tend to walk slower and smaller characters walk faster. In general, men have slightly slower gaits than women, and sad people walk slower than happy people.

One nice thing about working with a computer is that many programs enable you to scale the length of your animation. If your character is walking too slow, you can speed him up a bit by reworking the keys.

Keeping Your Feet on the Ground

The most important thing to remember when animating a walk is to keep your character's feet firmly locked to the ground. The friction between the feet and the ground propels him forward. If the feet slide around, the illusion of friction is lost and the animation will not seem realistic. (If he's walking on banana peels or an oil slick, sliding may seem hilarious.)

How do you keep the feet locked to the ground? It really depends on your software and its feature set. Many packages have tools to assist you in this task; others do not. The following are a few of the more popular methods:

- **Inverse Kinematics (IK) with Locks.** Many packages with IK enable you to "pin" or "lock" an object, such as a foot, to a point in space or to another object—such as the floor. IK is one of the preferred walk-animation methods because it ensures that a character's grounded foot stays in the same spot for the duration of the step. Knowing that the feet are locked frees the animator's mind from annoying details and enables him to concentrate on animating the character.

- **Forward Kinematics with Locks.** When you use inverse kinematics, you move the end points of the chain, and the computer determines a "solution," rotating some joints automatically to keep the skeleton together. Sometimes this solution may not be optimal, forcing you to rotate the joints manually. Plug-ins such as Meme-X's Lock&Key for LightWave and Kinetix' Biped for 3D Studio MAX enable you to lock the feet to the ground and manipulate the skeleton with or without IK.

Tip

When you're animating multiple characters, it's always tempting to make them walk at the same rate to simplify the animation process—not a good idea. Giving your characters the same gait makes your characters look like they're marching in unison, which can detract from the shot. It's always best to stagger walk cycles and give characters different gaits. If one character is walking at 12 frames per step, give the other a gait that's slightly slower or faster—maybe 10 or 15 frames per step. By mixing it up, you make your shots more varied and interesting.

■ **Footstep Generators.** Some packages have what I call "footstep generators". The most popular of these are 3D Studio MAX's Biped and Softimage's Multiped. These plug-ins enable you to toss down footprints on the ground, up hills, down ladders, wherever you want. The program then automatically moves the character's legs and feet to match. Typically, the motion is generated by an algorithm that computes the character's physical weight and dynamics.

Using such a plug-in is a great way to get the first pass of a walk into the computer, but that's about all it will do. As the animator, you still need to control the process and add personality to the walk. You must go back over the animation and tweak the poses and motion on a second and third pass to add the flavor and individuality that makes your character unique.

■ **Inverse or Broken Hierarchies.** This method does not require IK and works with any package that supports forward kinematics. In a normal skeleton, the hips are at the top of the tree, with the spine and legs as children. If you don't have a way to lock the feet, this setup can cause problems, because moving the hips will move the spine, legs, and feet.

In the Inverse Hierarchy method, the hierarchy is turned upside-down and broken at the hips. The feet become the parents of the legs, enabling you to place the feet where you want them. Because they're the parents, you can rest assured that they won't move unless you absolutely want them to move.

What about the hips? In a hierarchy, because an object can't have two parents, the hips must be disconnected from the legs and are forced to float free above them. The hips are then animated so that they match up with the legs. Because exactly matching the hips to the legs can be problematic, this method works best for characters whose hips are hidden—a soda can with feet, or a character in a skirt. It also works well when using bones, as the character's skin tends to obscure most hip-alignment problems. Besides, viewers usually notice the feet slipping long before they ever notice

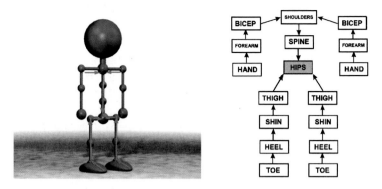

In a normal hierarchy, all joints point to the hips. Thus, by moving the hips, you move the entire body. This method can make it very easy for the feet to slip inadvertently.

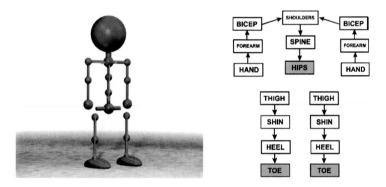

In an inverse hierarchy, the link is broken at the hips, and the feet become parents of the legs. The feet never move unless you tell them to, and they never slip.

that the hips are not quite connected; it's the lesser of two evils.

- **Using Guides.** If you're unable to use the preceding methods, you can always use *guides* to aid in the placement of the feet. In any package, you can place null objects, dummies, or transparent objects along the character's feet and use them as virtual place holders. If the foot moves inadvertently, you have a reference point that enables you to put the foot back where it belongs.

Some packages enable you to simulate an "onion-skin" effect by ghosting the previous frame which provides a good simulation of the traditional animator's light table. Because you can see where the feet are on the previous frames, it's easy to align them on the current frame.

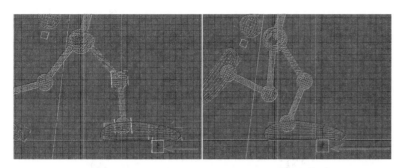

This box is being used as a guide in the placement of the foot. By aligning a reference point on the foot to the guide, you can be reasonably sure it won't slip.

Finally, some animators have been known to use wet-erase overhead projector pens to draw the guides directly on the computer screen. The marks can then be erased with a damp cloth. Still, it would be awful if you to grabed the wrong pen and made permanent marks on the screen, so be careful! A good substitute might be a sticky note placed on the screen and marked with a pencil.

To Cycle or Not to Cycle?

Because walking is a cyclical motion, it may behoove the animator to create the walking motion as a cycle rather than as straight-ahead animation. If done properly, a cycle can save an inordinate amount of animation time. One cycle can be applied to a number of different environments. Your character and his cycle can just as easily be placed in a cityscape as a country road, because the walk motion is essentially the same. Why duplicate your efforts? Classical animators use this trick a lot, simply repeating the same sequence of drawings and swapping only the background painting—placing the character in a different location. In 3D, you have the flexibility to change the cameras, lighting, and environment to make the shot look completely different.

There are downsides to using cycles. First, because the cycle is repetitive, it can seem sterile and flat, particularly when viewed for an extended period of time. Second, cycles work best on level terrain. If your character has to walk around a corner or over a hill, the cycle might not match up properly. It can be difficult in some programs to stop a cycle after it's started. For example, if your character walks into a room and stops, the cycle must be stopped and the character keyframed from that point.

This multiple exposure of a walk cycle shows that the body does not move forward; instead, the feet move beneath it. The red marks show how the foot on the ground moves the exact same distance on each frame to prevent slipping.

Animating a cycle is similar to making your character walk on a treadmill. The body does not move forward; the feet simply move beneath it. To maintain the illusion of walking, the entire character must be moved across the ground (or the ground moved past the character) at the exact same rate that the feet are moving. Otherwise, the character's feet appear to slip. Also, the foot on the ground needs to move the exact same distance on each frame. Again, if the length of the steps vary, the feet appear to slip.

The following exercises illustrate four ways you can go about animating a two-legged walk. They are certainly not the only ways to animate, but they do touch on many of the major points discussed in this chapter. Pick and choose those techniques that strike your fancy and match your chosen software's features. You can also use them as jumping-off points for creating your own techniques.

Exercise #1: Animating a Walk Cycle Using Forward Kinematics

On the CD

If you don't have a character, you can use one from the CD. On the CD is a character named TINKRBOY.DXF or TIN-KRBOY.3DS; you can use either if you want.

In this exercise, you animate a walk cycle without the aid of Inverse Kinematics or locks. Many animators consider this method to be the long way around, but it's kind of a fail-safe technique; it should work with almost all packages.

This cycle is timed at 16 frames per step—32 for the whole cycle. At video rates, that's just over one second per cycle. Film animators can reduce this to 12 frames per step. You're doing this example with a simple skeleton, but the techniques should transfer well to any two legged character. The ability to lock your character's feet to the ground is important, but not necessary, as I'll explain along the way.

To begin, load up your character and hierarchical skeleton in your favorite 3D animation program. Create an animation that's 33 frames long. I've added the extra frame to the end as a target for frames in the second half of the cycle. It will not be rendered.

Start by animating the hips and shoulders.

It's best to start here, because all other motions derive from the hips. The hips have two separate, overlapping rotations that are mirrored by the shoulders. The first rotation is along the vertical axis of the spine and follows the position of the legs and feet.

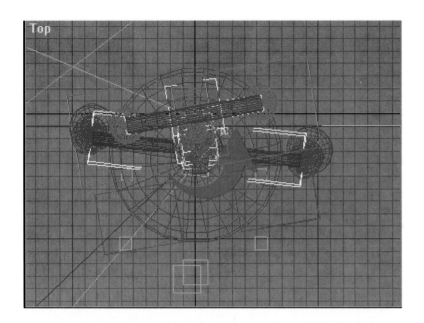

1. Start the walk with the right foot; the right hip must go forward, as well. On frame 1 of the animation, rotate the hips around the Y axis so that the right side is forward. From the top view, rotate the shoulders to mirror the hips' rotation.

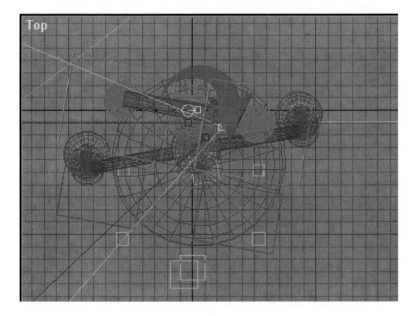

2. Next, go to the halfway point (frame 17) in the cycle and rotate the hips and shoulders in the opposite direction. Remember, they should still be mirroring each other.

continues

3. Go to one frame past the end of the cycle (frame 33), and copy the first frame's keys here. This frame is a target for the frames that are in-betweened on the second half of the cycle.

4. Next you need to create the sway of the hips. Go to the frame in the middle of the first step (frame 9). If your rotations are correct, the hips and shoulders should be parallel when viewed from the top.

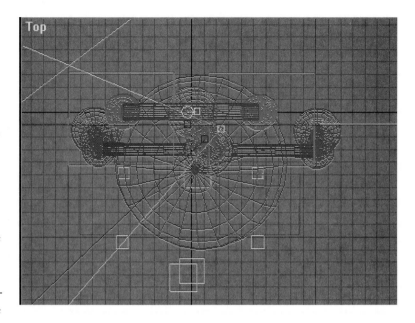

At this point, the passing position or the point of highest leg extension, the body rests on the right leg and the left leg pulls the hips out of center.

5. From the front view, rotate the hips around the z axis so that the right hip is higher. Adjust the spine and shoulders so you get a smooth line of action and the shoulders mirror the hips.

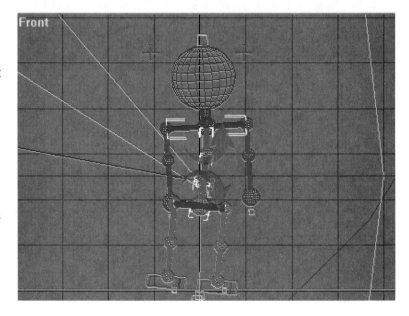

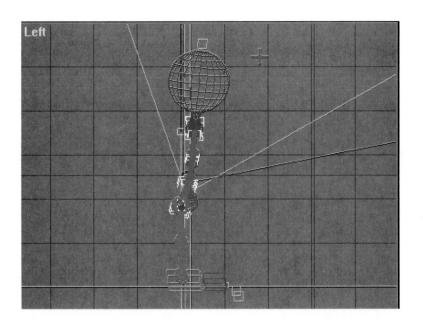

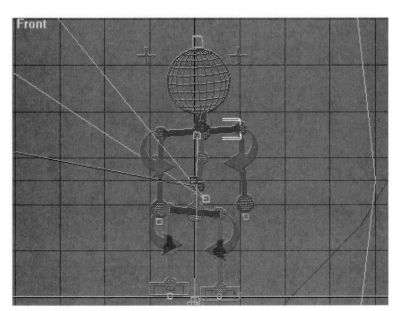

6. Go to the middle frame of the second step (frame 25) and reverse the rotations that you just made at the middle of the first step. The body will rest on the left leg at this point, and the spine will curve in the opposite direction.

7. Next, adjust the spine on the first frame to give it a forward lean and a nice curve.

8. Finally, go back to each keyframe and adjust the legs and arms so that they hang vertically throughout the cycle.

9. Play back the cycle. If it looks smooth and balanced, move on to the next step. Otherwise, tweak the keyframes until you have a nice, smooth motion.

You now need to move the legs and feet—the trickiest part of the process.

continues

10. First, set up the extreme poses. From a side view, go to frame 1 and set the first pose, where the legs are at maximum extension. Copy these keys to the end of the cycle, at frame 33.

11. Next, go to the middle of the cycle (frame 17) and mirror frame 1 so that the left leg is forward. A ghosting feature would help considerably in this process.

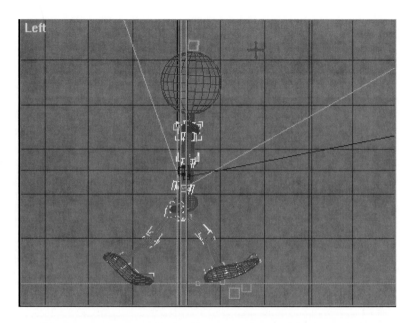

   To aid in the animation process, use a guide to help position the feet. If you are using locks, you probably won't have to do this step; if you inbetween the foot linearly at the two extremes (with no slow-ins or slow-outs), the foot will move across the floor automatically. Still, a guide acts as a nice double-check.

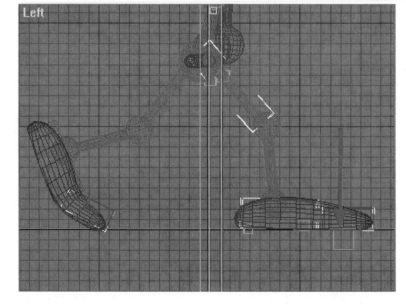

12. To create the guide, model a box and place it directly beneath the floor near the character's forward foot. If it's below the floor, it won't show up at rendering time. You could use a null object.

13. Go to frame 1 and move the guide horizontally to the place where the toe hits the ground.

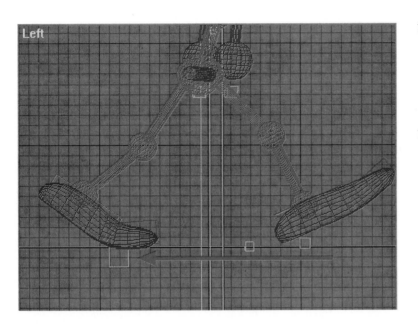

14. Next, go to the middle of the cycle (frame 17) and position the guide at the exact same place on the toe as you did in frame 1.

15. Set up the guide so that it inbetweens these two positions at a linear rate. The guide will tell you exactly where the toe needs be at any point in the step. (If you have an IK system, you can pin the foot to the guide for a sure-fire solution.)

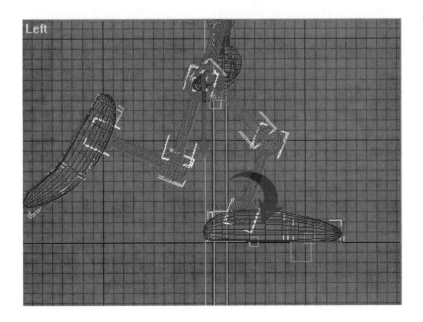

16. Now, you need to tweak the poses. Because you know where the feet need to be, you can concentrate on the legs. About a quarter of the way through the first step (frame 5) is the recoil position—where the leg absorbs the shock and bends to its lowest point. Move the hips down so that the shin is forced to rotate forward a bit, giving the knee a nice bend.

continues

17. Next, the body recoils upward into the passing position. Move the hips up so that the forward leg is fairly well extended. It's very important to keep the knee bent slightly to make the action look natural.

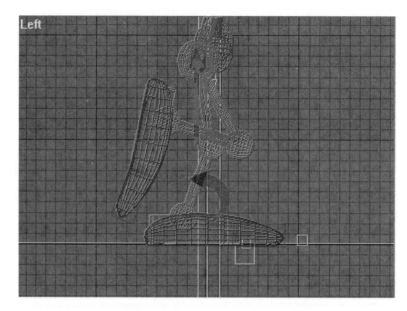

18. At this point, the weight of the body is on the ball of the foot. The heel lifts off the floor as the body falls forward. The hips are moving downward at this point. There may also be problems with the free foot as it swings forward; if you have extra-big shoes, they'll hit the floor unless you bend the toes slightly.

19. The first step is now complete. Create a second guide and repeat these procedures for the left foot on the second half of the cycle. Be careful to make the second half as close to the first as possible. Render a test and go back to tweak any inconsistencies.

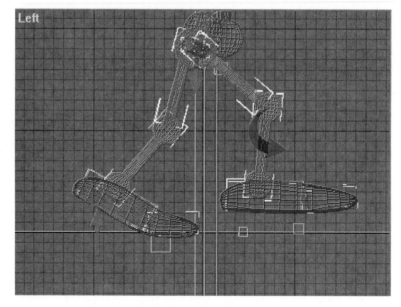

Now you need to create the motion of the arms and head. In the simplest case, the arms swing back and forth to maintain balance in opposition to the legs. The arms also drag behind the action a bit, placing the arms' extreme poses a few frames behind the legs.

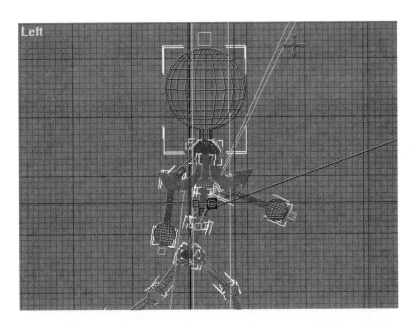

20. Rotate the arms into position on the first frame. Because the right leg is forward, the right arm is back, and the left arm is forward. This pose is not an extreme pose, but it is close.

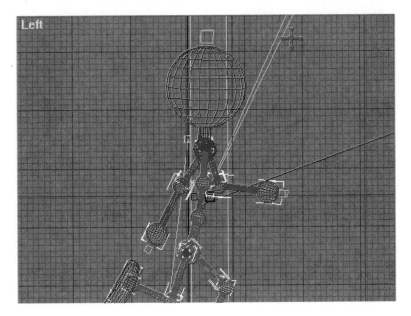

21. Next, go a few (2 to 5) frames in to view the arm's extreme pose. I chose frame 5. On the left arm, rotate the forearm back to a nice extension. On the right, rotate the forearm up slightly.

22. Go a few (from 2 to 5) frames past the start of the second step and mirror the extreme from the previous step. Finally, copy the keys on frame 1 to the last frame, so the arm will swing through to the end of the cycle.

23. Now you need to depict the head. Go to the keys at the start and halfway through each step and rotate the head so that it remains vertical and the eyes are facing forward. The head can bob from side to side a bit, as long as it's not too distracting.

You can also make the spine bounce up and down a bit. Remember the effects of drag that we discussed in the last chapter. This applies to the spine as well. If you want, you can make the spine flex between curved and straight, dragging behind the up and down motion of the hips by a few frames. As the hips go up, the spine is compressed into a curve. When the hips come down again, drag causes the spine to straighten out.

Now that you have a convincing cycle, to get your character off the treadmill and out into the world. To do this, you can do one of two things: either move the character along the ground, or move the ground under the character. Moving the ground is best when you want to use a panning camera that is locked on the character; because the character is still, the camera can remain still. Moving the character is best in cases when you want the camera stable and the character to walk past.

In this example, move the ground. If you used a guide to assist in your animation, the task is simple. Find the absolute position of your first guide in frame 1, then again when it stops in the middle of the cycle.

In my shot, for example, the guide moves along the X axis. The first position of the guide along X is 300 units. At frame 17, the guide is at 100 units; the character's foot moves a total of 200 units per step (300 minus 100 equals 200.) This value is known as the *stride length*. Doubling it equals 400 units for the total cycle. On the first frame, move the floor to the starting position. On the last frame (frame 33) move the floor 400 units along the X axis. Inbetween these frames linearly. That's it. The shot is done.

On the CD

On the CD is a finished movie of the walk. The title is WALK01.AVI through WALK04.AVI or WALK01.MOV through WALK04.MOV; you can watch it as a reference, if you like.

Exercise #2: Animating a Walk Cycle with Inverse Kinematics

You can animate a walk using inverse kinematics in many ways. In this exercise, you create a cycle by locking the feet to a path. As in the previous example, you still need to move the cycled character across the ground at a steady rate to complete the exercise. In this exercise, you work with a skeleton, or you can use a character that you've built, or use one from the book's CD. Of course, every system's IK sets up differently, so if you use one of the models off the CD, you will have to set up your joint limits and constraints within your software before starting.

1. The first thing you need to do is get the feet moving in a nice, steady cycle. One of the easiest ways to do this is to move the character's ankles along a path. Draw a simple path, shaped something like the one shown in the following illustration. It should be completely flat along the bottom.

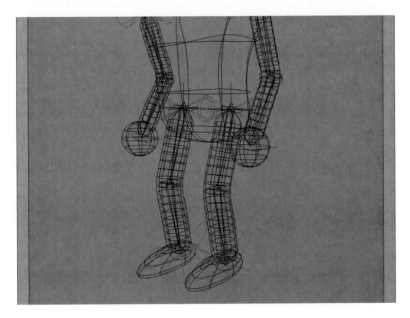

2. Duplicate this path. Move both paths so that each is positioned neatly over the right and left foot, respectively.

continues

3. Attach the left leg's ankle to the left path. If you run the animation, you'll see the leg move in a cycle.

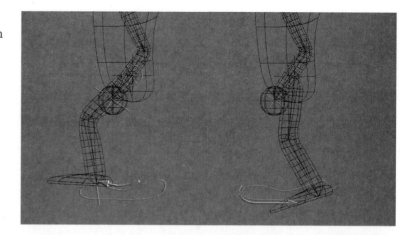

4. Attach the right ankle to its path in the same manner. If you run the animation, you'll notice that the ankles and the attached feet move in lockstep, so that the character looks like he's hopping. To fix this situation, move the right foot's start point 180 degrees back along the path, so that it is exactly opposite the left foot's start point.

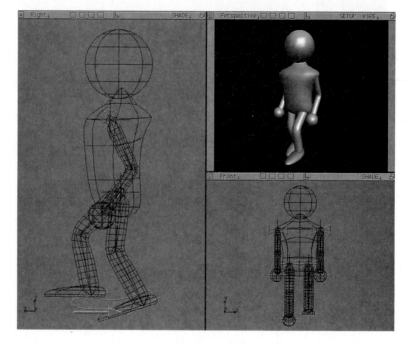

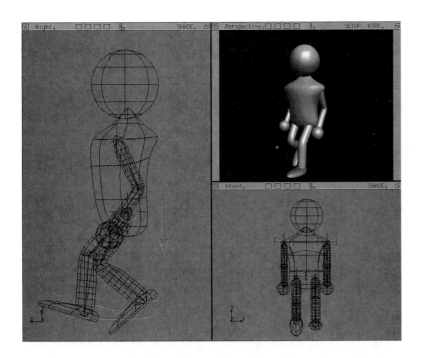

5. Now move the upper body up and down to match the rate of the walk cycle. Because the ankles are locked to the path, the feet should remain still, but the IK system will bend the knees automatically. As in any walk cycle, the low point of the body is at the recoil position, and the high point is at the passing position. Make sure the body cycle connects smoothly.

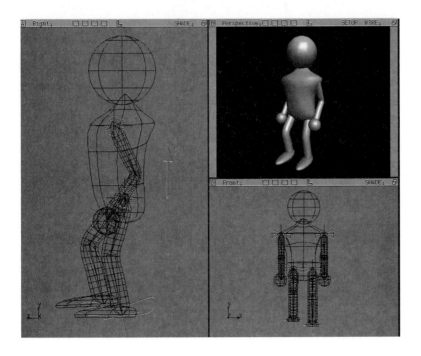

continues

6. Rotate the hips back and forth to match the rate of the body.

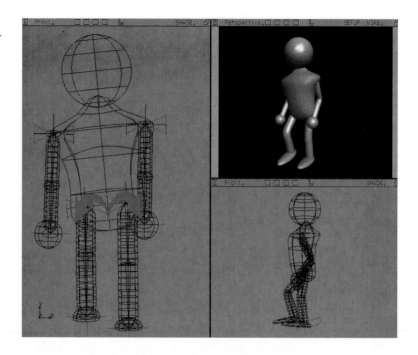

7. You're almost there. Rotate the feet and create keyframes so that they remain flat on the ground when the leg is down, and rotate them so the toes don't drag when the leg is up.

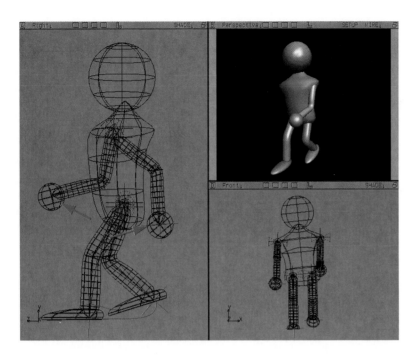

8. Add a bit of swing to the arms and bob to the head.

That's about it. As in Exercise #1, you must move the ground to match the character or vice versa. You can use the instructions for that exercise on this one.

Exercise #3: Animating a Walk Using Inverse or Broken Hierarchies

In this example, you put feet and arms on a soda can and animate a walk using inverse hierarchies. This method works well in almost any package. One nice thing is that this method locks down the feet quite easily and forces you to move the hips properly. Also, you animate this walk straight-ahead rather than in a cycle. Animate this walk at 12 frames per step for film (15 frames per step for video).

You must begin by getting the hierarchies set up properly. In this example, I'm using box bones to animate the feet, but the principles apply to segmented characters as well. If you have a segmented character, you can set up the hierarchies and animate the segments exactly the same way as the bones.

 On the CD

For this exercise, you can use a model on the CD; use either SODACAN.DXF or SODA-CAN.3DS. Each has two pairs of arms and legs; one is a solid mesh set up for use with bones, the other is a segmented model with seams, in case you don't have bones.

continues

digital character animation

1. Set up the bones (or segments) on the right leg so that the toes are at the top of the hierarchy. The order of the hierarchy is as follows: toes parent the heel, then shin, then thigh. Do the same for the left leg.

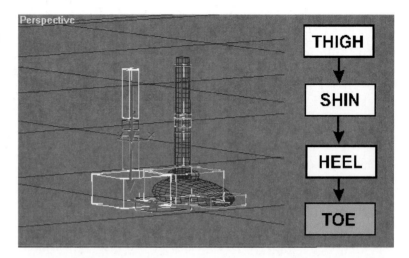

Because the soda can does not need to bend, leave it as one solid object.

2. The arms do need to bend, so use bones to animate the solid meshes. (If you use segments, simply link the segments to the can hierarchically.) The can will be the parent of the arms. Link the arms to the can at the shoulders.

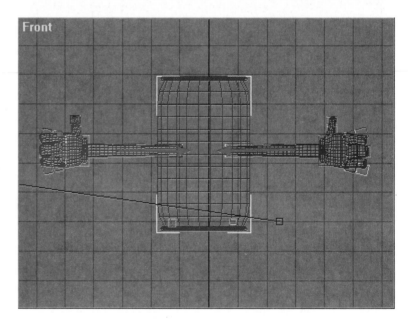

You now have three separate objects: two legs and a can with arms.

Your main task is to animate the legs and feet. Leave the can out of the shot for this part of the process, because it won't be needed until later.

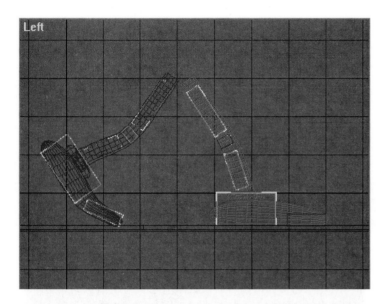

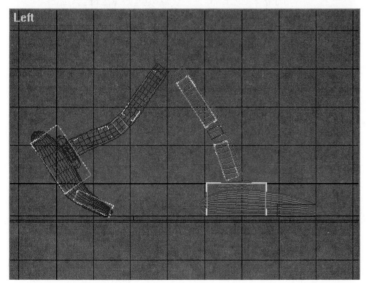

3. Position the legs in the extended position, with the right leg forward. To adjust the positions of the legs, move the toes first, and then work your way up the chain from there. The position of the legs determines the stride length. Also, be sure that the tops of the legs are not too far apart, where the "hips" would be.

4. Next, create a little ruler to help maintain this same stride length throughout the shot. Model a rectangular box that is the same length as the stride length. The corners of the box should touch the heel of the forward foot and toe of the back foot. Use this on the second step to position the feet properly.

5. Now you can animate the rest of the walk. On the right leg, rotate the toe and move the foot so it contacts the ground. From this point, the foot remains stable until the next step is taken. Notice how you can rotate the joints of the leg without affecting the position of the foot. The feet stay put and no slipping occurs.

continues

Exercise #3: continued

6. Jump forward to frame 13—the beginning of the next step. Move the left foot into the extended position, and rotate (don't move) the toe of the right foot to the proper position. Use the ruler you created to align the feet properly.

   The length of the ruler is the stride length, and the corners are where the toes and heels will be positioned.

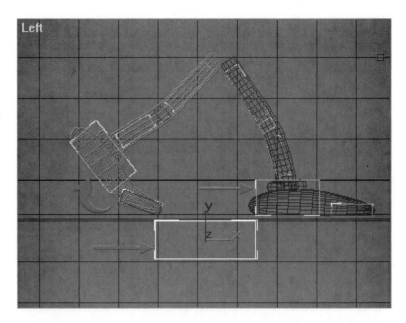

   Now, go back through the first step and align the rest of the keys.

7. Align the passing position. Go to frame 7, which is halfway through the first step, and rotate the right shin at the ankle to make the leg almost vertical. Next, rotate the left leg so the foot is somewhat vertical and position the thigh by rotating the knee. The tops of the two legs should be about equal, with the left slightly lower.

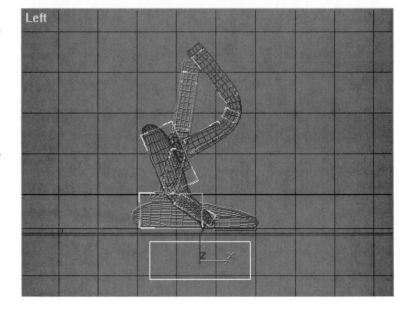

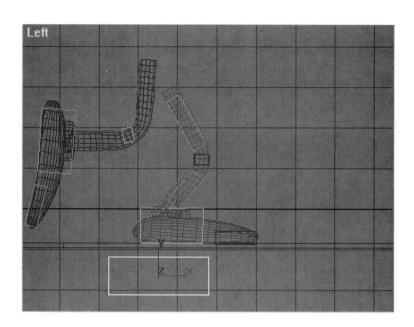

8. Next, go to frame 4 and get the recoil position. Again, rotate the right leg at the ankle so that the knee is bent. Rotate and align the left foot so that the leg is free.

9. Finally, create a key near frame 10, where the left foot swings forward. Because the hierarchy is backward, positioning the free leg may be a little tricky.

10. Play through the first step and tweak the keys.

11. You now have the first step. By repeating the preceeding steps, you can continue on and create as many more steps as you want. Go ahead and animate three or four more steps. When you're finished, you should have a pair of legs walking across the floor.

Now that you have the legs and feet, all you have to do is place the body above them and rock it back and forth along with the "hips." Because your character is spineless, you don't have to worry about shoulders.

continues

12. On the first frame, position the can so it is above the legs, with the tops of the legs slightly protruding through the bottom of the can. Rotate the can forward slightly to give it a natural stance.

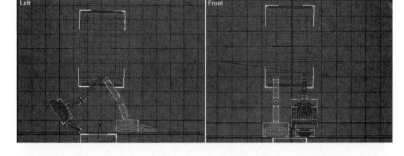

13. Move to the next set of keys, at the recoil position (frame 3). Position the can above the legs, but lower. If you animated the feet and legs properly, you should naturally see how to position it.

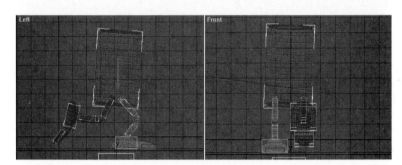

14. Next is the passing position. In this position, the left side is slightly lower at the hip, so rotate the can slightly in this direction.

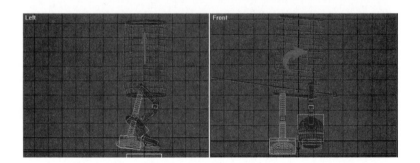

15. Continue through the rest of the shot, positioning the can above the legs and rotating it from right to left along with the hips.

16. Play back the animation to make sure that the can remains centered above the legs.

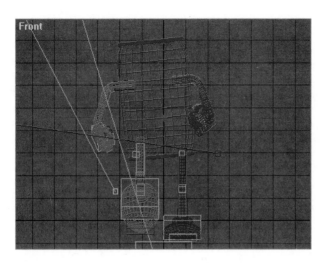

17. Now, animate the arms. As in the previous example, you need to have them drag slightly behind the action of the legs. When the right leg is forward, the right arm is back, and vice versa.

18. Finally, render the animation and tweak as necessary.

Exercise #4: Animating the "No-Feet" Walk

The "no-feet" walk is very simple—never show the feet. By shooting your character from the waist up, and bobbing the upper body at the same rate as if it were walking, you get a pretty good illusion of a walk. Many seasons of *The Flintstones* got away with this trick, and so can you.

For emphasis, I've deleted the legs from this robot so the effect is clearly seen.

On the CD

ON the CD is a finished movie of the walk. The title is SODAWALK.AVI or SODAWALK.MOV; you can watch it as reference.

On the CD

For this exercise, you can use the robot model from the book's CD. The model is called TINROBOT.DXF or TINROBOT.3DS.

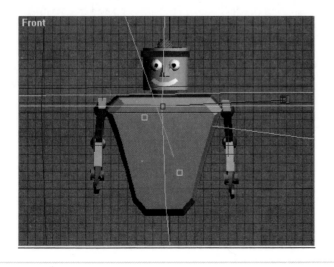

continues

1. Shoot your character
   from the waist up, and
   position the lights so that
   there are no tell-tale
   shadows that would show
   that your character has
   no legs.

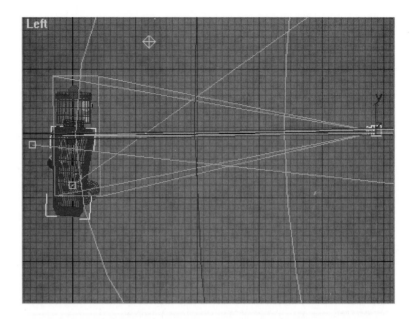

Now you're ready to start moving
the body, which is just as simple as
the first step. You can move the
body along the background as if it
were walking, or you can move the
background.

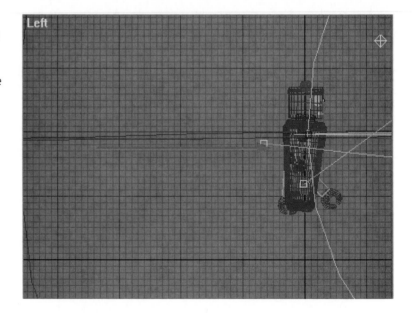

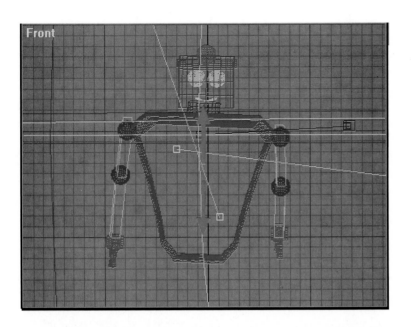

2. Bob the body up and down to match the character's gait—once per step. For example, if he takes 20 frames per step, then the body needs to go up and down at the same rate.

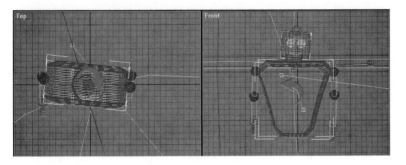

3. Rock the body back and forth to simulate the sway of the hips. The length of this cycle is about the same as two steps. For example, if our character walks at 20 frames per step, it would be a 40 frame cycle.

You also need to move the arms and head. Because the audience will not see the legs, you don't have to be as precise about the arms as you were in the previous exercises.

4. Swing the arms back and forth in sync with the apparent motion of the legs.

5. Keep the head pointed forward. You can rock it slightly from side to side to keep it balanced.

6. Render a test and tweak as necessary.

Animating Four-Legged Walks

If you think mastering a two-legged walk is difficult, a four-legged walk is doubly troublesome. First, the anatomy of most four-legged animals (as well as birds and dinosaurs) is quite different from primate podiatry.

Take a horse, for example. A horse actually walks on its toes. Whereas the human heel actually touches the ground, the horse's "heel" is far above the ground—where the human knee would be. A horse's knee is actually even higher up, as are the thigh and hip. The front legs are similar to human arms. Again, the horse walks on his fingers and his wrist is far above the ground.

To create a realistic four-legged walk, you need to study the movements of real animals. Take a video camera to the zoo, or rent a nature documentary and go through the animal's movements frame by frame.

In addition to normal walking, a four-legged animal has several different gaits. The animal varies the timing and rhythm of its steps as it moves faster and faster. These gaits are the walk, trot, canter, and gallop. Some animals, however, might only do a subset of these. The elephant, for example, always walks—it never changes its gait. It simply walks slower or faster.

In the walk, the horse's legs behave very much like the arms and legs of a human—if the right rear leg is back, the right front leg is forward, with the opposite happening on the left. This positioning changes as the strides change. By the time the horse has reached a full gallop, the front legs are in sync, going forward and back nearly in unison. The back legs operate the same way.

The walk.

The gallop.

Another way to view a four-legged walk is in a more cartoony way. Think of the old vaudeville act in which two guys get into a tattered old horse suit. On stage, the horse literally walks like two people stitched together. You animate the walk like a double two-legged walk, forcing you to have different joint constraints and body construction.

A cartoony four-legged character is much simpler to animate, because you can set up its walks like a double two-legged walk.

The back legs on this dog are not realistic; they bend the same way human legs do. Still, the cartoon nature of his design enables the animator to move the dog this way and get away with it.

Conclusion

This chapter covered the basics of animating a character to walk or run. Although walking and running look easy when humans or animals do it, animating these motions requires much time spent studying and interpreting. It is important to develop the gait of your characters, though, because the way they walk conveys a great deal about their personalities.

CHAPTER 8

Anthropomorphic Animation

O ne of the most compelling reasons directors have for choosing digital character animation over other forms is the computer's capability to closely mimic reality. Not only has this capability given digital characters some very nice jobs in Hollywood, but it also has taken Madison Avenue by storm. The capability to breathe life into a very realistic looking product—such as a cereal box or ketchup bottle—gives 3D animation a leg up on the competition.

In the days when cel and clay animation were the only options for bringing inanimate objects to life, animators had to go through all sorts of gyrations to make a product look "real." Any cel animator who has cut and pasted photographs of a product's logo onto a stack of cels, knows what I mean. Advertisers typically want the animated logo to be realistic and accurate; enter digital animation.

Breathing life into an otherwise inanimate object is known as *anthropomorphic animation*. It need not be restricted to advertising product shots; it has a number of uses. Think of the trees that sprang to life in *The Wizard of Oz*. If that film were done today, Dorothy would be hipper and more sarcastic, but those anthropomorphic trees would probably be digital. Animators have had a long history of bringing inanimate objects to life—from Fleischer's cartoons of the 1930s to the present.

So how do you breathe life into something that doesn't have arms, limbs, or even a face? Through strong poses and good timing, which are the essence of good animation. Animating something as simple as a cereal box will give you good insight into the pure art of timing and motion that every animator should master.

Types of Characters

I generally find that anthropomorphized characters fall into two broad categories. For lack of better terms, I call them "static-shaped" and "squishy" characters, and you learn more about their unique properties in the following pages. In production, the distinction between these two methods of character animation may blur a bit, but the directorial choice remains one of absolute realism versus surrealism.

Static-Shaped or Jointed Characters

The *static-shaped character* is modeled fairly realistically and moves only in the ways it would move in the real world. A perfect example of this kind of character can be found in Pixar's *Luxo Jr.*, directed by John Lasseter. In this film, a desk lamp is brought to life. The lamp moves at three joints, but the timing of the motions makes it convincingly lifelike. The lamp remains real and the lamp's parts never change shape. They move and rotate as a Luxo lamp's parts normally would.

Static-shaped characters are great for mechanical or quasi-mechanical objects with lots of joints, such as an industrial robot or a tin toy. If your character doesn't fit in this category, you'll need to create a squishy character.

Squishy Characters

Squishy characters are animated by what I call the "squish" method. It aims to break the laws of physics and gives your character an ability to stretch and squash that it would never have in the real world. A box has no real "joints" to speak of, so you must use the squish method to give it some.

Squishy animation can be used in a variety of situations, and a good example is the television commercial where the bottle of shampoo springs to life.

A shampoo bottle sprung to life. This bottle normally would be fairly rigid, but when animating it, the animator can take liberties and change its shape.

Conceiving Your Characters

Typically, when working with an anthropomorphized character, the task of modeling is fairly straightforward. How much time does it take to model a cereal box? The real trick is in figuring out who your character is and how to move it around convincingly.

One method that might help is to determine what type of animal your character most resembles. With its four legs, a coffee table might be thought of as a dog, or a garden hose might be thought of as a snake. Boxes lend themselves to bipedal motion—the bottom corners of the box being the feet and the top corners being the shoulders or hands. Your character's size also determines how it moves. Silverware sprung to life should move much faster, relatively speaking, than an anthropomorphic Chrysler Building.

Another question you face in the design and concept stages is whether to give your character a face. As you're well aware, most emotions can be portrayed through body posture alone, but if your character speaks, the face question becomes important. You could add lips and a mouth, but this is the easy way out. If you're clever about these things, you can make your character speak without adding such artificial devices. For instance, the end of a vacuum cleaner's hose could be used as a mouth. Just by flapping a can's lid up and down, you can create some surprisingly convincing lip sync.

This cola can has arms and legs, but are they really necessary? Sometimes, it's more challenging to go without such artificial devices and animate the shape itself.

The Big Secret: Timing

Animating a faceless, limbless object can be difficult, but it is also one of the best exercises an animator can undertake. Any emotions or attitude you bring out of a character will be directly related to the timing and poses you give the character. Animating this type of creature can be fun because you're not encumbered by the expression on the character's face, the positions of the fingers, or whether the feet are placed realistically. The poses are typically broad and easy to create.

The big secret in this type of animation is the timing. If you nail the timing and use lots of anticipation and overshoot, you should be fine. Really, the basic animation tools discussed in Chapter 6— squash and stretch, anticipation, overshoot, and moving holds—are all you have in your animation arsenal. Because the character doesn't have such things as eyes or hands for the viewers to watch, they'll be very focused on the character, its poses, and the timing. Any timing glitches will be more noticeable, and bad timing will turn into *really* bad timing. Anthropomorphic animation makes a great exercise for any animator.

Animating a Jointed or Static-Shaped Character

Generally, when you are animating a static-shaped character, you find that the joints are the only points of motion. Because you can't change the character's shape, most squashing and stretching of the shape itself is ruled out. You have to find the essence of the character in anticipation, overshoot, and moving holds. You also have to determine which parts of the object represent the body, the head, and the other parts found in a living being. For example, imagine that the quintessential desk lamp comes to life. The light source can be considered the face and the reflector can be thought of as the head. The body continues down to the base.

Exercise #1: Animating a Static-Shaped Robot Arm

Here is a good exercise to help you understand how to animate a static-shaped character. Load the robot arm model from the CD and create an animation of the robot arm coming to life, noticing the ball, picking up the ball, and tossing it off screen. Here are a few pointers to guide you in the animation:

 On the CD

On the CD is a model of a robot arm and a sphere in a file called ROBOTARM.3DS or ROBOTARM.DXF. Load this file into your 3D program and examine it. Suppose you wanted to create an animation of the arm noticing the sphere, picking it up, and tossing it off the screen.

This robot's arm is a nice example of a jointed, static-shaped character.

Think of this joint as your character's waist. It enables your robot arm to "bend over" or "stand up," so to speak.

Think of this joint as your character's head. By rotating it, your robot can shake its head yes and no, and observe the ball.

The claws can be thought of as a mouth. Much like a dog carries things in its mouth, your robot arm can pick up the ball in its "mouth."

The robot can also rotate at its base, turn around, or wag its "tail."

Animating Squishy Characters

Making your squishy character change shape as it bends and moves will break the wall of ultra-realism, but the technique can give your character more personality. More variables exist in this type of animation than with static-shaped characters, so your options are vast.

Just how you change your character's shape depends on the features and capabilities of your animation software. Because every package is different, the names and implementations of each tool may be slightly different from what's mentioned here. Not every package has every tool, so use the ones you have to the best advantage. Don't complain about the tools that are missing; complaining stifles and wastes your creative talents. Sometimes, creating a novel solution with a limited toolkit can be just the ticket to a great animation.

Using Simple Deformations: Scale, Bend, Twist, and Tapers

Sometimes simple is better. Simple shapes such as boxes lend themselves to simple animation methods. Every decent package that I am familiar with enables you to scale an object along any axis and animate the scaling. This animation method might be all you need to give your character squash and stretch and to create a convincing animation.

Scaling can pose problems because you can easily lose volume and make your character look like it is shrinking and growing rather than squashing and stretching, much like the techniques covered in Chapter 6. For example, if you stretch a character along the y axis, you should shrink it along the x and z axes to maintain its volume.

A normal cereal box.　　　　The box squashed by scaling.　　　　The box stretched through scaling.

Other techniques, such as bends, twists, and tapers, can give a more dynamic flair to your character by making it appear to be very flexible. If you're animating a simple box, you need to give it enough detail so that it deforms smoothly without showing the underlying structure. If you build it with splines, you can get away with a few subdivisions; however, a polygon-based box requires more.

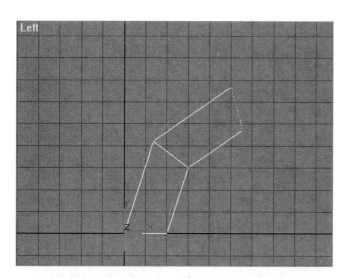

A polygonal box illustrates the need for subdivisions.

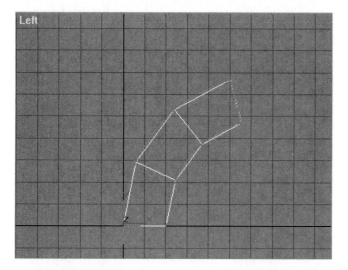

The more subdivisions the box has…

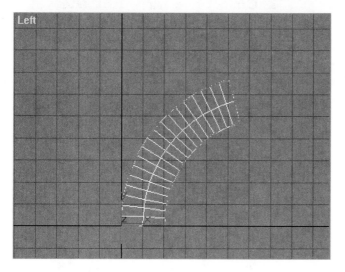

…the smoother it bends.

The bend modifier is great for giving the character a waist. Depending on the axis of the bend, the character can bend forward, backward, or side to side.

Using a simple bend modifier, you can give a box a waist, and bend it forward…

…or backward.

Twisting a character is great for creating the illusion that it possesses hips and shoulders. In humans, the hips and shoulders twist back and forth during a walk, and this movement can be effectively simulated even in an animated box by using a twist. If the character needs to look over its right shoulder, twist the top half of its body around to the right.

A simple twist modifier enables your character to look to the left…

…or to the right.

Tapers are good for giving your character a feeling of weight and volume. Think of a character jumping and landing on the ground.

You might want to scale the character as it hits the ground to give it a nice squash and a feeling of weight. By adding a bit of taper to the character, you can place more of that weight near the ground. The taper modifier is also good for cases where the character needs to stick out its chest.

Using a taper, you can push the character's volume around, and make it appear to do such things as stick its chest out…

…or bulge…

…or seem surprised.

Tools such as scale, bend, twist, and taper are quite handy, but they work best with simply shaped objects such as a cereal box or a television set. They do have their limitations; for instance, they can be imprecise when it comes to the exact placement of the feet. If you're trying to do a walk strictly by using twists and bends, there's no real way to lock the feet to the ground. An alternative to using a walk might be a series of leaps or hops that don't depend on exact foot placement.

The following exercise illustrates how much personality you can get from a simple box by using nothing but timing and posing techniques.

Exercise #2: Animating a Box with Simple Deformations

1. First, you need to model a simple box the size and shape of a cereal box. Be sure to give the box enough detail so that it can twist and bend smoothly.

continues

2. Place your box in the shot with the camera at a three-quarter view.

3. Next, use a deformation tool to twist the top of the box so that it looks to the right. This motion should take about half a second. Be sure to anticipate this move with a small twist to the left for a few frames and overshoot the pose by a few frames. Hold this pose for a half second with a moving hold.

4. Again, using anticipation and overshoot, twist the box to the left so that it looks over its shoulder. Make this turn a few frames faster than the first—about one-third of a second. After the box is looking over its left shoulder, add about a one-half-second moving hold to the pose.

5. Now twist the box back to the right so that it "looks" directly at the camera. Hold this pose for a few frames.

6. Now animate a strong anticipation so that the box is leaning back and preparing to run out of the scene. It should take a third of a second to hit this pose. Hold the anticipation for a few frames with a moving hold.

7. Move the box off the screen by running, hopping, or sliding.

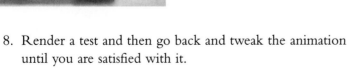

8. Render a test and then go back and tweak the animation until you are satisfied with it.

On the CD

A movie of this exercise can be found on this book's CD. You can find the file in two formats: CEREAL.AVI and CEREAL.MOV. If you need a reference to help you with completing this exercise, load this movie and watch it.

Using Lattice Deformations

Another easy method to shape and stretch characters is by using lattice deformations. With a minimum of fuss you can create nice, squishy deformations. To animate the character, you animate the lattice's vertices; the character's corresponding vertices follow along. If your object is too complex to be contained in a box, you can add multiple lattices, or they can take on more complex shapes if your software allows it. In fact, you can animate some very complex characters by using lattices and lattice-like deformations.

Generally, the reason you use lattices is to reduce the number of vertices you need to control. Again, the theory of simplicity applies. By moving one or two control points, you can completely reshape dozens of the object's vertices. Some people create a big problem for themselves by making their lattice nearly as complex as the model itself, which is self-defeating. The idea is to reduce the lattice to its simplest form to keep the animation easy. If you can get the effect by moving one point rather than ten, your job will be easier, and chances are that the animation will look smoother and more natural.

Keep your lattices as simple as possible.

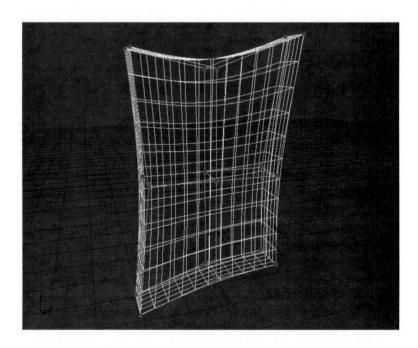

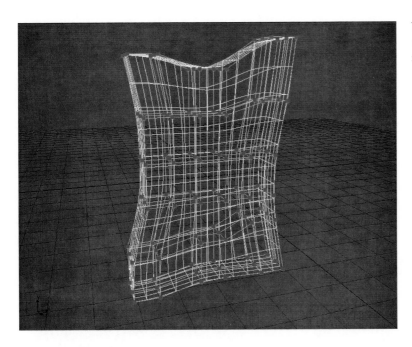

Too much detail in a lattice means more detail to move and this is self-defeating.

Bending Along a Spline

A good way for animating snakelike objects is to use a spline as a deformation tool. Use the spline as one axis of the character. When you bend and manipulate the controlling spline, your character will follow. Controlling your character with a spline is as easy as controlling a few simple vertices.

A spline can control snakelike objects, such as this vacuum hose. The vacuum itself was animated using bones.

Using Bones

Bones are probably an animator's best tool for bringing inanimate objects to life. With them, even the simplest of objects can be given plenty of motion. Again, for most situations, it's best to keep the skeletons simple. For a box, you could use as few as four bones, one for each corner, although eight would be more practical because you could place two bones on each corner and connect them to give your characters knees and elbows. Bones are great because you can apply IK to them, which makes posing very easy and enables you to lock the feet in place during walk cycles.

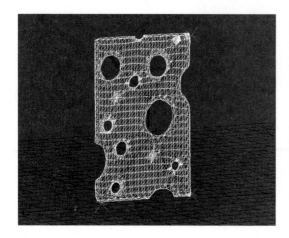

A boned skeleton for a simple slice of Swiss cheese.

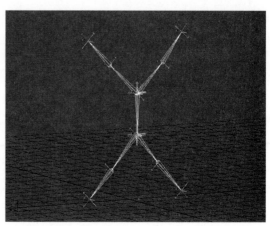

Just the bones, no cheese. Notice how simple the skeleton is.

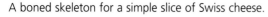

Exercise #3: Animating a Slice of Swiss Cheese

On the CD

On the CD, you'll find a model of a slice of Swiss cheese. The file is in 3D Studio and DXF format; look for either SWISS.3DS or SWISS.DXF. For best results, load this model into your 3D animation package for this exercise.

Because it is rectangular, a slice of cheese is very similar to the box you just animated. However, this time animate the character with bones. (If you don't have bones, you might want to try this exercise using a lattice deformation.) For this example, I used Digimation's Bones Pro, which uses simple boxes for bones. Don't let this throw you off because you can use almost any skeletal deformation system to do this exercise.

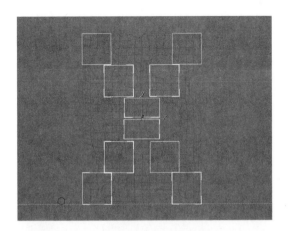

1. First, you need to construct a skeleton to use
   in manipulating your
   cheese. This figure illustrates a wireframe of the
   cheese with box bones.

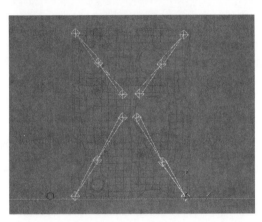

Or you can use an
equivalent skeleton with
skeletal-type bones. Use
whatever type of bones
your package supports
and whatever you feel
comfortable with. Create
the skeleton and assign it
to the cheese so that the
mesh deforms smoothly.

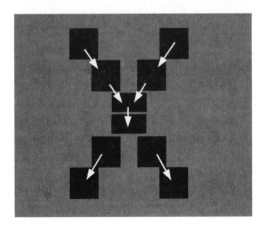

2. Now you can make the
   cheese walk or do a little
   dance. The way you do
   the animation depends on
   your package. If you have
   IK, it's a matter of locking the foot bones to the
   ground and animating,
   but there are other ways.
   I animated this example
   using an upside-down
   (broken) hierarchy. In this
   case, the hierarchy looks
   something like the one
   shown in this illustration.

continues

Exercise #3: continued

Notice that the upper body is connected to the hips, but the thighs are not; they use the shins/feet bones as their parents. Again, you have many options. If you want to use a more connected hierarchy, that's fine too.

3. Now you are ready to animate the walk. If you mastered the walks in Chapter 7, "Walking and Locomotion," this will be fairly easy. I won't bore you with the details; I'll just show you how the bones move as well as the cheese itself. The following are some stills.

The cheese completely rendered.

The bones by themselves.

Exercise #4: Bringing the Vacuum to Life

On the CD

This book's CD contains two sets of movies: SWISS.AVI and SWISS.MOV (showing the rendered cheese) and SWISS-BON.AVI and SWISSBON.MOV (showing just the bones). Load the files into your 3D package and watch them as a reference, if you like.

The following is a more advanced exercise for readers who have a package that supports bones. In this exercise I'm just going to give you the raw materials and some ideas for finishing the animation instead of walking you through the steps.

Take a vacuum cleaner and a vacuum hose, place them in a scene and have them interact with one another. Use bones to animate the vacuum cleaner; you can use splines, a lattice, or bones to deform the hose.

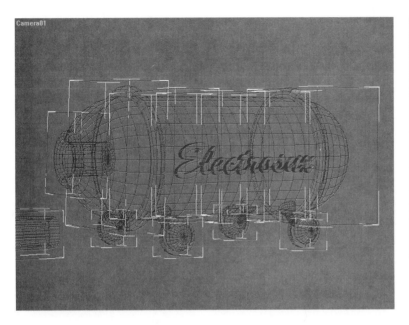

The mesh for the vacuum cleaner.

On the CD

The book's CD contains the files VACUUM.3DS and VACUUM.DXF, which are raw mesh files. You'll need to bone them and animate them yourself. There are also two movies for you to use as reference: VACUUM.AVI and VAC-UUM.MOV and VACBONE.AVI and VAC-BONE.MOV. As in the Swiss cheese example, the first movie shows the rendered shot; the second movie shows only the bones.

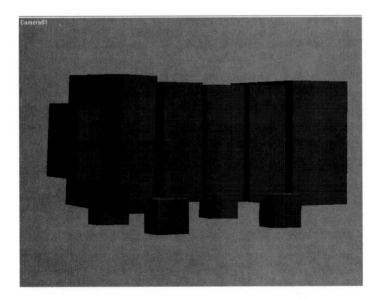

One way to animate the vacuum is to use one bone for each foot and a few more for the tank. This example was animated by using Digimation's Bones Pro. The boxes represent the bones.

continues

Exercise #4: continued

Also, it's not absolutely essential to keep the whole thing together in one hierarchy. When I animated a test of this shot, I found that using a broken hierarchy worked just as well as IK, the preferred method. I had the foot/wheel bones as separate objects and placed them under the tank at the right places. The struts were affected by the bones on both sides and stretched to match.

The following are some stills from the sample movie.

The vacuum walks in from off-screen.

The vacuum notices the hose and sniffs it.

The vacuum gets an idea, turns to the camera, and wags its tail.

Tip

The sample movie on the CD is just one example of what you can do with two simple characters. My advice is to be creative and have fun. The vacuum's personality can be just about anything. The only "face" you have is the hose socket in the front of the tank. Use it to your advantage.

As for the hose, a spline deformation may be a good way to move this mesh around. If your package doesn't support spline deformations, bones will work just fine. In the example on the CD, the hose was animated with bones.

The hose suddenly springs to life, startling the vacuum.

Like a snake, the hose strikes, causing the vacuum to run away.

Conclusion

The anthropomorphic animation techniques presented here will give you a good starting point from which to go. With digital animation you have virtually no limits as to how realistic you can make your characters behave. Remember to be creative and have fun with your characters as you animate them. Think about the type of personality you want each character to have and animate that.

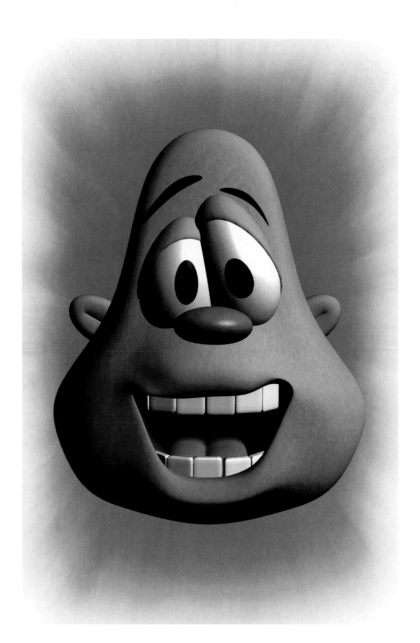

CHAPTER 9

Facial Animation

A nimating the face is one of the most challenging and rewarding tasks you will encounter as an animator. We as humans are all experts in the subtleties of expression and emotion. We know instinctively when a bad actor is on the screen, typically because his emotions seem forced rather than genuine. The same goes for animation; great facial animation looks seamless and does not draw attention to itself, whereas bad animation seems curiously "off" for some unknown reason.

Animating the face requires a good eye and a thorough knowledge of acting and emotion. While you are in the learning process, keep a keen eye on people, their faces, and how they express themselves. A good background in classic films—particularly those of the silent comedians, who had to express themselves purely through facial expressions and body language—can prove invaluable to the animator.

Additionally, good software tools are a must. You will need a package that can build and animate complex shapes with a minimum of fuss. A well-modeled head that is flexible and animates simply will save yourself a couple of bottles of aspirin down the road.

Preparing a Face for Animation

We'll cover the subtleties of animation, expression, and emotion later, but the most important step is to prepare your digitally modeled face for animation. Your software will, to a great extent, determine how you actually animate the face. If you are using shape animation, you must have a face that you can easily sculpt and reshape. If you are using bones, for example, you must properly attach the bones to the face. The following sections are a simple guide to the fundamentals of animating with both bones and shapes.

Using Shape Animation with Faces

Shape animation is one good way to animate faces. A good package enables you to animate many different poses of the same object. This process is known by a number of terms, the most popular of which is *morphing*. Setting up your model for animation is simply a matter of modeling a library of the appropriate poses. This method works for both spline and polygonal models. Some packages force you to create separate objects for the shapes, whereas some enable you to create shapes by using one model. Most software packages require that the models being morphed contain the same number of vertices in the exact same order—a task easily accomplished by modeling a single stock, expressionless face, copying the expressionless face, and reworking it into the many expressions and facial poses you need.

One of the downfalls of shape animation is that it seems like you never have enough poses. In real life, the human face can make an infinite number of expressions, so you'll have to pick your battles and model the broad expressions you need most. This really depends on the character and the project. If your character suffers from terminal happiness, for example, then creating shapes for a sad face are not necessary. Many of the delicate subtleties can get lost when you use such stock poses. Strictly morphing between poses can also look mechanical, so having a few different versions of the same pose can be one way to avoid this problem.

"Morphing" by Any Other Name
The word "morphing" is one of many terms software packages use to describe animating between different shapes of an object.

In Softimage, it is called Shape Animation. Within that, Softimage has a feature called Shape Weights that enables you to combine multiple shapes to create new shapes.

In Alias, the feature is known as Shape Shifter, and it, too, allows you the freedom to combine multiple shapes to create new shapes.

In 3D Studio MAX and LightWave, the feature is simply called morphing. LightWave has a new plug-in called Morph Gizmo, which will let you mix multiple shapes.

In Animation Master, shape animation is done through muscle motions. Each individual shape is called a muscle frame.

More advanced software—such as Softimage and Alias Poweranimator—enable you to combine and weight different shapes to create new and novel poses. You could model individual shapes for expressions such as anger, fear, joy, surprise, disgust, and so on, and then combine them for a pose that is 30 percent surprise and 70 percent joy. If you want to transition that expression to 100 percent joy, simply animate the surprise shape down to zero while moving joy up to 100 percent. You can combine two, three, four, or as many shapes as you want. All you really need to animate is the relative weights of the shapes, making it much easier to create the perfect pose for a given moment and also requiring that fewer poses be modeled. Some packages even enable you to attach these weights to virtual sliders so that you can "dial in" your poses, which makes generating poses at animation time downright easy.

Exercise #1: Reshaping a Spline Face

If you choose to use shape animation, you need to get used to shaping and reshaping the face into expressions. If you built the human head in Chapter 4, "Modeling Heads for Animation," you should be able to follow along with this exercise by using that model. If you prefer to use a different head, however, the same principles apply to other types of heads as well.

After the face is modeled, it should have a fairly neutral expression. Forming expressions is as simple as modifying the vertices and splines that comprise the face.

continues

1. Push the vertices in the top right corner up and out to make a sneer—the same effect as the zygomatic minor, or sneering muscle.

2. Select all the vertices around the lips and scale them together to tighten and purse the lips—the same function as the orbicularis oris muscle.

3. Select all the vertices in the lower half of the face and pull them downward. This has the same effect as dropping the jaw.

As you can see, a well-constructed face works along many of the same lines as the human face, making it possible to form just about any facial expression without too much difficulty. If you want, you can continue to work on these shapes and save them for use during animation.

Animating with Multiple Shapes

If you have a package such as Softimage or Alias, you can combine multiple shapes into one. This allows you to model fewer expressions and still have a wide range of motion. For this example, I'll focus specifically on Softimage's shape weights, which give a good example of this technique. In Softimage, each shape in the library is represented as a curve. In this example we have 10 shapes (and 10 curves)— each representing a mouth

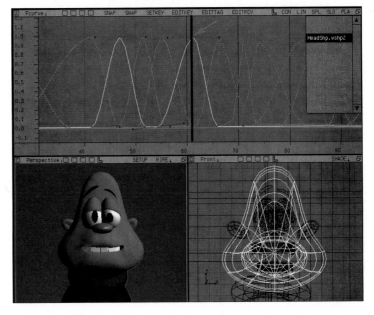

Here, the character's lips are poised to make the sound of the letter F. At frame 61 this shape is at 100 percent.

shape used for lip sync. Manipulating the curves animates the corresponding shapes. The red arrow indicates the position on the timeline.

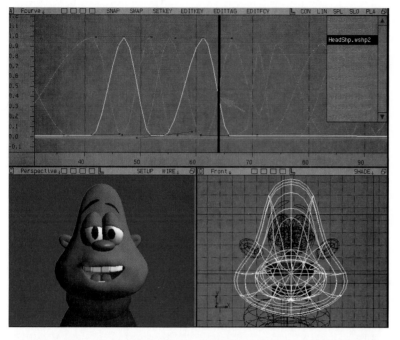

At frame 64 the curve is now at 50 percent, and the curve for the next shape is rising from zero. Notice how the character's mouth shape is halfway between this shape and the next.

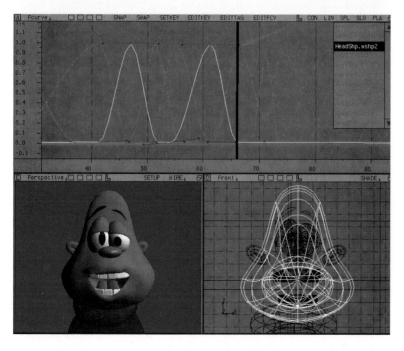

At frame 67, the second curve, for the "A" sound, is at 100 percent, and the first curve has tapered off to zero. Although this example is simple in that it uses only two shapes, you can use this technique to mix any number of shapes in any combination.

Direct Manipulation

Some packages enable you to directly manipulate and animate the vertices of the model over time, making it easier to animate subtle tweaks in the poses. This method is similar to animating with clay; it's the least efficient because you have to re-create every expression at every keyframe. It can be resource-intensive on the workstation as well. Layering direct manipulation on top of another method, such as shape animation, however, is a good compromise that enables you to customize stock poses.

Some packages take this notion a step further. Softimage, for example, gives you the ability to give names to groups of vertices. Called Clusters, these groups can then be selected and animated by name. You could name a cluster "Left Eyebrow" or "Right Lip Corner," for example, and then animate the eyebrow rising or the corner of the lip turning into a slight frown. This makes direct manipulation much easier to manage—the simple fact that each cluster has a unique name lets you track of things at animation time.

Animating Faces with Bones

Using bones as effectors to animate the face is another popular method. The bones are placed at the main control points of the face, essentially where the major muscles anchor to the skin. Animating the bones causes the surface of the face to stretch and follow along. As with using bones to manipulate the body, you need to carefully set up facial bones to avoid unwanted bulging and crimping. If you use bones, be sure to test them over a wide range of expressions before animating. Otherwise, unexpected and unrealistic results may occur, and you may be forced to backtrack. Although most polygonal animation packages use bones, they work great on spline faces as well.

Another important thing to remember when using bones is getting the bones to move along lines that are tangent to the surface of the face. Because the face is slightly curved, moving a bone linearly can cause unwanted bulges. One way to avoid the bulging is to place each bone's pivot at a point within the face. That way, bone movement can be expressed as a rotational movement rather than a linear translation. Because rotating the bones automatically moves them along an arc, the bones follow the surface of the face more closely. By carefully adjusting their pivots and axes of rotation, you can make the bones move along the same lines as the major facial muscles that pull the face.

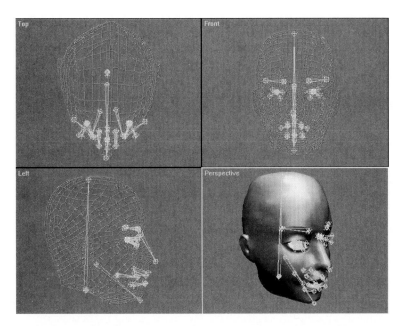

A face with bones used as effectors. The bones are placed so they affect the face where the major muscles anchor to the skin.

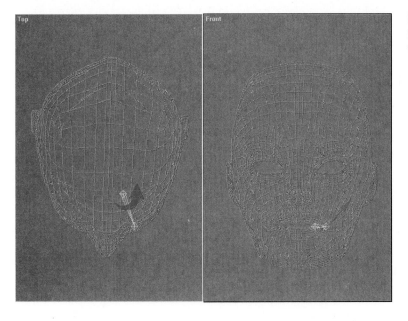

Bones should move on pivots, rather than linearly, so that they track the curvature of the skull.

You also can use bones to create stock poses—just as you can by using shape animation or morphing. All you need to do is create a library of "poses" for the bones as keyframes on the timeline. By copying these poses along the timeline, you can create the broad strokes for the major expressions and then adjust the positions of the bones individually to add the subtleties.

If you use bones to animate a face, proper placement of those bones is essential. Here is the basic face that we will use in this example. This face is made out of polygons, but the same principles apply equally to any type of geometry. For this exercise, you'll need a package that enables you to assign specific vertices to specific bones. If your software doesn't do this, you can use the bone positions in the exercise as a starting point.

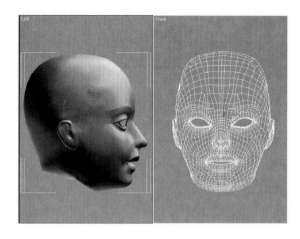

1. Place a large bone in the center of the head to define the skull. If your package does not enable you to assign the vertices manually, you may need several bones to fill the volume.

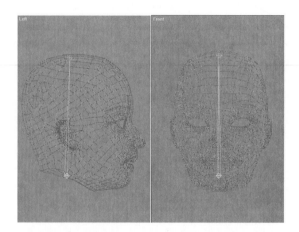

2. Assign the vertices that represent the solid portions of the head to this bone. (You will assign the fleshy areas of the face later.) These vertices remain rigid, so exclude them from other bones.

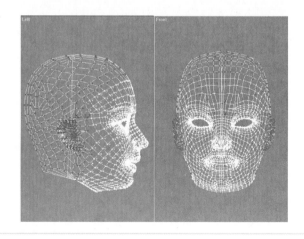

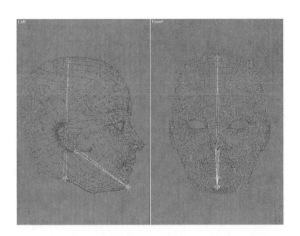

3. Add a jaw bone, pivot it somewhere near the bottom front corner of the ear, and extend it to the chin. Assign the vertices of the chin and lower face to the jaw bone.

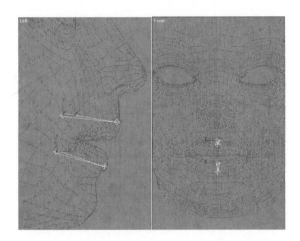

4. Now for the lips and mouth. Add two bones, one each in the center of the top and bottom lip.

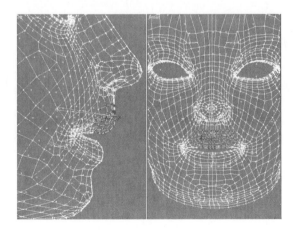

5. We want each bone to affect only its chosen lip. For the top lip bone, include only those vertices on the top lip. Do the same for the bottom lip's bone and vertices.

continues

6. Now you need to add two bones in the corners of the mouth. Make sure these bones pivot along the same axis that the zygomatic major, the smiling muscle, pulls. Rotate the bone to see whether it moves roughly along the surface of the face. From the front, the bone should pull the corner of the mouth to the side and slightly up, just like when a person smiles.

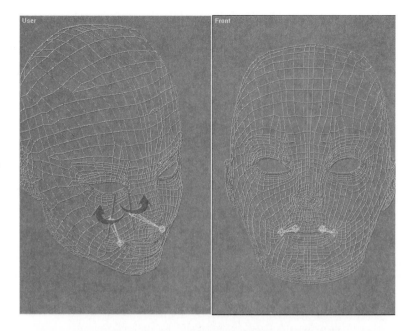

7. Add four more bones, each halfway between the corners and the middle of the mouth. To keep transitions smooth, these bones should each have an area of influence that slightly overlaps the adjoining bones. These bones should pivot so they move outward radially like the muscles of the face (refer to the arrows in the figure).

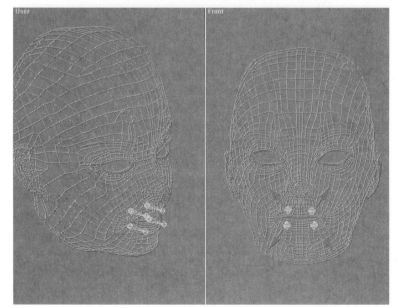

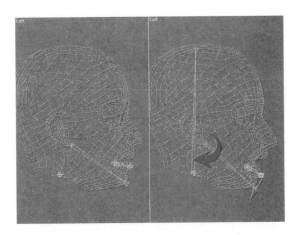

8. All the bones along the lower lip mimic muscles that are attached to the jaw. Link or constrain these bones to the jaw bone so that when the jaw pivots down, the bones and the vertices they affect move with it, forcing open the mouth.

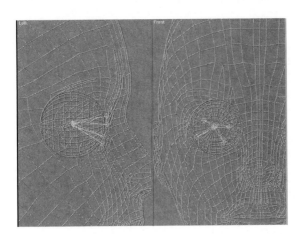

9. With the lower face done, concentrate on the eyes. Placement of the bones around the eyes is similar to the mouth, but one or two bones per lid are sufficient. Pivot the bones along the center of the eyeball so that the lid moves along the eye's surface. I unhid the eye (green sphere) so you can see how the bones are placed.

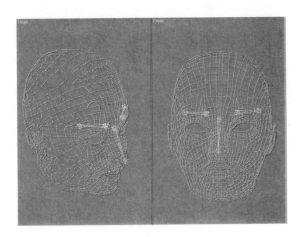

10. You probably will want to add a bone for the nose to help keep it rigid, as well as add bones for the eyebrows and maybe even a bone or two to help puff out the cheeks during a smile.

continues

11. Finally, create a test animation to check for flexibility of the face. If you find dents, bulges, or crimping, reassign the vertices to the proper bones so that everything moves smoothly. Once you're happy with how your model moves, be sure to save your work. You can then use this file as a starting point for all animations with this face.

Lattices and Metamation

Lattice deformations are also used occasionally for facial animation. Many packages restrict you to rectangular lattices, which really don't work for faces because the face is hardly rectangular in shape. The face is fairly complex, so a more complex lattice is required.

One variant of lattice deformation is LightWave's Metamation. A second cousin to lattice deformations, this unique feature relies on LightWave's Metaform automatic smoothing feature. When modeling, you create a simple, low-resolution object out of a handful of polygons. You then smooth this object by using Metaform to create a high-resolution model suitable for rendering. At animation time, the low-res model becomes a lattice or "cage" used to deform the high-res model. The points of the cage are typically manipulated using bones, but the cage itself is what determines the deformation of the final model.

In Metamation the cage (yellow) is a lattice animated with bones. The detail is filled in automatically at rendering time (gray), avoiding the crimping and bulging inherent with animated polygons.

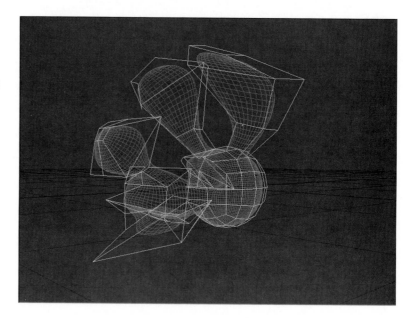

Head Turns

When animating the head and face, the first thing you need to learn is how to move the head naturally. Suppose you want to turn your character's head to the left. Your first instinct might be to rotate it along a horizontal straight line, making the head movement look mechanical. In real life, heads dip slightly below horizontal as they turn, making a shallow arc.

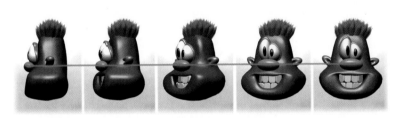

Heads do not turn on straight lines.

Instead, they dip slightly in the middle of the turn, forming an arc.

While on the subject of head turns, here are some extra little tricks that will make them more realistic. People tend to look in the direction that their head is turning, so it's best to lead the head turn with the eyes. If the head is turning left, the eyes will turn left before the head moves. Also, when the pupils move, they move on arcs as well, dipping in the middle of the turn much like the head. A final tip is that the eyes usually blink while the head turns. These little details can add extra life to your character.

The eyes usually point in the direction of the head turn, and a blink in the middle of the action adds some life.

Blinks

Blinks go a long way to adding life to your character. You should generally have your character blink every few seconds if only to show that he is alive. The timing of the blink itself depends on your character's personality or mood. Typically, I find that five frames is usually adequate for most situations, although four frames can make a character look more alert. If a character is large or tired, more frames are needed.

This figure illustrates the standard timing for a blink and should work for most situations.

This blink's timing is fast, but it makes the character look more alert.

This blink is for a very large or very sleepy character.

For practice, take one of the heads you constructed in the previous chapters and make it do some head turns—one with a blink and one without.

Creating a Library of Poses

No matter what animation method you choose, you should build a stock library of expressions from which you can draw when creating your animation. These libraries can grow to be quite large and can be time-consuming to model, but they invariably save time in the long run. If you have 20 or 30 expressions, you can store them as individual keyframes or on disk as individual shapes, depending on your software.

As mentioned earlier, by using Softimage's shape weights, you can combine multiple shapes by assigning each a percentage or weight. Alias Poweranimator's Shape Shifter feature works along similar lines and enables you to model as many expressions as you want and then combine them by percentages. The feature also enables you to break down expressions into their component parts—one set of shapes for the eyes, another for the mouth, and so on.

If you animate with bones, the positions of the bones at each keyframe determine the individual expression. By copying these keys to other parts of the timeline, you can make animation easier. You can separate the components of each expression and copy them where needed. For example, you can manipulate and copy the keyframes of the bones that control the eyes separately from those that control the mouth.

One easy way to create a library is to simply create keyframes (or groups of keyframes on the timeline) which then can be copied.

A convenient place to store these keys is in the negative frame numbers before frame zero. That way, you don't have to worry about offsetting your animation. If your timeline doesn't support negative frame numbers, you can block off the first hundred frames as a place to store the keys. Instead of your animations starting at frame 0, they can start at frame 10 or frame 100, for example.

Choosing the Right Poses for Your Library

When creating a library, what sort of expressions do you want to model? You can choose from a number of basic expressions as well as the mouths used to animate dialogue. Also, as you animate a character, you may create new expressions that strike you as ones that you may need to use again. There are, however, a few basic expressions that you can use as a starting point.

Basic Whole-Face Facial Expressions

The face can make an infinite number of expressions; luckily, they fall into some broad categories—anger, disgust, fear, joy, sadness, and surprise. We'll detail them here, but you must recognize that they are extreme expressions only—primary colors among the many hues of expression. You could never animate with these six alone, but these basic "faces" can take you a long way toward understanding the underlying mechanics of expression.

Anger: The eyes are open, but the brows are down. The mouth is usually open with the lips tensed and teeth bared. The jaw may be lowered.

Disgust: The whole face is tightened with the eyes squinting and the mouth closed and pulled toward the nose.

Fear: The mouth is wide open and pulled back at the lower corners. The jaw is dropped, and the eyes are wide.

Joy: The mouth is pulled upward into a smile, exposing the upper teeth, forcing the cheeks up. The brows are usually relaxed.

Sadness: The mouth is pulled down at the lower corners and may expose the lower teeth. The eyes squint and, when crying, may be closed.

Surprise: The eyes are wide open, and the brows are raised but not furrowed. The mouth is relaxed, and the jaw is slack.

These six expressions also make a good basis for your library because they are so extreme. If your face can effectively convey these expressions, it should be able to carry any other expression equally as well.

However, don't kid yourself into thinking these six expressions are all you need. There is a plethora of other expressions: aloofness, bitterness, conceit, despair, exuberance, fury, glee, hunger, impatience, jealousy, kindness, love, modesty, nervousness, passion, quizzical, reflective, sarcasm, and thirst—to name only a few. Most of these expressions are much more subtle than the basic six and may not always be absolutely clear; they must be judged in context. Add the mouth shapes used when speaking to these expressions and you have zillions of combinations.

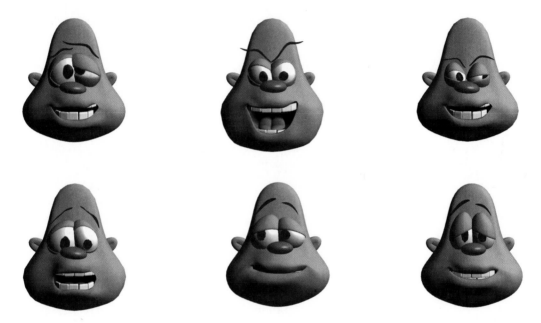

Faces can portray so many other expressions that it's hard to count, but here are just a few.

Upper- and Lower-Face Combinations

Another way to break down the expressions is to separate them into two zones: the upper and lower face. This way, you can create different sets of keys and combine them—angry eyes with a happy mouth, for example. If your eyes are external—built from separate objects—you can copy the keys for angry eyes and combine them with the keys for a happy mouth. If your character has internal eyes, you might want to use direct manipulation or clusters—one set of cluster keys for the mouth, one for the eyes.

By keeping the eye and mouth expressions separate, you can play musical faces.

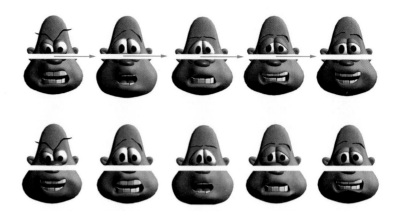

Mix the expressions any way you like to get new and novel expressions.

With the face having so many expressions and subtle changes, how do you know which expression to use? Much of that determination comes from study and experience, trial and error. Experimentation is part of the equation. If a shot isn't working, try starting from scratch instead of trying to fix it. Look at reference material on videotape, particularly the silent classics. You can also use your own face as reference. Another good idea is to keep a small mirror handy when you animate. That way, you can see the desired expressions you want your character to perform by observing yourself.

Exercise #3: Building a Library of Facial Expressions

There are a number of ways to animate facial expressions, including bones, shape animation, or morph targets. Using your favorite method and one of the full-body characters you've built, create a library of a dozen facial expressions for use later.

1. To do this, create a basic animation file that is 12 frames long. These frames are not meant to be viewed as an animation. Instead, they are a library that contains your facial expressions. These can then be copied to other parts of the timeline to create the actual animation.

2. On frame one, create a keyframe that replicates the shape for anger. How you do this depends on the animation method you've decided to use. If you're using bones, rotate the bones to duplicate the mouth shape for anger and manipulate the eyes and eyebrows to get angry eyes. Save all of these modifications as keyframes at frame 1.

3. At frame two, create a face for disgust and save those keyframes. Continue on through the rest of the basic six expressions as outlined above.

4. Finally, create six more of your very own. The expressions you choose depends entirely on your character and your personal whims. Have fun with this task.

Save this file. You now have a stock library of expressions you can use later.

Animating the Face

Now that you have a library of expressions, you can use them as building blocks to create animations. The theory is that you copy the keyframes representing each shape to where you want the pose on the timeline, letting the computer do the inbetweens.

Automatic inbetweening is another issue. Many times, the computer's inbetween will not look correct or you may need to tweak a final pose. You need to plan for this possibility when animating. Also, expressions aren't always formed at the same time. Just like when animating the body, you often need to use the techniques of overlap, follow-through, squash, and stretch for the face.

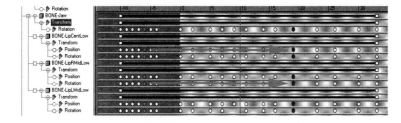

Creating facial animation is as simple as copying the keys from your library to the proper point on the timeline.

To get the motion right, you should animate the face in several passes. First, block in the major facial expressions and poses. Second, go back over the animation several times to add subtlety and detail—add facial ticks, follow-through, overlap, and so on. These little details, not the broad strokes, infuse your character with life.

If you're using bones to manipulate the face, for example, each bone's position is represented as an individual key. Let's say we're going from sad to happy over the course of one second. In real life, the eyes would probably brighten half a second before the lips actually smile. In this case, you may want to copy all the keys for the "happy" face to the proper point in the timeline and then offset only those keys for the bones representing the mouth by a half second. If you're using shape animation, you'll probably want to keep upper and lower facial expressions separate. That way, you can weight the upper and lower parts of the face differently to add some nice overlap. To add more subtlety, you may want to push up the right corner of the mouth a few frames before you push up the left corner of the mouth. Overlap, anticipation, and follow-through are not just animation principles that apply to the body; they apply to the face, as well.

A simple happy to sad done with one straight inbetween; it looks somewhat mechanical.

If you add some overlap—making the eyes dim first, for example— you can make your character more lifelike.

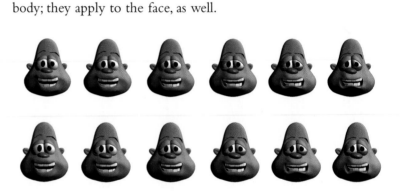

Exercise #4: Animating the Face

Using the stock library of expressions you created, animate a three-second shot with a character who goes from sad to happy to angry.

1. To do this, you first need to load the file containing the library of expressions you created in the previous exercise. Because the first 12 frames of this file contain the library of poses, you'll need to start animating after frame 12. You could start your animation on frame 13, but that's not an easy number to remember, and it's also unlucky. Instead, start your animation on frame 100. That way, you can add a one to the frame count.

2. This means our three-second animation will be 3×30 frames/sec, or 90 frames long. (If you're animating to film, it would be 3×24 frames/sec or 72 frames long). Add to this

the 100 frame offset to get an animation time that runs from frame 100 to frame 190.

3. At frame 100, copy the keyframes for a sad face to frame 100. If you're using bones, these will be the keys representing the positions and rotations of your bones. If you're using shapes, these will be keys for the shape.

4. Go to the middle of your range, frame 145, and copy the keys for happy.

5. At the end of the animation, frame 190, copy the keys for angry.

6. Render frames 100 through 190 and view your test. You will notice the animation looks rather stale. This is because we have straight inbetweens without anticipation, follow-through, or variation in the timing of the poses.

7. Go back over the animation to make it look more lifelike. I will leave the specifics up to you because experimentation will tell you more about which changes work and which don't. As a starting point, you may want to add a few blinks and maybe some head motion. You should also alter the timing of individual parts of the face. Maybe the right corner of the lip moves a few frames ahead of the left; maybe the eyes precede the mouth when going from sad to happy. Consider these tips and choose the ones that seem to work for your character.

8. When you're done, render a final test.

Animating Lip Sync

Animating lip sync can really frighten the beginning animator—and rightly so—because it is one of the most difficult techniques for an animator to master. Live-action people have it easy; they just point the cameras at the actors and ask them to speak. Re-creating natural lip movements in animation, however, requires a great deal of time, patience, and analysis. In addition to getting the mouth shapes and positions right, you must also be concerned with the acting and body motions associated with the dialogue. Like any hard task, however, lip sync animation is grounded in some very simple techniques. Practice those techniques, and you are well on your way to mastering lip sync.

Using the Body Effectively in Dialogue

Before we go any further, it must be stressed that animating effective dialogue is not simply getting the lips to match up with a soundtrack; it's also the acting and body motions that go along with the dialogue. When an audience member watches a scene, he's not just looking at the lips; he's also looking at the rest of the face, the body, the gestures, and the acting of the character as a whole. If your character doesn't move, it looks like a doll with lips right out of a bad episode of "Clutch Cargo." Getting the lips right is important, but it's only part of a much larger equation. The poses and attitudes that the body takes are just as important to the audience's interpretation of the character's demeanor as the dialogue you are animating.

A happy face on a sad body. This juxtaposition makes the exact emotion unclear.

A happy face on a happy body. This is very clear. The body's attitude plays a big part in showing emotion.

When talking, many people use their hands to clarify and emphasize the major points of their speech. Getting this part of the animation correct is a lesson in acting. If you want to see how *not* to animate, watch some really nervous or first-time actors. They usually are very self-conscious—stuffing their hands in their pockets, wringing their hands nervously, or hanging their hands loose at their sides.

In real life, body language precedes the dialogue by anywhere from a few frames to as many as 20. Generally, a slow, dimwitted character has more time between his gestures and his dialogue than a sharp, quick character. Speedy Gonzales has considerably less lead time on his gestures than Forrest Gump. Someone giving a long, boring speech will be much slower than a fire and brimstone evangelist.

Make an effort to ensure that the gestures you create fit the dialogue smoothly. The first gesture every animator learns is the ubiquitous finger point for emphasis, followed soon after by the fist pounding into the palm. These gestures certainly have their place, but it is within a much larger palette. Simply watching people in their natural habitat is always your best reference. I've also noticed that guests on those trashy afternoon talk shows seem to gesture quite voraciously. If you can stand it, spend an afternoon watching trash TV for additional reference.

Recording Dialogue

In animation, dialogue is almost always recorded before the characters are drawn. Dialogue looks more natural when the animator follows the natural rhythms of speech. Voice actors have difficulty matching previously animated dialogue while trying to make the dialogue sound natural, which is why recording the speech before the animation begins is essential.

Directing a voice session is an art in itself, and the voice actors must know the scene and the setting. This knowledge enables the actors to inflect different tones and pauses into their speech. As well, it is useful for timing purposes for the actors to act out character movements as they record the dialogue. Another method that may prove useful is to give the actors a storyboard so that they can visualize the shot as they record the dialogue.

After the dialogue is recorded, the animator is responsible for breaking down the track frame by frame into individual phonemes—the most basic sounds of human speech—to be animated. The easiest way to picture a phoneme is to think of each discrete sound that makes up a word. The word "funny" for example has four phonemes—the "f" sound, the "uh" sound, an "n" sound, and finally, a long "ee" sound. Reading a dialogue track can be a tedious task. The dialogue must be broken down frame by frame and written by hand onto exposure sheets. Computer animators have the advantage of using digital audio software to read their tracks, and some packages, such as Alias Poweranimator and Animo, can actually break down the track automatically.

Tip

If the voice actor acts out character motions while he records dialogue, videotape the voice session. You can then play back the tape to provide additional reference for your animation of both dialogue and gestures.

digital character animation

The exposure sheet is used to break down the dialogue track frame by frame. Here a character is saying, "Give it a shot" (highlighted in white). The exposure sheet can also contain other information. To the left of the dialogue is a column to write down notes on how you want your character to act—to blink or bob his head, for example. To the right of the dialogue are notes indicating which mouth shapes to use.

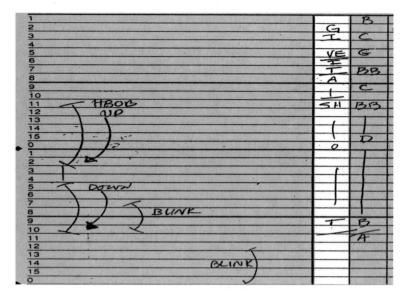

The Eight Basic Mouth Positions

Before reading the track you must understand how your mouth moves when you make sounds. There are dozens of different mouth shapes made during the course of normal speech. Animators usually boil these down to a handful of standard shapes that are used repeatedly. Depending on the style of animation, some animators get away with as few as three or four shapes, and some use dozens. For most situations, you can get away with approximately eight basic mouth positions. These eight positions usually provide adequate coverage and enable you to animate most dialogue effectively.

To see how these positions work, watch yourself in the mirror while you talk. Make the sounds used by each position. If you talk naturally, you'll begin to see how the shapes work and how they all fit together into a continuous stream. The shapes and the rules that govern them are certainly not strict. Different accents and speech patterns may cause you to substitute one shape for the other in order to achieve a more convincing look.

Position A is the closed mouth used for consonants made by the lips, specifically the M, B, and P sounds. In this position, the lips are usually their normal width. For added realism, you could add an additional position with the lips slightly pursed, for sounds following an "ooo" sound, such as in the word "room."

In position B the mouth is open and the teeth are closed. This position is a common shape used for consonants made within the mouth, specifically sounds made by C, D, G, K, N, R, S, TH, Y, and Z. All these sounds can also be made with the teeth slightly open, particularly in fast speech.

Position C is used for the wide open vowels such as A and I.

Position D is used primarily for the vowel E, but it can also be used on occasion for C, K, or N during fast speech.

In position E the mouth is wide open in an elliptical shape. This is the position used for the vowel O, as in the word "flow." Sometimes, particularly when the sound is at the end of a word, you can follow this shape with the one in Position F to close the mouth.

In position F the mouth opening is smaller, but more pursed. Position F is used for the "oooo" sound, as in "Food," and for the vowel U.

In position G the mouth is wide open with the tongue against the teeth. This position is reserved for the letter L. It can also be used for D or TH sounds, particularly when preceded by A or I. If the speech is particularly rapid, this shape may not be necessary, and you can substitute Position B.

In position H the bottom lip is tucked under the teeth to make the sound of the letters F or V. In highly pronounced speech, this shape is necessary, but the shape could also be replaced with Position B for more casual or rapid speech.

Exercise #5: Creating Mouth Shapes for Lip Sync

As outlined previously, there are a number of ways to animate facial expressions, including bones, shape animation, or morph targets. By using your favorite method and one of the full-body characters you've built, create a library of mouth shapes to use when animating lip sync.

continues

Exercise #5: continued

1. Create a simple animation file that is eight frames long. These frames are not meant to be viewed as an animation; instead, they are simply a library with eight slots in which to place your eight basic mouth shapes. Some packages, such as Animation Master, enable you to save each shape to disk. If this is the case, save your shapes to disk rather than in the timeline.

2. On frame 1, create a keyframe that looks like mouth shape A—with the lips closed. How you do this depends on your chosen animation method. If you're using bones, push together the bones controlling the lips and save keyframes for the bones. If you prefer shapes, reshape your model to duplicate this pose and save it to disk or as a keyframe, depending on your software.

3. At frame 2, create mouth shape B and continue throughout the rest of the shapes, one per frame for a total of eight shapes.

You now have a library of stock mouth shapes you can use to animate dialogue.

Reading the Track

Now that you understand the basic mouth positions, it's time to break down the track. If you have animator's exposure sheet paper, use it. Otherwise, get a pad of lined paper on which to write your track, using one line per frame. (If you prefer, you can create a spreadsheet for this purpose and do it digitally.) Load the dialogue in a sound editing program. A number of sound editing packages are available, and you should choose one that enables you to display the time in frames, as well as to select and play portions of the track. The capability to label sections in the editor is also handy.

Plenty of sound editing programs are available for the Mac and PC. Macromedia's Sound Edit Pro is a good choice for the Mac.

For the PC, Turtle Beach's Wave for Windows and Cool Edit, a shareware program (available at www.shareware.com) are good choices.

First, match your sound editing program's timebase to the timebase you're animating—30, 25, or 24 frames per second, for example. After your timebase is set, selecting a snippet of dialogue enables you to listen to the snippet and read its exact length on the editor's data window. The visual readout of the dialogue gives you clues as to where the words start and stop. Work your way through the track and write down each phoneme as it occurs on your exposure sheet, frame by frame. This is a tedious but necessary chore.

Some packages, such as ElectricImage and 3D Studio MAX, enable you to play back audio in sync with the animation. This feature is particularly helpful because it gives you the ability to skip the step of reading the track and simply eyeball the sync. Still, it's always a good idea to have read the track methodically before animating so that you know exactly where all the sounds occur.

When reading the track, be sure to represent the sounds accurately. In human speech, most consonants are short and usually don't take up more than one or two frames. Vowels, however, can be of any length. If a person is shouting, for instance, you may have vowels that top 30 frames in length. In these cases, it is important that you don't hold the mouth in the exact same position for more than a second—it would look unnatural. Instead, create two slightly different mouth positions and keep the mouth moving between them so that the character looks alive.

Exercise #6: Reading a Track

Let's take a line of dialogue and read it for animation.

1. On the CD-ROM, choose the audio file called DIA-LOGUE.WAV if you use a PC or choose DIALOGUE if you use a Mac. Load the appropriate file into your favorite sound editing program. The dialogue says, "Hello. How are you feeling today?" At 30 fps, the dialogue measures 72 frames.

continues

Exercise #6: continued

2. After you the load the file into your sound editor, this dialogue file looks something like this.

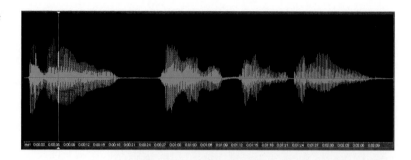

3. Highlight the first 18 frames of the sound file. This is the word "Hello." Play back this section.

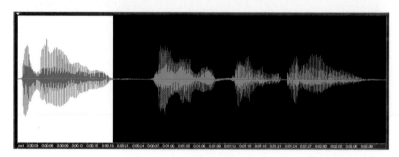

4. Try highlighting smaller sections to get the individual phonemes HE - L - OOO. Notice how the HE and L sounds take up only the first four frames of the sound, whereas the OOO sound takes up 14 frames, indicating the amount of time vowels take compared to consonants. Notice, too, that vowel sound waves are usually taller and louder than the consonant's.

5. Work through the entire track, writing down the positions of each phoneme. The following is a graphic representation of where the phonemes fall.

6. On paper, you should have something similar to the list shown in table 9.1. (Note that in the table I've also marked the mouth shapes and where they should start.)

Table 9.1
Reading the DIALOGUE Track

FRAME	PHONEME	MOUTH SHAPE	FRAME	PHONEME	MOUTH SHAPE	FRAME	PHONEME	MOUTH SHAPE
1	H	D	25			49	EE	
2	E		26	H	D	50	EE	
3	L	G	27	H		51	NG	B
4	L		28	OW	E	52	NG	
5	OH	E	29	OW	F	53	T	
6	OH		30	OW		54	AH	C
7	OH		31	AH	C	55	AH	
8	OH		32	AH		56	D	B
9	OH		33	AH		57	A	
10	OH		34	Y	F	58	A	C
11	OH		35	OO		59	A	
12	OH	F	36	OO		60	A	
13	OH		37	OO		61	A	
14	OH		38	OO		62	A	
15	OH		39	OO		63	A	
16	OH		40	F	H	64	A	
17	OH		41	F		65	A	
18	OH		42	F		66	E	D
19	(silent)	A	43	EE	D	67	E	
20			44	EE		68	E	
21			45	EE		69	E	
22			46	L	G	70	(silent)	A
23			47	L		71		
24			48	EE	D	72		

Now that the track is broken down, you can begin to animate the character speaking the line.

Animating the Dialogue

In cel animation the body movements are invariably drawn first. After the acting is perfected, the mouths are drawn. The animation is done in this sequence because the animator never knows the exact position of the head until the animation of the body is complete. Digital animators don't suffer from this limitation. They have the flexibility of animating the mouths at any point in the process. Many times it's done first because it's easier to check the sync on an immobile head.

However you approach it, dialogue animation should be done in layers. Dialogue animation is a cyclical process of blocking in the major moves and then tweaking each layer over several passes. One approach is to first animate the lip shapes and get them to sync to the dialogue. After that, tweak the facials to match the emotion of the character and then do the body motions and the acting. After all this is done, go through each element again until the whole shot is seamless.

Exercise #7: Putting It All Together

If you've been doing the exercises, you should already have a character with a library of mouth shapes. Depending on your chosen method, these shapes can be bone positions, shapes, morph targets, or whatever suits your needs. Load this character in your 3D animation program and follow along.

Using the track that you just read, let's go through the first word of the track, "Hello."

1. The H and the E sounds are really one vocalization and can be best represented by mouth position D. At frame 1, create a keyframe that represents the mouth position by copying the shapes out of your library or from other parts of the timeline, depending on your package. Next, you have the L sound at frame 3. Again, copy the appropriate keys for position G to frame 3. At this point, let the computer calculate the inbetween. You can tweak the animation later. Finally, the OH sound. Because this is fairly long, you should probably close the mouth from position E to position F over the course of the sound. At frame 5 or 6, make a key for position E, and then at frame 12 or so make a key for position F.

2. At the end of "OH," close the mouth. Closing the mouth is not a requirement, but, again, let the computer do the inbetween for you. You can tweak it later.

3. As you can see, matching animation to the dialogue is a matter of placing the keyframes at suitable positions on the timeline. Go through the rest of the dialogue and finish animating the mouth positions.

4. Render a test.

5. After you're finished, you'll have a nice animation of only the lips. To check the sync, load the rendered test and play it along with the sound track. How you do this depends on your platform and its capabilities. On the desktop, the testing is most easily done within a nonlinear editing package such as Adobe Premiere.

6. If you followed the read of the track fairly closely, the lips should sync on the first try. If the whole track looks off, you may first want to jog the audio forward or back by a frame or two to see whether you can sync the dialogue without reanimating the shot. If a single word or syllable is off, you need to go back, adjust the appropriate keys, and render a new test.

After you match the lips to the dialogue, you need to animate the acting of the face and body. Because there are no hard and fast rules to follow for this part of the exercise, the rest of the exercise is open to your own interpretation.

There are, however, a few guidelines to follow when animating the face and body:

■ Play the dialogue a few times while acting out the shot to get a good idea of exactly how you want your character to act.

■ Body motions tend to precede spoken dialogue by a few frames. If you decide to use any gestures of the head or hands, make them fall before the word they accent.

- To keep the face from looking like a doll, add a blink or two within the shot.

- When animating the body, be sure to remember such things as anticipation and follow-through to keep the character looking natural.

- Experiment and have fun animating. There is one example of the animation on the CD-ROM. It is called DIA-LOGUE.AVI or DIALOGUE.MOV.

Practice the Fundamentals

This chapter has discussed the fundamentals of dialogue animation. The fundamentals are easy to understand and grasp, but getting your animations to look good requires some more work. Now it is time for you to practice, practice, and practice some more. You should record some tracks of your own and animate more characters. There are, however, ways to get dialogue other than hiring a voice actor. Aardman Animations in Britain did some wonderful clay animations using "found" dialogue. The company recorded people speaking in normal conversation and then edited these tapes down from several hours to a few minutes in length and used it as the basis for an animation. Nick Park's Academy Award winning short *Creature Comforts* is a classic example of this technique. Another way to practice is to lift dialogue from a famous film. Robin Steele at Colossal Pictures did a great little series of shorts called *Stick Figure Theater*, which animated dialogue from famous films such as *The Graduate* using nothing but stick figures. It looked great and was very funny. Of course, if you want to distribute such a film commercially, you may run into copyright problems and need to get all sorts of permissions. For practice use, however, it's not an issue. Wherever you obtain your dialogue, have fun when animating.

CHAPTER 10

Advanced Tips and Tricks

So far, you have been dealing with individual characters in very simple situations. The animated world, however, is usually much more complex. The real world is full of objects needing to be picked up, carried, and tossed. Your characters need to look at their world as well—another subtle form of interaction.

Your characters can also show a wider range of emotions than what we've been dealing with so far. They can react violently in a cartoon "take," or they can laugh and cry. You now need to start thinking about how to get your characters to interact more with each other and their environments and show a wider range of actions. This chapter covers some methods for doing this.

Picking Up and Holding Things

One particularly vexing problem faced by digital animators is the simple task of getting a character to pick up a coffee cup and hold it in his hand. Generally, the animator wants the object to follow the character's hand pretty much everywhere it goes.

The first instinct is to construct a simple hierarchy—the cup being the child of the hand. A parent-child hierarchy, however, can prove troublesome because it runs smack into some package's limitations. Most packages don't enable you to create and break hierarchies on the fly during an animation. Some exceptions do exist, such as Meme-X's Lock and Key plug-in for LightWave, which enable you to change hierarchies on a frame-by-frame basis. For most packages, however, your character's hand is either the parent of the cup for the entire scene or they remain separate.

Lifting an object off the table can pose some tricky problems. How do you keep the object with the character?

You can use a few techniques to get around the problem of keeping an object with the character. These methods apply not only to picking up things with your character's hands, but also to things such as hats, belts, backpacks, and any other thing that needs to look like it's attached to your character and needs to move with him.

Animatable Locks and Pins

In addition to using parent/child relationships, locking or pinning features found in some IK implementations can also be used to help your character hold on to something. Rather than pinning your character's feet to the floor, you can pin the coffee cup to your character's index finger, for example, and it should go wherever the finger goes.

Some of these locking or pinning features, however, do not pin objects to each other; rather, they pin objects to a distinct point in space. In the coffee cup example, your character's hand might be pinned to the point in space just above the counter where the coffee cup was sitting, making it very difficult for your character to take a sip. If this is the case, you'll need to resort to other methods.

Animating in Groups

Another simple way to keep an object in a character's hand is to move both the hand and the object at exactly the same time along the same path. This method works only for hands and arms that can be animated using IK. In this method, you simply select the object and the hand and move them both. The arm uses IK to animate the shoulder and elbow joints automatically, and the hand follows a path through space. If your object and your hand move at exactly the same time, the object will appear to be fixed to the hand. Of course, if you move the arm using another method, such as forward kinematics, the object will slip from your character's grip.

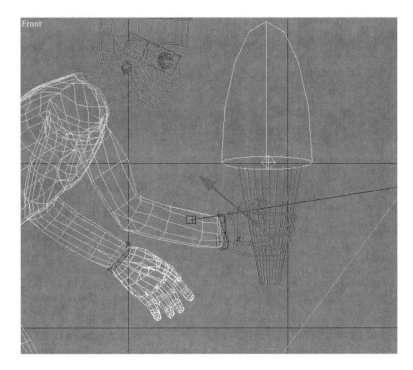

If you select the object and the hand at the same time (highlighted in red), you can move them together as a group (arrow). You must let your Inverse Kinematics system solve for the position of the arm, however.

Segmenting the Shot

If you don't have the luxury of IK or animatable locks, you can still get a character to pick something up and hold it. One way is to divide up your shot into segments. Suppose you have shot number 27, where the character picks up a ball on frame 100 and places it on the table on frame 150. You simply divide the shot into three segments: 27A, 27B, and 27C. In the middle segment (27B, from frame 100 to frame 150) the ball is hierarchically linked to the character's hand. In the other two, before he picks up the ball (27A) and after he sets it down (27C), the ball is not linked.

Segmenting the shot means breaking it into sections.

When the character picks up the ball, you make a seamless cut to a new shot, identical to the first, enabling you to attach the ball to the hand.

When he sets it down again, you cut once more to another identical shot, enabling you to detach the object once again. Making the cuts seamless, however, can prove tricky.

If this is meant to be one continuous movement, you may run into problems when you make the cuts between the shots. You need to make sure the overlap and follow-through of all the other elements of the character's body sync up perfectly. The easiest way to maintain the synchronous movement is to animate the entire shot as a single shot first, and then segment it, linking and unlinking the held objects last. By using this technique your shot should remain seamless.

An easier way to keep the action seamless is to actually cut to a different camera angle to hide the parenting change. You could have the character reaching for the object, cut to a shot of his hand touching the object, and then cut back to a shot of him picking up the object. Using this method, you eliminate the need to keep the cut perfectly seamless and hidden.

If you can't get the transition to be seamless, cutting to a new shot might do the trick.

Hiding and Unhiding Two Objects

If your package enables you to animate the hiding and unhiding of objects, you can simply do some digital sleight of hand and have two identical objects in the shot. The first object has the hand as a parent and moves with the hand; the second object is a completely unlinked object that has no relation to the hand whatsoever. The object in the hand is hidden, so it is not rendered while the other object is free. As soon as the free object is picked up, it is hidden and the object in the hand is revealed. If you match the positions of the objects, you should not have any problems. If your 3D package does not enable you to hide objects in the middle of the animation, you can simply animate the object's transparencies so that one object becomes transparent while the other becomes visible.

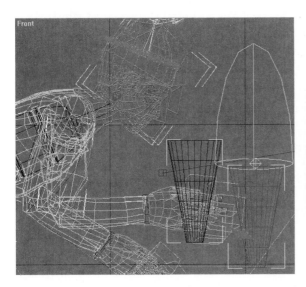
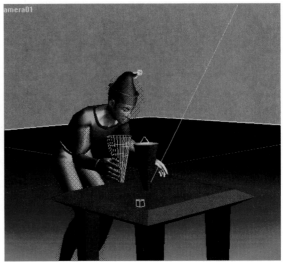

In this frame, the object linked to the character's hand is hidden (shown in wireframe); the one on the table is visible.

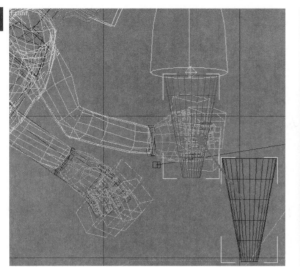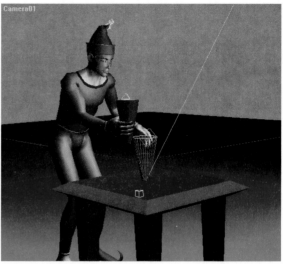

When the character picks up the object, you hide the object on the table (wireframe) and reveal the one in his hand. The object on the table hasn't moved; it has simply become invisible. You still have two objects, but the audience sees only one.

Doing It Frame by Frame

Finally, if you want, you can keep the object separate from the body entirely and keyframe the held object, frame by frame, so that it matches the character's hand perfectly. For short shots this should not be a problem, but if you have the character holding the object for more than a few seconds, you're in for quite a bit of work. If your character needs to hold an object for an extended period of time, you should probably consider using one of the other methods outlined previously.

For practice, use one of those methods to create a simple animation where a character picks up an object and sets it down somewhere else. You might want to try more than one method to see which one works best with your software.

Riding Things

What happens when your character gets into a car, hops on a motorcycle, or rides a horse? This situation is the exact opposite of the previous one—rather than the small object being picked up and carried by your character, you have your character being picked up and carried by a larger object. Again, many of the same principles apply, only this time in reverse.

Your character riding in a car presents the same problems as when he carries something, only in reverse.

You can "pin" or "lock" your character's feet to the object so the character moves with it. If your character is sitting, you can lock down his hips in the same manner.

You can move the two together as a group. If your character is flying his Space Speeder through the cosmos, his hips or feet move along the same path as the spaceship as it flies through space.

You could also segment the shot, giving yourself time to attach or detach the character from the vehicle.

Finally, for short shots, you could simply keyframe the character frame by frame so that he matches up perfectly with whatever he's riding. As you can see, the same principles apply, only in reverse.

Keeping an Eye on Things

Another problem arises from the more subtle interaction of your character with his environment—that is, looking at it. People are very astute when it comes to your character's eyes and where those eyes are looking. If your character is supposed to be looking into another character's eyes, but his gaze is off, it will look like he's staring into space and not paying attention. If he is looking at a fly buzzing around the room, his eyes need to remain fixed on the fly.

Another little tidbit of human interaction is that even when a person moves his head slightly—to accentuate a part of speech, for example—his eyes tend to remain fixed on their target. Of course, large head turns and blinks usually mean a shift of focus for the eyes as well. More to the point, how does the animator keep his character's eyes "on target?"

"Look At" Functions

Some packages have functions that enable you to constrain an object's direction so that it's pointed at another. Some packages call this function a "look at" controller because it forces the object to always face or look at the object to which it is constrained. When such a controller is applied to the pupils of the eye, for example, the eyes automatically rotate to track an object. One good example is a fly buzzing around the room. By constraining the pupils of the eyes so they always "look at" the fly, you can make the fly go all over the place and the character's eyes always follow it. This example is extreme, but the principle applies even on a situation as simple as two people talking face to face, with each character's eyes fixed on the other. You simply have each character's eyes look at the other character's face.

A much more flexible way to use the same function is to create an invisible null or dummy object to help define your character's focus. Simply make your character's eyes "look at" this invisible object. You can then move the object anywhere in the scene, and rest assured your character's eyes will be pointed exactly where you want them.

I am calling this feature a "Look at" function. It has many names, however, and is a good example of the same feature being called many different things in different packages. Here are a few other ways to get this same effect:

- In Softimage it is a constraint found under Motion/Constraints/Direction.

- In 3D Studio MAX, it is called a "Look At" controller and is found in Track View

- In LightWave you could use the IK target function.

- In ElectricImage it is called "Look at Object" and can be found in the Project Window.

In this scene, the character's pupils are fixed to the red sphere with a "look at" controller.

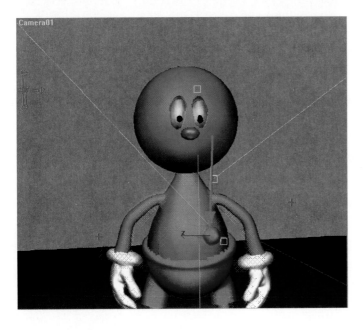

When the sphere moves down, the pupils follow, remaining fixed on the sphere. Making the sphere invisible enables you to use it to guide the eyes in any shot. Simply place it where you want your character to look, and the eyes will follow.

Pointy Objects

Another way to keep the eye on target is to stick pointy objects in your character's eyes. No, I don't want you to maim your characters. By pointy objects, I simply mean an invisible object used as a guide to assist in pointing the eyes. Usually you use a thin cone or a cylinder that has a transparent texture applied to it so that it doesn't show up when rendering.

To create such a guide, model a long, thin cone or a cylinder and attach it to the pupil via a hierarchy or a constraint. The guides will then point into space like searchlights, showing the direction of the character's gaze. If the pupil turns, so will the guide, giving you a very good idea as to where the eyes are pointed and helping you to aim them at their target.

In this wireframe view, you see how these simple cones help position the eyes.

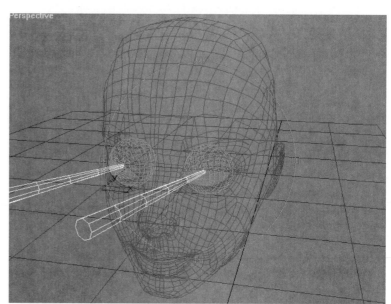

If you apply an invisible texture to the cones, they disappear after rendering.

Takes and Double Takes

One of the more fun tasks of animation is the chance to do a cartoon "take." How you do the take depends wholly on your character and the situation. Remember, a take is simply your character's reaction to something unexpected. The reaction can be wild, wacky, and completely over the top as in a classic cartoon, or it can be more subtle. Sometimes a small and subtle reaction has a much greater effect than a reaction that's extremely exaggerated. Realistic characters usually do not go into bug-eyed hysterics, for example. There are no rules, however, and wild takes can be very effective, particularly at times when you need maximum contrast.

The two broad categories of takes are a normal take and a double take. In the normal take, the character reacts almost immediately. If his hand gets whacked with a mallet, for instance, the reaction is probably immediate, hence the take. In a double take, the reaction takes a while to set in, and you can see the transformation as the character realizes what has happened. Handing your character a check for a million dollars is a great set up for a double take. It takes a while to realize just how much money that is, but once it sets in, the character's reaction can be huge.

In a take, you start with a normal pose.

How do you actually animate a take? To some extent that depends on the type of take you're animating. Look at a typical wild take and see what it's made of.

The take is a few simple poses timed for maximum impact. First, you have an anticipation, where the head squashes down before going into the take. A huge action such as a take demands quite a bit of overshoot, so you probably need another pose at that point. Finally, you have the take itself.

The head then squashes into the shoulders, anticipating the take.

The timing of a take really depends on the action. In the double take, the slow realization can be milked for up to several seconds. Before the take itself, there will be an anticipation of anywhere from 4 to 20 frames; the more violent the take, the bigger the anticipation. After the anticipation, the character goes into his take, overshooting the final pose by a few frames. Once into the take itself, you might want to vibrate the head and facial features a bit to keep them looking alive. Even after the take, you may want to continue your character's reaction, making him collapse into a quivering glob of jelly.

Finally, the head rises up into the take, overshooting this final position before settling in.

Be aware that a take is simply a reaction, and the size of the take is directly proportional to the situation. A small reaction needs only a small take—as small as a simple blink. Your character does not need to go into jaw-dropping, eye-popping takes at every twist and turn of the plot. Instead, save the big take for the big moment. When it happens, the take will be that much stronger.

You don't need a face with bulging eyes to do a take. This faceless little vacuum does a nice simple take in reaction to the hose.

Staggers

What happens when you hit your character on the head, stretch him to the point of breaking, or simply take him for a ride along a bumpy road? In each of these situations, you might want your character's motion to vibrate or stutter. To get this type of motion, you need to use a stagger.

A stagger is a timing and positioning effect. You simply move the object back and forth between staggered points—generally taking two steps forward for every one back. If you had points A, B, C, and D in a line, the object would move from A past B to C, then back to B then on past C to D, then back to C, and so on. This sequence gives the object a less linear movement, producing a stuttering effect. The same type of motion can be cycled as well, for something similar to a character's head ringing like a bell. Be careful when doing such effects because strobing can become a serious issue. A liberal dose of motion blur, however, covers this quite well.

You can also play with the spacing of the stagger to enhance or diminish its effect. For a deeper stutter, animate three steps forward for every two steps back. For a more subtle effect, animate five steps forward for every one step back.

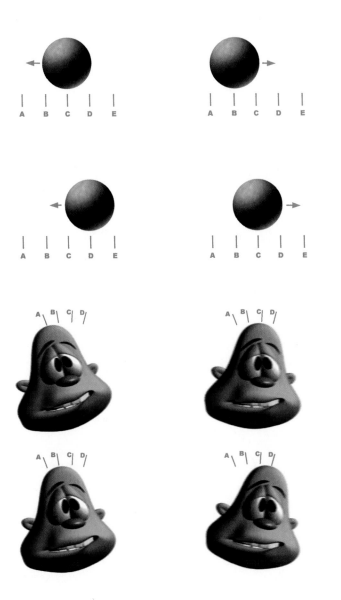

When animating a stagger, it's a simple back and forth motion—taking two steps forward and then one step back, for example. This simple stagger goes from A to C, back to B, forward to D, back C, forward to E, and so on.

The same principle applies to rotations, as in this vibrating head. The positions in this animation would be: A C B D B C A. The resulting animation can then be cycled. This type of motion can strobe very easily, so a good dose of motion blur will help smooth things out.

Animating Laughter

When animating laughter, you first must realize it is an action that involves the entire body. The head, shoulders, chest and belly all play a role in creating a laugh. There are as many laughs as there are personalities, but these generalizations will help guide you.

When laughing, your character will usually take a deep breath, followed by a series of short exhales as he laughs. The deep breath

When laughing, your character should throw his head back as he takes a deep breath.

He then exhales as he laughs, his head bobbing up and down...

...and up again as the head moves forward.

The character's actions should all happen in time with the dialogue track for the duration of the laugh.

pushes the shoulders and head back, which come forward again during the laugh. As the laugh progresses, the head and shoulders bounce up and down along with the contracting belly, which on heavy characters, can jiggle quite a bit. As the head moves forward, staggering the timing of poses can make the laugh a bit more realistic.

Breakdown of a Laugh

The absolute guide for timing the laugh is the dialogue track. Each laugh has a unique rhythm that you can usually notice quite easily if the track is read properly. Making sure your character's laugh is in sync to the track helps you to pull off the shot.

Conclusion

These are but a few of the many tricks that people use to spice up their animation and make it more lifelike. As you can see, many of these tricks, such as those used to help your characters pick up things, are just simple ways of using your software to your advantage. Part of the fun of being a good animator is thinking up devious ways to use the tools to get the best effects easily. The better you know your tools, the easier it will be to think up new and novel ways to use them.

CHAPTER 11

.

Creating Digital Sets and Environments

Now that you understand the fundamentals of character animation, you need to understand how to place your digital characters into environments. These environments may be totally real, such as when your digital characters are composited into a live-action film or commercial.

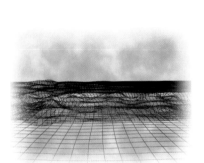

These environments can also be completely unreal, as in a cartoon world. Worlds such as these are subject to your own whims and design choices. Whatever kind of world you create, you can use a variety of techniques to make your animations easier to create and faster to render.

When building environments for your characters, you should think of the environments as digital sets—binary backlots, if you will.

The Importance of Art Direction

The process of deciding exactly how your film will look is called *art direction*. The art director's decisions affect everything in the film—from color to lighting to textures to the choices of furniture, props, and design styles. When making these decisions, the art director must ask many basic design questions, such as

- Is the furniture going to be '50s Moderne, Bauhaus, or Victorian?

- Is the look of the film realistic or stylized?

- What about color? Reds? Grays? Blues? Avocado? Pastels?

All these decisions (and many others, of course) determine to a great extent how your film appears on the screen.

These decisions also determine how the audience perceives your film. If your characters are in a happy place, white light, pastels, and rounded furniture may be the ticket. If the place is scary, dark textures, a smoky atmosphere, dim lights, and dilapidated furniture would probably be good choices. Not only do the characters and their actions set the mood, but the design of the environments they live in plays an important role as well.

A good reference library is essential to all visual artists, and animators are no exception. For set design, there are scores of books on industrial design, architecture, furniture design, fabrics, and other related subjects. Just leafing through books such as this can spark your imagination and help you synthesize a unique look for your film. Photographic reference is also a good idea. If your film is about horses, for instance, take your camera to a stable and photograph horses for reference.

Color is very important, and a good art director will invariably have a good sense of color. The color and textures you assign to your characters must not only match the character's personality, the colors and textures must also let your character read in every situation he encounters. If your character is wearing a polka dot shirt and he steps in front of a striped wall, the resulting combination might be too much for your audience to handle.

One easy way to do keep your characters and your sets from clashing is to use colors that complement each other, but are far apart on the color scale. You might want to give your characters warm colors (reds and yellows) and your digital sets cool colors (greens and blues). This is, of course, a very simplistic way of assigning color, and for the sake of space, I must defer to those whose expertise is color. Color is a very deep subject, and there are entire books written about color theory. I suggest a trip to the bookstore or library for more in-depth information about the many subtleties of color and how it affects people's perception.

In pre-production, some directors go as far as to create a "color script" for their films. This is done by roughly coloring in the storyboard panels of the film with markers and pinning them up on a bulletin board. The director can then step back and see how the color flows throughout the film. A jarring shift in color, say from green to red, may jar the audience. This can be used for shock value, or it might be an unwanted effect. The color script will help you decide this. Getting the color of a film to flow smoothly will give it a subtle sense of continuity.

Furniture and Props

How you model furniture and props depends to some degree on your modeler's capabilities. If you have a modeler good enough to create convincing creatures, you should have no problem creating perfectly acceptable props and furniture. Modeling props is a straightforward task and is just a matter of following the art direction you've set.

Stock libraries of objects can also be helpful because they are a big time saver. Think of them as digital clip art. A number of software vendors ship libraries of objects on the CD with their software, and there are many companies, such as Viewpoint, Acuris, Zygote, and REM Infographica, that create and sell digital models as a business. There are also repositories of objects on the Internet at places such as Viewpoint's Avalon site (www.viewpoint.com).

Many of these objects, however, can seem somewhat stale and generic. To add fuel to the fire, stock objects travel quickly, and many have been used in countless other productions as well. To get a more unique look, you should spend some extra time creating textures that differentiate your library of stock objects from everyone else's. If you've ever reupholstered a couch, you know how much a change in color or texture can affect its appearance.

Another route you can use when creating furniture and props for your environment is to customize the stock objects themselves by adding, deleting, or resizing elements, such as armrests or table legs. You can also rescale or change the proportions of the object itself by using simple tools such as bends, tapers, or lattice deformations. A simple taper added to a stock object can give it an off-kilter, cartoony appearance, for example.

To change the look of this stock couch…

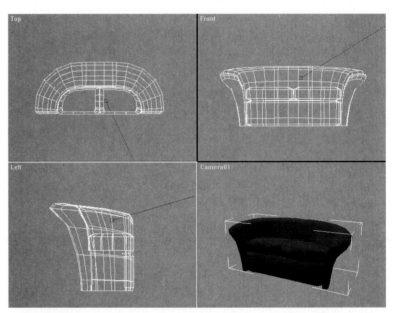

…I simply surrounded it with a lattice…

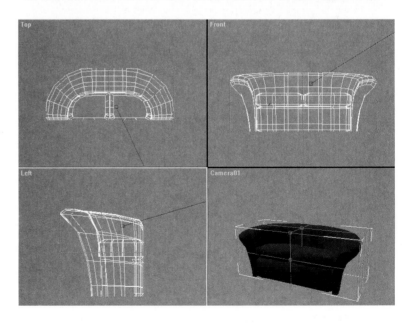

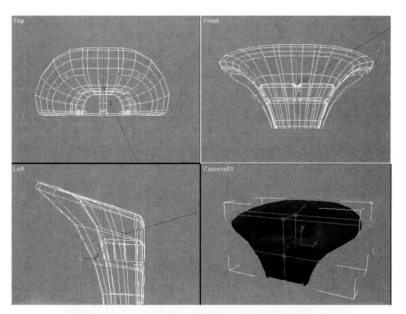

...and reshaped it to give it a more cartoony look.

These pieces of furniture were pulled from a stock 3D object library.

By adding new textures, reshaping the furniture, and swapping the lamp for a new one, you can achieve a whole new art direction.

Walls and Floors

For interior sets, most floors and walls are flat and can be modeled out of simple boxes or planes. Just as in a live-action movie shoot, you need only to place walls and sets in front of the camera. Many times, a single plane for the wall and another for the floor are all that's needed. Don't confine yourself to thinking you need to keep your set rigid. If turning a wall a bit makes the close-up shot look better, go ahead and turn it. As long as you maintain continuity, little tweaks can help liven every shot.

This looks like a nice interior shot on a late afternoon.

Pull the camera back and we break the illusion. The wall and floor are simple planes with texture maps, and the baseboard is another simple object.

Interiors need not be limited to simple flat surfaces, however. The inside of a factory, for example, will have all sorts of pipes, wires, machines, and other assorted contraptions, all of which need to be designed and modeled. With its complex curved surfaces, something as ordinary as the inside of a car can be a modeling nightmare. (In fact, Alias' modeling tools were originally created in the mid-1980s to help automobile companies design cars.)

When modeling a complex interior, you still need to be concerned only with what the camera sees. If your film takes place inside a house, you'll need to model interior walls and furniture, but you really don't need to model the individual shingles on the roof. The camera never sees this. Again, as in live action filmmaking, sets can be moved and changed depending on the requirements of the shot. If you need a high angle shot, for example, you might have to remove the ceiling of your set to move the camera to exactly the right place.

This interior is more complex than a simple wall and floor and will take more time to model.

From the outside, you can see the roof is a bit too big and the floor doesn't quite line up to the edges of the walls. The camera will never see this, however.

You can also move and rearrange your digital sets as the shots dictate. To get this high angle shot, for example…

…you might have to take off the ceiling and remove a few beams so that they don't block the camera.

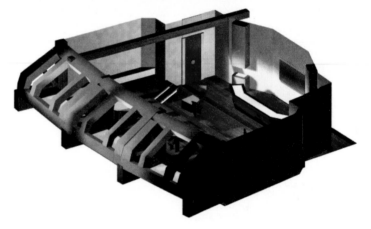

Creating and Manipulating Textures

To create textures for your walls and floors, stock image libraries can be a very good source. Many 3D packages ship with stock textures, and these are a good starting point for creating your own textures. Like stock models and furniture, you'll probably want to manipulate your textures to give them just the look you want. Photoshop or another image manipulation package will help you do such tasks as color correction and other image manipulation chores. A green marble texture is easily manipulated to make blue or red marble using Photoshop's Color Balance feature, for example.

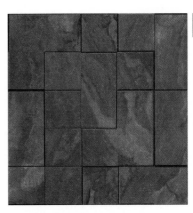

This basic marble texture was pulled out of a stock image library (Pixar's One Twenty Eight CD). It is a simple generic texture that can be customized to fit your own tastes.

You can customize this texture in Photoshop by simply changing its color.

Or by changing its color and breaking it into smaller tiles.

Another way to gather textures is with photography. 35mm film can be transferred to PhotoCD very easily, and this is a great format for storing large quantities of photos. These photos can then be the basis of your own personal library.

A flatbed scanner is another good investment if you want to create your own textures. You can break out the paint and brushes, for example, and create some custom textures to give your film a more painterly look. Conversely, a 64 box of crayons might be all you need to create the textures for a children's film. You can scan anything that's flat. Fabrics, blocks of wood, and wallpaper are all examples of flat objects that can be scanned.

Or by changing its color, adding noise, blurring, and pixelating it. As you can see, the basic texture is only the starting point for creating your own new and novel textures.

Textures can be found just about everywhere. To get the texture for this luncheon meat, I tossed a slice of cotto salami on a flatbed scanner.

Sky

You can model the sky in a number of ways. The easiest is to take a simple sphere or hemisphere and texture map a sky inside it. If the sphere is sufficiently large, the camera will always pick up the sky no matter where you are inside. Remember, however, to make sure that your sky texture does not accept shadows. If your character accidentally casts a shadow on the sky, the illusion is lost—the audience sees the sky as an object. Shining a very wide spotlight directly at the dome can also get rid of unwanted shadows and also give the sky a nice, even illumination.

Some packages, such as 3D Studio MAX and Softimage can generate the sky automatically. You simply assign a bitmap to the environment or apply a procedural shader, and the software does the rest. This automation can save you a lot of time and headaches.

Mapping a cloud texture on the inside of the hemisphere is an easy way to make a sky.

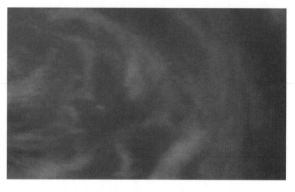

From inside the sky dome, the texture looks like the sky, no matter where you point the camera.

Some packages offer procedural clouds and environments. This one was created by using a custom shader for Softimage's Mental Ray.

Ground

Unless your animation is set in outer space, chances are you need to model some ground to support your characters. Ground can be covered with anything from dirt to grass to ice to carpet, but modeling it is pretty much the same.

Ground is easily modeled as a flat plane, but totally flat ground can get boring and stretches into infinity. An infinite horizon can cause other problems because you can always see the edges of the plane, forcing you to use fog or other distance cues to hide it. You need to create something that can break up the horizon. Mountains in the distance, a sky dome, or some other horizon breaker can work as well.

This completely flat ground plane shows exactly what it's made of—a boring, flat plane with the edges and corners showing.

One of the ways to hide such a plane is with a distance cue, such as fog. The fog, however, can make your film very moody.

A second approach is to add terrain in the background to break up the horizon. That way, the edges of the set are hidden, and the horizon is more interesting.

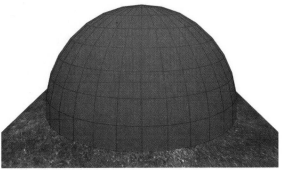

Another method would be to add a sky dome. Here, the sky dome is seen from the exterior.

From the inside, the dome gives a nice, circular horizon.

Many packages offer a randomization or a noise routine to jumble the height of the vertices within your models. Applied to a flat plane, a noise routine can easily make a nice, bumpy ground cover. Another way to create ground is by using a displacement map. Simply paint the terrain you want in a paint program and use it as a map to displace your ground plane.

Trees and Ground Cover

Nature is very complex, and natural items such as trees and grass are not exceptions. But getting a tree to look natural can be a very difficult modeling task. To assist in this task, a number of programs on the market such as Tree Pro for the Macintosh or Animatek's World Builder for the PC can help you generate realistic foliage. You can also buy pre-made 3D foliage from any number of modeling companies, such as Viewpoint, Acuris, and REM Infografica. You can model the trees yourself, but you need to use caution. Trees made from geometry can prove costly in terms of modeling and rendering time—particularly if you need an entire forest. Modeling trees takes time.

You can model detailed trees such as these or purchase them from any number of 3D model vendors.

If faced with this time constraint, you could make an art-direction decision and go with a stylized tree, which might save time and headaches. Stylized trees can also give your film a more personalized look. Who says a tree has to look real? Why can't it be flat, drawn in crayon, or look like a lollipop?

Ultra-realistic trees are nice, but stylized trees can also give your film a different direction and are a lot easier to model.

If your characters are going to be outside, you're going to need some sort of ground cover, and natural ground cover can be a lot more challenging than carpet or parquet flooring. Dirt and rocks are fairly easy because they can be made as solid objects, with creative texture mapping supplying most of the detail. The North Pole is easy to create as well because ice is flat. If you have grass, however, animation can get a bit tough—grass gets squashed and pushed around by your characters. Grass is a lot like hair in that it has thousands of individual strands that all move individually. Consequently, one way to create grass is with a fur or hair-type shader.

You can use simple bitmaps to create rocks and dirt. As well, you can use this bitmap technique to create short types of grass.

Tall grass, however, is tougher. Because it's very similar to hair, a hair shader may be a good way create it.

When to Add Detail

Many times, you'll have a situation where the background is far away and the characters never interact with it. A mountain on the horizon is a good example. In 3D you could digitally build that mountain to scale, texture it with a nice dirt bitmap, and add realistic trees and rocks. Doing that, however, would be insane because you're adding detail and polygons that you'll never need. Your camera will never be close enough to the mountain to realize this intense amount of detail. Placing a photograph or a stylized texture map of the mountain behind the character would be much easier—and just as realistic.

Consider the situation in which the character climbs into his helicopter, flies to the mountain, and lands on it with one, seamless shot. In this case, you probably need that high degree of detail because the character is interacting directly with the mountain. However, the general rule is model only what you need.

Lighting Your Sets and Characters

Lighting is one of the most important aspects of filmmaking. In live action, lighting is half the shot. The same goes for digital film. Creating flat, white, supermarket style lighting for your digital characters is easy; however, flat lighting usually adds nothing to the drama of the scene. By adjusting the lighting of your shot to match its mood, you add tension and drama to your film.

There are many examples of how lighting affects mood. A character who enters the shot silhouetted only by his car's headlights will seem mysterious. Lights placed low will make a character seem scary. If your character is dying of thirst in a hot desert, adding a reddish light will make the shot seem that much hotter. Conversely, blue light will make a shot look colder.

The color of the lighting will also affect the color of everything in the shot. This can affect your overall art direction. A blue light in the shot will shift all colors toward blue, for example. You need to take this into consideration when designing your film.

Positioning Your Lights

The location of the lights in a scene determines how we perceive the character. Simply by rotating a single light around a character, we can see how light affects him.

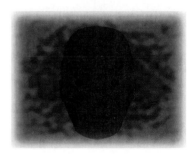

Directly behind the head: The light creates a silhouette of the head. If you use a volumetric light (discussed later in this chapter), you may also produce a halo around your character.

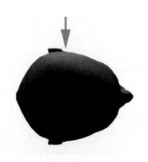

Three-Quarters Back: At 45 degrees behind the head, the light gives us a bit of detail, but most facial features remain hidden, thereby creating a moody effect.

Full Side: Directly to the side, the light gives a good definition of the contours of the face and a sense of depth.

Three Quarters Front: At 45 degrees to the front, the light is in the portrait position.

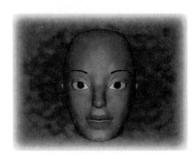

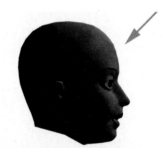

Full Front: When the light is at the same position as the camera, the lighting is relatively flat.

Underlighting: You can move the light down to create the classic underlighting effect. Keeping a light low results in a scary, film-noir effect.

Top lighting: Moving the light up results in a more favorable light. For classic portraiture, the light should be three quarters front and top lit.

The Basic Three-Light Setup

When lighting for film, many directors start with a basic three-light setup and work from there. This same setup is a good place for digital animators to start. The classic three-light setup consists of a key light, a fill light, and a backlight.

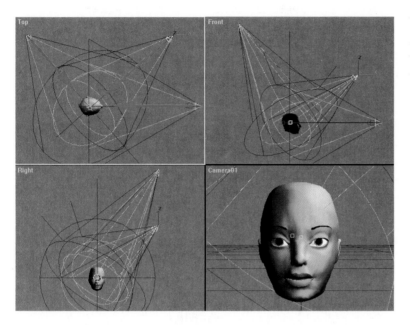

The three-light setup is a good starting point. The lights are (clockwise from top left) the backlight, the key light, and the fill light.

The key light is the primary light source and is usually the brightest. A good place to start with this light is three quarters front (in front of the character at 45 degrees to the right or left). The key defines the major direction of the light and is almost always the primary shadow light. The light is generally placed high, so that the shadows fall on the floor and not on nearby walls or props. The fill light's function is to soften the shadows created by the key, particularly on the face. Generally, the light is placed close to the camera, so that its lighting is flat and unobtrusive. The light is less bright than the key and does not need to cast shadows. (Usually shadow casting is an on/off toggle in your software's light controls. For the fill light, you can simply switch it off, so that it produces no shadows. The capability to toggle shadows on and off is one of the nice advantages digital lights have over the real thing.) The backlight's function is to add definition and outline to the subject, separating it from the background. The backlight is usually placed three quarters back and slightly higher than the key light.

The three-light setup is a good starting point because it will always give you good, serviceable, lighting. You can add other lights to the shot to illuminate or highlight other characters or areas of the background. The three light setup, however, is fairly neutral. If you want your lighting to be more dramatic, you can diverge from this basic setup.

If you want that classic film-noir effect, for example, you need to move the key and the backlight down to get strong underlighting. A late afternoon shot might best be indicated by a single red, dusty light shining through some venetian blinds. Another example of lighting for effect is light that filters through a keyhole, illuminating your character's prying eyes. The lighting in a discotheque will change and pulse to the beat of the music. And, finally, there's also daylight, which is simply a single strong light placed far away (much like the sun), washing the entire scene in light.

Volumetric Lighting

One way to create a mood through lighting is with volumetric effects. These effects enable you to simulate lights shining through a dusty atmosphere. Think of the lights at a smoke-filled rock concert. These lights are good not only for stage effects; they also help to pull off things such as fog and moody atmospheric effects. Dusty light filtering through venetian blinds on a late afternoon is a good example. Volumetric lights also help indicate the position and direction of lights. Think of how searchlights are used to indicate an important event is taking place.

Volumetric lighting simulates the effects of dusty, smoky rooms.

Faking Radiosity

One of the hardest things to fake in animation is the way light bounces off surfaces. Raytracing can mimic the way lights in the scene travel through reflective and refractive objects, but the problem is that a reflective surface can act as a light source itself, softening and filtering the light in the scene as a whole. Raytracing does not take this into account. Digital simulation of this effect is called *radiosity*. Radiosity, however, is not included in most renderers, and the calculations involved slow down rendering considerably.

One way to fake radiosity is to add a few more soft lights in your shot to mimic the effects of the hotspots in the room. A white reflective floor, for example, illuminates the underside of your character slightly. Simply adding a light beneath the floor, you can accomplish most of the same effects without the large rendering hit. The same is true for any reflective or bright surfaces; simply place a light of a similar color near the surface to mimic its radiosity.

In real life, the floor in this shot would reflect light underneath the character. Rendering the shot without radiosity, however, causes the feet to be unnaturally dark.

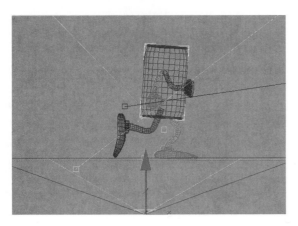

By adding a light beneath the floor, the radiosity effect can be simulated. To prevent the floor from blocking the light, simply exclude it from the light.

Now the underside of the character, particularly the feet, is more realistically lit.

Marrying 3D with Live Action

Many times you may want to marry 3D animation with live action. Classic examples of this are films such as *Casper*, *The Mask*, and *Jurassic Park*. Each of these films were created primarily live action, with the 3D animation and characters seamlessly composited in later. Done properly, your character will appear as though he were on the set from the get go. Knowing how to marry 3D animation to live action is an art in itself and takes years of experience to master. Still, the basic principles are easy enough to learn.

Keep Records

Preparation and planning are the keys to easy and seamless composites. If you can, it's always a good idea to visit the set while the live action is being shot. Matching the lighting is one of the most difficult things to do when compositing, so you should keep good records. Photograph the set for reference and make a detailed diagram of the lighting. Write down the positions and the angles of the lights as well as their intensity. One trick I've seen people use is to place a shiny metal sphere where the 3D character will be placed and then photograph the sphere from all angles. The sphere reflects the lights, and the photographs give you a good idea of exactly which lights are falling on your character. If the shot is outside, the lighting is less controlled. Still, you need to know the time of day, whether it's cloudy or sunny, and whether the director is supplementing the shot with additional lights or reflectors.

You also need to know which camera lenses the director is using for each shot, so that you can match the perspective and field of view of each shot. If the camera moves, it opens a whole new can of worms because you'll have to match the live action camera's motions with your digital camera's. There are a number of ways of doing this, such as using a motion control camera or tracking reference point in your scene.

Motion Control

On deluxe productions, you may have a *motion control camera*, which is a camera that can record and replay its every movement. This is great because you'll know exactly where the camera is at every frame. If your director shoots steadycam or handheld, you won't have motion control data, which introduces yet another factor. You'll need to find a stable point in the shot to use as reference to help track the camera.

To establish the reference point, you should take measurements of the objects and props used in the shot. Let's say you have a chair on the set that remains stable. If you have the exact measurements of the chair, you can create a rough model of it in your 3D program and place it in the exact same place on your virtual "set." You can then sync your 3D camera to the live action camera by making sure the 3D chair lines up with the photographed chair.

This simple plane provides a digital duplicate of the table top. By aligning it to the table in the background, we can rest assured our character will be positioned correctly. (Photo by Maestri Smith)

If you lack reference points—for example, if your shot is in an open field—you can put them in yourself. One useful trick is to place some ping pong balls on the ground in the live action shot. You can then place little spheres, or "virtual ping pong balls," in your digital set and use those as reference points to match your camera movements to the live action camera's, much like tracking a chair or a table. The only problem is that you have ping pong balls in your live action footage. These must be painted out digitally in post-production. It's a lot of work, but if your digital camera doesn't match exactly, your 3D objects will appear to slide.

Animating and Compositing

After you leave the set, it's time to animate. The animation can be tricky even if you don't move the camera. If you're animating a character, making it interact with the actors in the shot is an art in itself. Most good software packages enable you to load the live-action footage as background, which is critical because it enables you to see how your character is placed in relation to the live-action shot.

Loading the live-action images as a background within your animation program can provide valuable reference while you're animating.

Another problem that you must deal with is getting the proper interaction of characters with the live-action environment. Stand-in geometry should be used for those parts of the live-action scene that have any sort of interaction with the character. That way, things such as shadows and reflections can be created more easily.

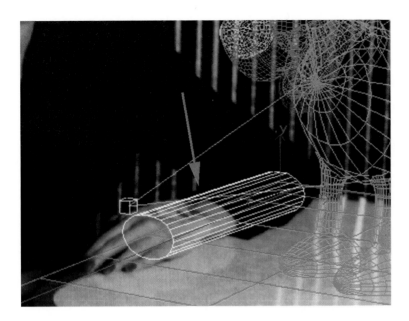

This cylinder is a digital stand-in for the forearm. Using the cylinder makes it easier to get the proper shadows for compositing later.

One nice feature, available in packages such as LightWave and 3D Studio MAX, is the capability to create "matte" textures and place them on an object (in LightWave this is called a front projection image map, but the theory is identical). This category of texture simply lets the background plate show through. For example, if your character runs behind a tree in the background plate, you can create a stand-in—a flat polygon the same shape as the tree in the shot—and then simply map the background to the tree. When the character runs "behind" the polygon, he's matted out. It's a nice trick that works well.

Using Objects

Let's take this still image of a row of houses and place a character behind it.

If the character is placed in front of the background, the houses will be behind him.

To get him behind the houses, create an object that matches the outline of the rooftops and place it in front of your character.

Here is a different angle of the previous illustration. The object is much like a low fence that the character is standing behind.

This object can then be textured with the background image for a seamless composite at rendering time.

If you want, you can also texture the object and the background with a uniform color. This will give you an image of the character that will composite seamlessly after the background color is removed. In Premiere, this background color can be removed by using the Chroma Key filter.

Mapping the background is the quick and dirty method because it doesn't allow for color correcting the two elements as they are composited. To allow for true color correction, you should texture the object with a matte-black, nonreflective surface or extract the alpha channel, effectively creating a matte to use later.

Shadows and Reflections

One of the most confusing aspects of compositing is creating proper shadows and reflections. Shadows really help lock a character into a shot. Mismatched shadows, however, make the character stand out like a nun in a discotheque. How do you make sure the shadows fall where they're supposed to?

The key is proper stand-in geometry and textures. The geometry will accept the shadows, enabling you to create a shadow plate. Reflective surfaces can also be simulated with stand-in geometry to obtain a reflection plate. To get everything right, however, you need to have stand-ins that closely mimic the actions and positions of your real-world objects.

Creating a Seamless Composite

To create a seamless composite, you need to have your cameras and lighting matched to the live action plate, as well as stand-in geometry to accept shadows and reflections. You also should render and test a wireframe or flat shaded test. The method shown here is the long way around. Many packages have additional features that may shorten a few steps, such as being able to render shadow and reflection buffers directly. This method, however, works for most any package.

1. Hide everything and render only your character...

2. ...along with an alpha channel.

3. Unhide the stand-in geometry—in this case, the table and the forearm. First, you need to create the shadow maps. Apply a white matte texture to all the stand-in geometry and render the shot against a white background. This process will give you the character and a shadow.

4. Next, texture only the reflective stand-in geometry with a reflective black texture. Render the shot against black.

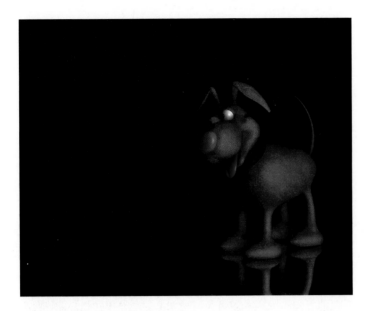

5. Now you have all the elements you need. Using the alpha channel extracted from our character, matte out the character in both the reflection and shadow plates. For motion shots, a package such as Adobe Premiere or After Effects can handle this task.

The following illustration shows the shadow plate...

…and the next illustration shows the reflection plate.

6. This picture shows the shadow and reflection composited into the shot. The reflection plate can be blurred a bit, and both should have a bit of opacity added to enable the background to show through.

7. Finally, add your character and composite the final shot by using your favorite compositing package.

Conclusion

These are the basics of compositing. These techniques cannot be used only with live action; they can be used for your digital sets as well. If your camera is fixed, your backgrounds will remain fixed as well—it might not make sense to render your backgrounds anew for every frame, particularly if the background is exceedingly complex. If this is the case, it makes sense to render the complex background only once and composite the characters into the shot much like with live action.

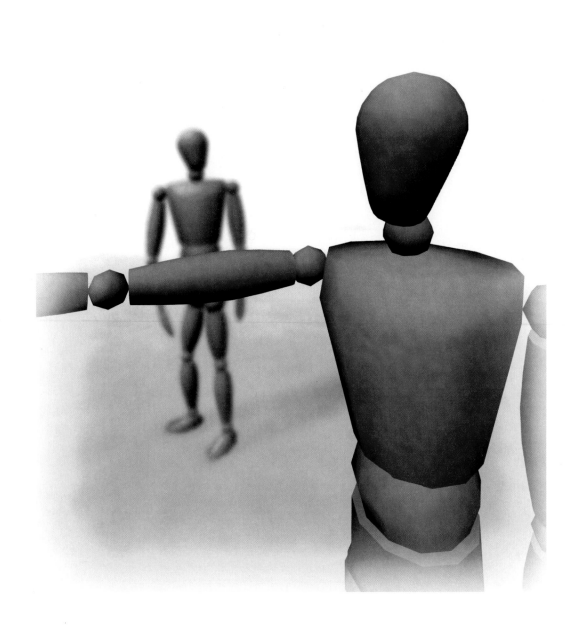

CHAPTER 12

Making a Film

Now that you understand the basics of digital character animation, it's time to consider making a short film. It is one of the best ways to challenge yourself as an animator because the process forces you to go through all the steps required to bring a film from concept to final execution.

Making a film is not to be taken lightly—it is not something that can be done in a few days. For a film that's a few minutes long, you should budget several weeks of full-time effort or several months of part-time effort to complete the job. Because a film can take so much time, it is an exercise in planning, discipline, and commitment; however, the rewards of making your own films can be great. Actually finishing a task that large gives you a tremendous sense of accomplishment. It also gives you a firm understanding of the process of animation as a whole.

Why Make a Film?

There is no real answer to this question, but if you have to ask it, maybe it is not a thing for you to consider. Generally, if you want to create animation, you'll want to make films as well. Making a film not only lets you tell a story, it forces you to understand the process as a whole. It also lets you have fun and create animation exactly the way you would want to see it on the screen without fear of network censors, the client, the ad agency, or anyone else who might have a say in the outcome of a commercial product.

If you create the film, you can be as surreal, as funny, as wild, as gross, or as action-packed as you want. Heck, it's your film; you call the shots. After they are completed, independent films can find their way to film festivals, video, or even the big screen. Many of today's best animation talents started with personal films that got noticed by someone. Getting noticed, however, should not be the prime motivation. You should simply create a film that appeals to your own sensibilities.

Whatever your reasons, my advice for your first film is to start small. The biggest mistake you can make is biting off more than you can chew. If you really wanted to, you could probably make a two-hour feature film in your spare bedroom. The problem is, making a film that long would most likely take the rest of your life to complete. A two- or three-minute film, however, is perfectly manageable, can still tell a great story, and can show off your talents quite well.

Creating Characters and a Story

The first step in the filmmaking process is actually deciding what your film will be about. The film will be based on two elements: the story and the characters. Both are important, and each tends to drive the other. There's no story without characters to inhabit it, and there are no characters without a story to show exactly who they are and what they did.

This chicken and egg syndrome means you should develop both character and story in parallel. Either you take a character you're familiar with and place him in an appropriate situation, or you take a situation and find the appropriate characters. Then, you refine the characters and the story so that the whole thing works as a film.

You've already built several characters as part of this book, and they might be exactly the characters you want to build a film around. Or you may want to start from scratch and design new characters that will work better in the context of your story. However you look at it, your character and his personality determine to a large extent how the story will play to the audience. If you cast Sir Laurence Olivier as Hamlet, the results would be quite different from casting Jerry Lewis in the same role. Conversely, Olivier as the Nutty Professor would certainly add a strange twist.

What type of story do you create? There are quite a few possibilities: the simple story with a full plot that has a beginning, middle, and end; a story that is only a collection of gags strung together, as in a Road Runner cartoon; or a vignette or a sequence of shots culled from a larger project. Whichever you decide, remember that any type of story should have conflict between characters as well as humor or drama.

Your story could be as simple as a child trying to open a child-proof container. Or you could turn that idea on its head and have the adult incapable of opening the container, while the child, the dog, and even the pet hamster have it all figured out. A character could be extremely hungry, so hungry in fact that he eats everything in sight—including himself. You could base your story on a traditional fairy tale—maybe the three little pigs who build houses out of straw, twigs, and bricks. If you want to add a strange twist to that concept, make them the three little lab rats who build mazes out of DNA. As you can see, the core idea of a film can be stated simply in one or two lines. This simple statement is called a premise. Creating a good premise is your first step to creating a good film.

Exercise #1: Creating a Premise for a Short Film

Brainstorming ideas is an exercise in pure creativity. Take a sheet of paper and fill it with one-line premises for films. The more premises, the better; if your ideas spill over to a second, third, or fourth sheet, that's great. You may even take several days to come up with the ideas, keeping a pad in your pocket to write down ideas as they hit you. At this point, you simply need to generate ideas for stories.

continues

Put these ideas away for a day or two and then go back and review them objectively. For each premise, try to picture exactly how the story might take shape. Maybe even go so far as to sketch out ideas for gags or situations. If the story points flow readily, chances are the premise is sound. If you can't picture how the premise could be made into a film, put that idea aside for another time or another film.

Ultimately, one of these many ideas will strike you as the idea for your film. After you have chosen your premise, you'll need to develop your story.

Developing Your Premise

As you can see, the possibilities for premises are limited only by your imagination. After you have a premise in hand, you need to ask yourself some serious and objective questions about how the film will be made. If it's a story about fish, for instance, you may need to animate water. If you do a story about a barber, you may need to animate realistic hair. Ask yourself if your software is capable of handling the types of shots and characters the premise demands. If it is not, you may want to choose another premise or put the premise into another setting.

You also need to think about length. Some stories cannot be told in three to five minutes, although you would be surprised by how much you can fit into that span of time. Focusing on one set of characters and one set of conflicts is best; however, simpler is usually better.

Beyond determining the length, you'll also need to flesh out your story so you know, beat for beat, the exact sequence of events, including the ending. Take the idea of the adult who can't open the childproof bottle. The story could be developed as a series of gags, with the kid, the dog, and the hamster opening the bottle as steps that lead to a climax. The climax could be anything—maybe the adult is driving himself crazy with frustration or maybe he has such a pounding headache that his head explodes. You could make a surreal *Twilight-Zone* ending, where the adult and his world are contained within another giant childproof bottle. Again, the number of possibilities for any story is infinite.

At this point, in addition to writing, you also need to be drawing. Animation is a visual medium, so you absolutely need to visualize how your film will take place. Even if you draw in stick figures, sketching out your ideas in storyboard form helps you understand exactly how gags and situations in your film will be staged. We'll cover proper storyboarding later, but at this point, thumbnail sketches should suffice.

One way to flesh out your story is to go through another brainstorming session to generate as many ideas as possible. If your premise is good, you can generate plenty of ideas—in fact, too many to fit within your time constraints. I've written premises for 11-minute cartoons that, when all the gags and ideas were fleshed out, clocked in at almost 20 minutes. The problem became one of too many ideas, in that almost half the cartoon had to be eliminated. Throwing out good material is always painful.

If you have too much material, you can think of it as either a luxury or a curse. If deleting the extra material from your story makes it incomprehensible, your story might be cursed with too much complexity. You probably need to take a step backward to rethink the premise or the major story points to get the film to a manageable length. If you can toss out material and still have a sound story, you have the luxury of too much good stuff. Hopefully, keeping only the best material will make your film that much stronger. Even if you have lots of great material, don't delude yourself into thinking it all needs to be put in the film. Every extra bit of material means an extra animation for you to complete. If you bite off more than you can chew, it can come back to haunt you later.

Exercise #2: Fleshing Out Your Premise

You need a stack of note cards or Post-It notes for this exercise. Select your favorite premise from the previous exercise. Using the premise as your guide, think up story points, writing down or drawing each point on a separate card.

These points can be as simple as "She walks down the street," and "Notices something in the window." If you have an idea for a visual gag, draw it on the card. Generate a large number of ideas at this point. If the ideas don't flow readily, you might want to select a different premise.

continues

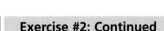

After you have as many ideas as you can think of, go through the stack of cards and organize the story points into a rough outline of the story. You can do this by pinning the cards on a bulletin board or laying them out on a table. After you've arranged these cards into an outline, you have a good idea of what your story will look like.

Creating Storyboards

After you have a firm idea what your story will be about, it is time to begin storyboarding your film. In animation, the story-board is the blueprint you use to construct your film. You would not pour the foundation of a house without a blueprint, nor would you make an animated film without a storyboard. You should always create a storyboard before you begin animation.

Conceptually, a storyboard is simple. It's a shot-by-shot or action-by-action diagram of your film. It's kind of like a strange hybrid somewhere between a script and a comic strip. Most commercial productions use the script to generate the storyboard, but this is not always the best way to proceed. If your film relies heavily on visuals—rather than dialogue—work the film out visually. A picture is worth a thousand words, or so the saying goes.

When creating a storyboard, it's best to get a small pad of paper or a stack of Post-It notes and rough out each shot, one per sheet. By having each shot on a separate piece of paper, you can add, delete, or rearrange shots quite easily. A large bulletin board will enable you to pin up your storyboard and see how it works.

A storyboard for your own film does not have to be a work of art. It is strictly a visualization tool to help you see how your film will flow, shot by shot. If you have trouble drawing, stick figures are perfectly acceptable—no one need see the storyboards but you. The film is what people see, not the storyboard. Of course, if you're showing the boards to a client, the storyboards will have to be presentable.

No matter how they are drawn, storyboards are the only way you can plan your film properly. Without storyboards you have

no idea how many shots you will need to animate, how long
your film will be, or what kinds of props and sets you will need
to build. Also, the storyboard is one of your last steps in pre-
production. It is very cheap and easy to change a storyboard. After
you begin animating, however, every change in your film becomes
costly and time-consuming.

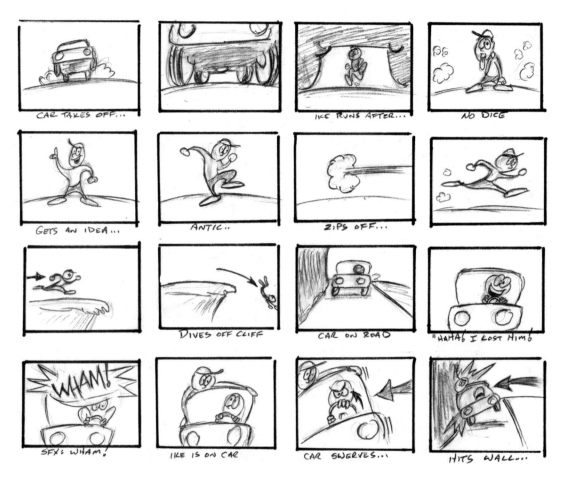

A storyboard consists of simple thumbnail sketches showing every shot of the film and the major actions
within those shots.

Exercise #3: Creating a Storyboard

Using the outline fleshed out from your premise, create a storyboard for your film. Simply work out the story points visually on
note cards or Post-It notes. Every shot in the film needs at least
one note card, and long shots will need a note card for every

continues

major action. When you're done, pin the drawings to a bulletin board and rework any shot that seems out of place. Pretty soon, you'll begin to see exactly how your film will flow, shot by shot.

Recording Dialogue

It is certainly not a requirement for your film to have dialogue. Many of the best cartoons have no dialogue whatsoever. If your film does have dialogue, however, you'll need to record voices after you're happy with the script and storyboard. In the voice session, you may want to have the voice actors read from the script verbatim, or you can have them improvise a few takes to see if you can get a more inspired read. Many times, good comic actors can add more life to the script than you ever imagined.

It's always a good idea to record the dialogue on a high-quality archival medium such as DAT. If you don't have access to a DAT machine, a reliable cassette deck or a reel-to-reel recorder will suffice. You can also record directly into most computers digitally at CD quality, but you still need a good microphone and mixer to get the sound to the computer. Also, a voice session can usually produce three or four times as much dialogue as you'll actually use, so if you record directly into the computer, be sure to have plenty of disk space handy.

Having a computer with a sound editing program also gives you the capability to edit your dialogue. You could, for example, take one sentence from the first take, another from the second take, and so on. If you get really good at editing sound, you can even cut words out of sentences.

Leica Reels

After you have your storyboard and your dialogue, it's a good idea to cut a Leica reel, also known as an Animatic. What you're doing is scanning your storyboard drawings into your computer and timing them to your dialogue tracks. The Leica reel will help you to further refine and visualize your film before you begin animation.

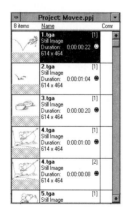

If you use Premiere to create your storyboard, simply load all your scanned storyboard panels into the project window...

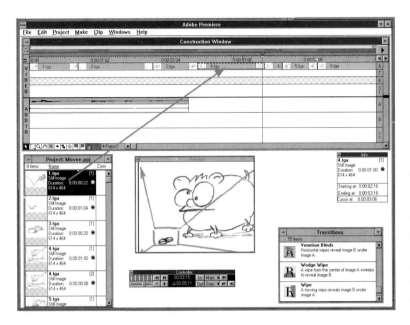

...and then drag these panels to the construction window. If you have audio, drag that to the construction window as well.

The Leica reel actually plays much like a very rough version of your film. The timing of the shots are in place; there can be dialogue or sound effects; and if you watch it, you can actually begin to see how your film will look and sound.

Exercise #4: Creating a Leica Reel

On the desktop, a package such as Adobe Premiere is a good choice for creating Leica reels. The procedure is relatively straightforward, and the principles apply to other packages as well. You need a scanner or a video camera with a capture card to get your storyboard drawings into your computer. If you have a full motion video card, you may want to scan these at a full 640×480 resolution and record the final product to videotape. This step is not critical, however, and you can scan at a lower resolution, say 320×240, and simply play the Leica reel directly on your computer monitor.

First, you'll want to scan your drawings one by one into your computer. It's easiest to name them in ascending order such as PANEL000, PANEL001, PANEL002, and so on. If your scanner has a sheet feeder, the automation process is helped considerably.

If you have dialogue, you also need to record the audio into your computer. If the audio is on tape, record the selected dialogue lines into your favorite sound editor one by one, making a separate audio file for each line of dialogue.

After you have these on your disk, you'll need to import all of the storyboard picture files into Premiere. If you have dialogue, import the sound files as well.

To adjust the length of a storyboard panel, simply click on the edge of the panel's picture in the construction window and drag it right or left. The length of the panel will appear in the info window.

continues

If your animation is to video, set Premiere's timebase to 30 fps; if your animation is timed to film, 24 fps is the proper timebase.

Now it's simply a matter of clicking and dragging the individual pictures to the video timeline and adjusting their lengths so that the film plays the way you want. In Premiere, when a still image is brought to the timeline, it defaults to a length of one second per image. By simply dragging the edges of the image on the timeline, you can add or subtract time to your film.

If you have dialogue, drag it to the timeline as well. Dialogue, however, is a fixed length. The only way to make it shorter is to cut words or sentences.

After you've worked your way through all the dialogue and storyboard panels, render your Leica reel and watch it. If you need to, go back and make timing changes. At this point you may also want to cut extraneous shots to tighten up the film or add needed shots to flesh it out.

The finished Leica reel will give you a good idea of exactly how long your film will be, as well as exactly how long each shot in the film will be.

Exposure Sheets

Creating exposure sheets, or X-sheets, is not absolutely required for a personal film, but it is something that is usually required for commercial productions. The sheets simply show a frame-by-frame timing of the shots, the readings of the dialogue tracks, and any transition effects, such as wipes or dissolves.

If you don't have dialogue, you should at least go back through the Leica reel you created and write down the exact number of frames each storyboard panel covers. This procedure will give you the timing for the shots and for each major action within each shot because you need to know exactly how long your film will be and how much you'll need to animate on each and every shot in the film. For shots with dialogue, you will need to track read the dialogue to exposure sheets before you animate, as outlined in Chapter 9, "Facial Animation."

Animation

After all this preparation, you're finally ready to actually animate your film. That's what most of this book has been about, and animation is one of the truly fun parts of making a film.

When animating your film, the temptation is to animate every shot in sequential order, from beginning to end. This method of animating, however, is usually not the best way to proceed. The beginning of the film is very important to the rest of the film, so don't animate it until you are comfortable with your characters—which will take a while. The first shot you animate should probably be an easy one somewhere in the middle of the film. That way, you can get a feel for the characters before animating the critical shots.

Rendering and Output

After your animation is complete, you need to render it and output it to film or video. Film always looks great, particularly on the big screen. Unfortunately, you can't simply hand someone a 35 mm print and tell them to go watch your film. Video is certainly a more practical medium, although it lacks the quality of film. You can also distribute your animation digitally on CD-ROM or over the Internet.

Output to Video

Output to video is the most common way to animate on the computer. Video output cards are reasonably priced, making it by far the cheapest way to get your film out to a format that people can use. You can simply print your video to a standard home video recorder, but this will not, by any means, give you the best quality picture. The output of some of the better cards is broadcast quality, so getting your animation to a high-quality video tape is simply a matter of hauling your machine over to the local post house and outputting to Betacam or a digital format such as D1.

Most post houses can output your digital frames directly to video. You simply back up your frames to an archival medium, such as Exabyte tape, and have your post house do the conversion and output for you. Typically, these frames will go directly to D1, which has a frame size of 720×486. The D1 format has non-square pixels, so you have to set your 3D software's pixel ratio to 0.9 when you render. Otherwise, your animation will appear to stretch horizontally by ten percent.

Exabyte is a de-facto standard, but it is not the only format the post houses accept. I know of post houses that can also accept a hard drive or a CD-ROM full of digital frames. Some service bureaus will render your animation for you, outputting it directly to video or film. You simply need to call around and find a company that has the services you need.

Output to Film

If you want to output to film, you open up a whole new can of worms. Film requires a much higher resolution image. The typical film recorder requires an image that's at least 2,048 lines high, as opposed to video's 480 lines. Images this size are ten times what's required for video and can blow your storage requirements through the roof. Not only that, film recorders can be expensive to rent as well. Some companies, however, have set up service bureaus and output film from your data on a per frame basis.

To get your images to film, the typical process is to back up all the frames on an archival medium that the service bureau can read. Exabyte tape is the most popular format because you can get almost 14 GB on a tape. Typically the bureau will have SGI machines, so you will need to provide the tape in Unix tar format. After the tape is in the proper format, you basically hand it to the bureau, and you get back a negative of your film and, of course, a bill.

Other ways to get images to film typically require guerrilla tactics, but they can work very well. One method is to print your film out one frame per page on a standard color inkjet printer and photograph the pages on a traditional animation stand. You would be surprised how good this can look. This method also gives you the option of using textured papers and drawing, painting, or further manipulating the printed frames by hand to give your digital animation a more natural look.

Another inexpensive way to output to film is to get a 16 mm or 35 mm animation camera and point it directly at your computer screen, photographing the images frame by frame. The big problem with this method is the refresh rate of your computer screen. Most computer screens refresh every 1/60 to 1/75 of a second. Unfortunately, this time span is very close to the average exposure time for movie film, which is typically 1/48 of a second or less. Such short exposures will generate flicker in your film. To eliminate the flicker, you need to make the camera's exposure time as long as possible—typically a second or more—to get a high number of screen refreshes for each frame.

Adding Sound Effects

Now that you have your film animated and rendered, you still need to do some post production to add sound effects and sync the dialogue.

Creating good sound effects is an art in itself, and if you have the budget, a good sound engineer is worth the money. If you don't have that sort of budget, there are plenty of sound effects CDs on the market with a wide variety of sounds, from realistic to cartoony. Hanna-Barbera has released some of its cartoon sound effects on CD through Rhino records. It is a great source of material for anyone who wants that classic cartoon sound. For realistic effects the Sound Ideas sound effects library has a good selection you can use.

There are also many times when you need sound effects that aren't in any collections. If this is the case, you'll need to create them from scratch. Basically, you set up a microphone and record the sounds you need. If you want the sound of breaking glass, for example, get a hammer and smash some pop bottles. (Wear safety glasses, of course!) You can be creative when choosing what types of objects you use to create your sound effects. Toys such as slide whistles, kazoos, and jaw harps make great sound effects. Also, atypical effects can make a scene much funnier. If a character runs into a wall, the sound of a bowling strike may be funnier than a simple thud.

One sound effect that is often overlooked is the ambient sound of the room. If you're in the city, the room may have the faint echoes of traffic in the distance. Country dwellers may have birds or crickets as their background. This type of effect will be barely audible, but will subtly add a sense of space and realism to the film.

How do you add sound effects? Well, a good recording studio with an engineer is the best way. Not only are you paying for the use of the studio's equipment, but you're also paying for the engineer's time and expert ear. If you can't afford the studio, video editing packages such as Premiere or Speed Razor enable you to add a track of sound effects over the dialogue and sync it to video. Other, more sophisticated, multitrack sound editing software is available, such as SAW Plus for the PC and Deck for Mac. These packages enable you to mix as many as 16 digital tracks in real-time. The sound can then be mixed to a simple stereo or mono track and synched to your film in Premiere, or at a post-production facility.

A Final Word

Well, that's about it. Those are the absolute, bare bones basics of making a film. Filmmaking is always a big challenge, but you'll get a great feeling of accomplishment after it's finished. The rewards can be great as well because you'll have a product that you can use to sell your skills and further your career. Even if you create your film simply for yourself, it will pay you back many times over.

Have fun animating!

Index

Numbers and Symbols

W

WALK1.AVI file, 206
WALK1.MOV file, 206
walking
  animating, 209-237
  animating cycle with forward
    kinetics exercise, 214-222
  animating cycle with IK
    (Inverse Kinematics) exercise,
    222-227
  animating cycle with inverse or
    broken hierarchies exercise,
    227-233
  animating no-feet walk
    exercise, 233-235
  arms, 208
  body angle, 208
  complexity of, 206
  cycles, 213-235
  extended position, 206
  feet and legs, 206
  footstep generators, 211
  forward kinematics with
    locks, 210
  four-legged animation,
    236-237
  free leg, 207
  guides, 212-213
  hips, 206-207
  hips disconnected from legs,
    211-212
  IK (Inverse Kinematics) with
    locks, 210
  inverse or broken hierarchies,
    211-212
  keeping feet locked on ground,
    210-213
  larger characters, 210
  maintaining balance, 207
  mechanics of, 206-208
  moving ground under, 222

  multiple character rates, 210
  normal gait, 210
  onion-skin effect, 212
  passing position, 207
  personality, 205
  preventing slipping, 214-222
  recoil position, 206
  running versus, 208-209
  segmented characters, 32
  shoulders, 206-207
  side view of head and
    spine, 208
  spine, 206-207
  stride length, 222
  timing, 209-210
  tools for, 205
  weight-bearing foot, 207
walls, 314-315
  photography and textures, 317
  stock image libraries, 316
  textures and manipulation of,
    316-317
Wave for Windows, 285
Wavefont, 3
**weight illusion through
motion exercise, 177-178**
weight-bearing foot, 207
well-designed characters, 9
**well-proportioned
characters, 10**
wigs, 146
World Builder, 320
wrinkles, 67

X-Y-Z

X-sheets, 348